Wine Touring & Tasting in the Mid-Atlantic States

Ian T. Hill

BETTERWAY PUBLICATIONS, INC.
WHITE HALL, VIRGINIA

Published by Betterway Publications, Inc.
P.O. Box 219
Crozet, VA 22932
(804) 823-5661

Cover design and photograph by Susan Riley
Typography by Park Lane Associates

Library of Congress Cataloging-in-Publication Data

Hill, Ian
        Wine touring and tasting in the mid-Atlantic states / Ian T. Hill.
           p.   cm.
        Includes index.
        ISBN 1-55870-190-7 : $12.95
        1. Wine and wine making--Middle Atlantic States.   I. Title.
        TP557.H54 1991
        641.2'2'02575--dc20
                                                                90-20953
                                                                    CIP

Printed in the United States of America
0 9 8 7 6 5 4 3 2 1

For Katherine

ACKNOWLEDGMENTS

I would like to sincerely thank the winegrowers of Maryland, Virginia, and North Carolina for their time and assistance. Without their hundreds of hours of informative, warm, and exciting discussions with me, this book would never have been possible. I salute their generosity, energy, and devotion.

I would also like to apologize, in advance, for any errors contained within these covers. In this young, evolving industry, the names, faces, and personalities associated with the various wineries, as well as their wines, are constantly changing. I have tried my best to develop the most current and comprehensive guide possible.

Nothing in this touring guide should be construed as an endorsement of drinking and driving. Please, for everyone's sake, exercise moderation when enjoying the wine roads of the mid-Atlantic.

CONTENTS

INTRODUCTION:
The Whys And Hows Of This Book

In November 1988, the Wine Institute in San Francisco reported that Washington, DC was the biggest wine drinking jurisdiction in America. On an average annual per capita basis, Washingtonians consume 6.4 gallons of wine per year, compared to a national average of 2.4 gallons per person per year. This level also outdistances residents in such major wine states as California (4.6 gallons per person per year) and New York (3.0 gallons per person per year). Each year, therefore, every Washingtonian enjoys roughly 205 glasses of wine.

Yet, even given this enormous wine market, if you asked the average Washington-area resident to name five wineries in his or her part of the country, the vast majority couldn't. As a matter of fact, Washingtonians can find more than sixty wineries practically in their own back yard, scattered throughout the states of Maryland, Virginia, Pennsylvania, and North Carolina.

In 1983, my wife, Katherine, and I moved to the Washington area from California. Having both grown up in the "Golden State," we had become devoted fans of fine wine and, during our courtship, spent many joyous days driving through California's wine country, enjoying the scenery, the people, and the wines. But upon our arrival in the east, we soon began to experience severe withdrawals. We longed to visit wineries and experience the excitement and learning that grow from talking with vintners and tasting their creations.

We had heard a little bit about wineries in eastern America. We knew that a long history of winegrowing could be found in upstate New York, for example. To our delight, in local wine shops, we would even notice a stray bottle of wine from Virginia or Maryland. Taking on the role of junior Sherlock Holmeses, Katherine and I followed these leads, made countless phone calls, dug up obscure reference books and, after some difficult investigation, made a few excursions out into the countryside to find these wineries.

In nearly every case, we were delighted with what we found. Our missions inevitably took us through beautiful, pastoral landscapes, rolling farm lands, and rugged foothills of ancient mountain ranges. Countless times, when we felt certain that we had taken a wrong turn or misunderstood directions, we would finally come upon a quaint, rustic farm with a lovely vineyard stretching across a hillside. Just as inevitably, we were welcomed by warm and friendly people, people who were delighted that someone had taken the time to seek them out and show interest in their work. And inevitably, once again, we would encounter a striking number of fine and interesting wines. We could not help but feel terribly excited that we were witnessing and experiencing the infancy of a new winegrowing region, a region with great promise.

Upon reflection, we found it both frustrating and ironic that, on the one hand, it was so difficult to find any information about the wineries in this region—their location, the grapes they grew, the wines they produced—while on the other hand, once found, these mid-Atlantic wineries offered lovely countryside, lovely people, and often lovely wine. Innumerable times, we would say to each other, "Why isn't there a touring guide that can tell us these things?"

Since none existed, we finally concluded that we might as well create one ourselves. That was in the fall of 1986. After logging some 7,000 miles and conducting nearly sixty interviews with wineries, we are delighted to bring you *Wine Touring and Tasting in the Mid-Atlantic States*.

HOW TO USE THIS BOOK

First of all, let it be said that this is not a "coffee table" book. While we hope that it is pleasing enough to the eye to merit space in your living room, we have designed this book to be more at home on the front seat of your car or, at least on workdays, in the glove compartment.

This guide has been organized to equip the reader with every tool needed to spend a day or a weekend touring wineries within easy striking distance of Washington, DC. Every winery in the states of Maryland, Virginia, and North Carolina has been included in the guide (as well as a few in southeastern Pennsylvania). For lack of a more precise descriptor, the label "mid-Atlantic" has been applied to this tri-state region.

The guide is divided so that separate sections are devoted to each state. Wineries in a given state have then been further grouped by subregion, so that convenient weekend outings can be planned to allow for an efficient visitation to that area's operations.

Each winery in the mid-Atlantic has an entire section devoted to it. These sections begin by introducing you to the individuals involved with that winery and present information on their backgrounds and how they became involved with winegrowing. The next part of each section focuses on that winery's vineyard. Unlike most touring guides, this one includes detailed, technical information on the vineyard's acreage by grape variety and discusses some of the strengths and weaknesses of each vineyard's micro-climate. Next, a focus on the wines of each winery is presented. Again, a detailed, educational discussion of each winemaker's preferred approaches to winemaking, the equipment he uses, and the practices he follows is included. Finally, the author's tasting notes are presented for each wine produced by the winery. Rather than scoring the wines on any particular point scale of quality, I have instead tried to accurately describe the style of wines produced and highlight those I think are especially noteworthy. People's tastes are very individual and very personal; I have tried, from the outset, not to impose my own opinions of which wines are "good" and which are "bad" upon others.

Tasting notes focus on wines produced largely from the 1986 through 1989 vintages. While this fact inherently limits the timeliness of these notes, the guide will retain its usefulness since it has focused discussion on the *style* of wine sought by each winery and the specific winemaking approaches used to achieve that style.

Each sub-section of the book contains a simple, easy-to-read map. By using the map to plot your course and the specific directions to each winery contained at the back of each chapter, the wine tourist will find this guide very user-friendly.

During interviews with the winemakers, each was asked which area restaurants and inns he or she would recommend to visitors. These recommendations are compiled and alphabetized at the end of the book. Phone numbers are included so that the wine tourist can do a bit of research and plan an outing that will couple, perhaps, a romantic stay at a bed and breakfast or a fine meal with their explorations of the mid-Atlantic wine country.

Finally, a few other helpful sections have been included to make the planning and execution of a weekend wine holiday as easy and informative as possible.

"A Primer on Wine Tasting" describes, in straightforward language, how you can taste wine in a way that allows for maximum appreciation of all the virtues a wine possesses—color, aroma, and flavor.

"Grape Varieties of the Mid-Atlantic" presents a brief overview of the specific grape varieties that play important roles in the mid-Atlantic industry.

"A Glossary of Wine Terminology" is included at the back of the guide. Throughout this book, whenever a technical viticultural or enological term is used, it is printed in italics. For a detailed definition of that term, simply turn to the back of the guide and look it up in the Glossary.

"A List of the Author's Favorite Wines" is also presented at the back of the guide. Once again, the goal is not to impose my opinions upon the wine tourist. (You are encouraged to think critically on your own and formulate opinions of your own favorites.) However, for those whose palates happen to agree with mine, this list serves as a quick reference.

With all that said, enjoy! And may all your ventures into the wine country of the mid-Atlantic be enjoyable, restful, educational, romantic, and of a nature that restores balance and harmony to your hectic lives.

A PRIMER ON WINE TASTING

Almost everyone can remember the first time they saw someone, most likely a self-proclaimed "connoisseur," taste wine in a serious manner. Whether in a restaurant, at a party, or in a local wine shop, we remember him dramatically swirling his wine in the glass, carefully scrutinizing the liquid against a bright light, thrusting his nose deep in his glass and inhaling noisily until it seemed the wine he was smelling might be sucked up his nostrils. And then, best of all, he sipped the wine, paused to ruminate, then began the excruciating process of sloshing, swishing, practically gargling the wine throughout every corner of his mouth. After what seemed an endless amount of such antics, he swallowed . . . hopefully. (Depending on the setting, he may have even spit his wine into a nearby bucket!)

Thoughts that raced through your mind at that time probably blended an ounce of intimidation with a pound of sheer hatred. This ritual can probably be blamed for a great deal of the general public's distaste for wine "snobs," for it epitomizes the mystery and intrigue often associated with wine tasting.

But before we unfairly condemn this poor soul, let it be said that every step he engaged in fulfilled a specific and meaningful purpose. While there will always be those who attempt to use the act of wine tasting to impress those around them, the majority of wine tasters are simply practicing their hobby, and trying to critically appreciate the nectar of the gods: wine.

What follows is a brief guide on how you can taste wine, critically evaluate it using not only your taste buds but your eyes and nose as well and, most important, do so without risking the loss of your friends and loved ones. Fear not, serious wine tasting can be accomplished without calling a great deal of attention to yourself and without causing all of the activity going on around you to come to a screeching halt.

THE GLASS

To begin, wine should always be tasted out of a glass that is tulip-shaped, with a deep bowl and a fairly small-diameter opening. This shape allows for wine to be swirled without spilling and permits the aromas of the wine to be concentrated — held captive in the glass.

When wine is poured for a tasting, the glass should never be filled to more than one-third of its capacity. (I'll tell you why in a second.) Finally, the glass should always be held by its stem or base so that the warmth from your hands does not affect the temperature of the wine in the glass.

USING YOUR EYES

Your eyes are the first organs used to analyze wine. Simply by looking carefully at a wine, it is possible both to detect certain flaws as well as simply enjoy the infinite range of color that can emanate from a glass.

Since your glass is only one-third full, you can tilt it and spread the contents into a broad "disc" within the glass. By holding the glass either up to a light or, better yet, against a plain, white tablecloth in a well-lit room, you may review its appearance. First of all, ask yourself whether the wine is clear and clean. If so, all is well so far. If not, the wine may or may not be giving you the first clue that something is wrong. If, for example, the wine is cloudy or opaque, it almost certainly is very flawed and undrinkable. If, however, there is a small deposit in the bottom of the glass, this is probably just one of the many solids that may fall out of a wine and form a sediment during the aging process. Small crystals are actually potassium bitartrate, an acid, which in no way indicates that a wine is flawed. Other sediment may look muddier and, again, does not indicate a flawed wine. (Since, however, sediment can affect the taste of a wine when it is stirred up, it is recommended that wine with known sediment be stood up for several hours before serving to allow the matter to sink to the bottom of the bottle, then be decanted carefully into another clean bottle, leaving the sediment behind.)

Next, take a look at the wine's color. Color is often a good indicator of how well a wine is aging. White wines, for example, when young can be nearly colorless, a light yellow-green in hue, or possess a rich, yet vibrant yellow/gold color. When whites are older, however, they can turn a deeper, richer gold, bronze, or even brown. Young reds often possess bright purple, ruby, or garnet color. As reds age, the purple hue gives way to richer, deeper shades of red, and begins to show a brick or orange color around the edges. To keep things simple, look at the color of the wine in the glass in relation to the vintage date on the bottle. If, for example, a wine that was bottled just a year or two ago is already showing color-signs of age, it may be headed for an early grave.

USING YOUR NOSE

As we all know, the human senses of smell and taste are intimately linked. Indeed, the act of smelling wine is, in some ways, even more enjoyable than tasting, given the amazing sophistication of the olfactory senses.

Grasping the wine glass by its stem, the next step is to slowly swirl the wine. (Hint: If you want to be sure not to spill, keep the glass on the table while you are swirling it—this eliminates any out-of-control up or down motion.) Swirling allows the wine to come in better contact with the air, and aeration or oxidation allows the aromas and bouquet of the wine to develop.

After swirling, stick your nose down into the glass, and inhale gently but deeply. Fine wines will fill your nose with rich, enticing aromas of fruit, flowers, spice, perhaps oak. The level of excitement usually depends on the intensity and complexity of these smells. Very young wines may not display much smell at all, their "closed in" character a natural phase of development. Poor or flawed wine will usually be quite unpleasant to smell—literally stinky. Such wines may smell sulphurous (an indication that too much sulphur dioxide may have been used as a preservative), like a rotten egg (from hydrogen sulfide and mercaptans, which form during a poorly run fermentation), or like nail polish (the result of acetic bacteria infecting a wine and causing it to turn to vinegar).

It is at this point that one first encounters the difficult task of trying to describe sensory impressions. It is never easy to describe to someone what something tastes like or smells like. The only method is really through analogy. By applying adjectives to your perceptions, wines can be described as being like "something." The most common comparisons when smelling are with various fruits or flowers. For example, a Riesling may exhibit delicate honeysuckle aromas, mixed with scents of apricot and peaches.

TASTING

The final step is the actual tasting. By taking a healthy swig (a small sip is really not sufficient) and allowing it to sit in your mouth for a time, you can consider and evaluate the flavors being presented by a wine. Some tasters will "chew" the wine, allowing it to turn around and around in the mouth. This is actually a very appropriate practice, for it allows the wine to coat every part of the tongue (which has different types of sensory detectors—sweet, salty, acidic, bitter—located on different parts of the tongue). Some will also draw in a small bit of air through the mouth before swallowing, gently aspirating the wine with more oxygen. While this act can make a slight bubbling noise (annoying to some), it is also a good way of helping a wine to "open up" its flavors to the taster.

Here again, describing the wide range of sensations being experienced in the mouth is not easy. Wines will have a "mouth feel," either lush, full-bodied, and viscous, or thin and watery, or anywhere in between. Similarly, flavors of fruits and many other elements may present themselves. Complex, well-aged Cabernet Sauvignon, for example, may be described as displaying deep black currant and cassis fruit, with accents of mint, leather, and tar, all wrapped in smoky, spicy oak. Finally, your mouth will respond to the presence of alcohol by feeling a certain heat after swallowing, and to the presence of tannin by a puckery, drying astringency on the tongue, lips, and teeth after swallowing.

If many wines are to be tasted, you may wish to spit out the wine into a receptacle provided by the host. (This is fine—really. Winemakers and professional wine critics could never do their work if they actually consumed all the wine that passed their lips!) If one person has been given the responsibility of driving to and from a winery or party, that person might decide to only swallow a small amount of the wine actually tasted.

Whether swallowed or spit out, the tasting does not end here, however. Pay close attention to what happens after the wine has left the mouth. Do the flavors persist for a long time? Or do they quickly disappear? Does an unpleasant flavor quickly develop after swallowing? This characteristic of a wine is called its "finish." A lengthy and pleasing finish is certainly desirable in fine wine. Flawed wines will tend to leave a chemical aftertaste.

There, that wasn't so bad, was it? The overall goal when tasting wine critically is to increase your appreciation of it. Fine wines will offer the taster a sense of harmony and balance. Color will be bright and clean and pleasing, aromas will be attractive, enticing, and complex, and flavors will follow closely what was promised in the "nose." By thinking about all three during a tasting, you learn to consider and examine. You learn not only more about your own preferences, but can also begin to really appreciate the vast differences between grapes and wines.

A FEW FINAL SUGGESTIONS

None of us is super-human, we all have our limits. Therefore:

• It is not recommended that you plan to visit more than four wineries in a given day. The number of wines being tasted can add up quickly and can end up impairing both your enjoyment and your safety. Plan on having a good meal or a picnic at some time during each day of wine touring.

• Don't be afraid to take lots of notes during your visits. Again, during any given day, many wines will be tasted and memories of preferred wines can fade quickly. Besides, the act of writing down your impressions of wines really helps in developing a useful, workable wine vocabulary.

• Men and women both should not wear too much cologne or perfume on the days you plan to go wine tasting. If you (and the person next to you, for that matter) really want to appreciate the wonderful and subtle aromas wines have to offer, give your nose a break and don't introduce competing scents.

Major Grape Varieties Grown In The Mid-atlantic

There are literally thousands of varieties of grapes. But only a relative handful have been found, through the generations, to be capable of yielding juice that can be made into fine wine.

One of the most exciting aspects of wine touring in the mid-Atlantic is that, in this relatively small geographic region, you can encounter an amazing and diverse array of these fine wine grapes. The reason: The climate is so diverse that it can support such a variety.

The climate across Maryland, Virginia, and North Carolina can be harsh in winter, extremely harsh, but not as cruel as that seen farther north in Pennsylvania and New York. It can be devilishly hot in summer but, again, not as extreme as neighboring states to the south. The growing season is predictable only in its unpredictability. Droughts during summer are not uncommon, but neither are seasons of excessive rain. Almost always, though, the growing season is long enough to ripen wine grapes. In other words, the mid-Atlantic offers a middling sort of climate. Because of its variability, the land can support virtually every sort and variety of grape and, surprisingly, does so with a high degree of success.

All grapes belong to the group, or genus, called *vitis*. Within this genus are a number of species. The best known and, most agree, the noblest, is that called *vitis vinifera*. Along with nobility, though, comes the disadvantage of tenderness. Vitis vinifera varieties that originated in Europe and go by such familiar names as Chardonnay, Cabernet Sauvignon, and Pinot Noir are recognized as being especially sensitive to the vagaries of climate and soil and need extra attention in cultivation.

On this side of the Atlantic, however, early settlers from Europe found a great number of grape varieties growing naturally in the countryside. These "native-American" grapes have since been studied and grouped into several additional species including *vitis labrusca*, *vitis riparia*, and *vitis aestivalis*. Toward the southern parts of the east coast, another native species thrived, belonging to the family *vitis rotundifolia*. These species, in contrast to the vinifera, were very hardy and tenaciously vigorous; after all, they flourished in the wild.

Now, enter man. Virtually no species grow in the mid-Atlantic today (or anywhere else, for that matter) that don't bear the significant imprint of mankind. Some of these imprints are the result of natural breeding, some are the result of a horrid accident, and others due to the careful and painstaking research of botanists and other scientists.

First, the natural breeding. When the European colonists began to settle in eastern America, they often brought with them cuttings from their own vinifera vineyards back home in France, Spain, Italy, and Germany. These tender vines found the going very rough during hot, humid summers which gave rise to fungus, mildew, and disease, as well as during bitterly cold winters that often snuffed them out completely. As these early vineyards struggled and ultimately failed, they did manage to naturally cross-pollinate with many of the native species growing in nearby forests. These "native American" hybrids, natural crossings of vinifera with several native species, resulted in the development of many of today's best-known eastern American grapes including Concord, Delaware, Dutchess, and Niagara. These hybrids were very hardy and produced, from a winemaking standpoint, grapes vastly superior to their native parents.

Next, the accident. One of the many pests of the grape vine is the microscopic louse, *Phylloxera vastatrix*. This insect slowly feeds on the roots of grape vines, causing them to lose vigor and eventually die. Centuries of natural selection in this country caused hardy native species to be totally immune to the effects of phylloxera. Unfortunately, when world travelers happened to bring cuttings of American vines (with their soil infested with phylloxera) to Europe, the Europeans found, to their great dismay, that vitis vinifera vines were not so lucky. During the last half of the 19th century, this louse spread throughout the land, destroying thousands of acres of the greatest vineyards in France, Spain, and Italy. Just when all seemed lost, a few creative growers hit upon the idea that, if vinifera cuttings were grafted onto hardy American vine rootstock, phylloxera could be quelled. They were right, and today almost every vinifera vine in the world is grafted onto rootstock of some American variety or another.

Finally, the scientific approach. It didn't take the modern scientific and agricultural communities of Europe and America too long to understand that the same hybridization that had occurred naturally in eastern America could also take place in a controlled setting in a laboratory. Two main factors stimulated extreme interest in hybridization in the middle part of this century. First, it was commonly believed that vitis vinifera varieties could never be successfully grown on a commercial level in the eastern U.S. or other inhospitable climates in Europe. Second, the native-American hybrids simply did not produce wine of the quality desired by those used to drinking vinifera wines. The strong, grapey, "foxy" flavors associated with Concord and Catawba grapes was simply too assertive for "European" palates. So it was theorized that by carefully crossing various native species with vinifera species, new grape varieties could be developed which combined the hardiness and durability of the natives with the flavor qualities of the vinifera. Numerous scientists, mainly French, with names like Baco, Seyve-Villard, Seibel, Vidal, and Burdin developed a plethora of, for lack of a better term, "French-American" hybrids. So many were developed that, for a time, they simply bore the name of the hybridizer and a number. Over time, the better ones have been isolated and have had more colorful names applied to them like Chancellor, Seyval Blanc, and Villard Noir. In more recent years, other hybridizers in Germany and in this country at the Geneva Experimental Station in New York have continued to develop other vinifera/native hybrids such as the variety called Cayuga White. These exciting grapes and the promising wines they produce have been largely responsible for stimulating a resurgence in the eastern wine industry in the last thirty years.

For a variety of reasons, all four of these "families" of grapes can be found in the mid-Atlantic, adding immeasurably to the interest of this as a winegrowing region. Contrary to dire predictions that persisted up until just a few years ago, vinifera varieties have been cultivated successfully by more and more growers in Virginia and Maryland due to a number of important scientific advances:

• Better understanding of the importance of site selection allows growers to identify and plant their vines in locations that promise healthier growing conditions.

• Modern fungicides allow growers to keep damaging mildews and diseases in check during hot, humid summers.

• Equally advanced insecticides keep pests at bay.

• Viticultural techniques such as hilling up dirt around vines as insulation in winter and delaying pruning until spring help tender vines better survive extreme cold and variable springs.

Still, many growers experience occasional problems growing vinifera in this region. Mother Nature has the last word when it comes to deciding when it will or will not rain, when frost will form in the spring, and how cold it will get on any given day in the winter. Thus, many growers happily plant French-American hybrids alongside their vinifera vines, secure in knowing that the hybrids will hold up through thick and thin. Many are so pleased with the performance of these grapes that they bottle their wines as 100% varietals. Others, increasingly, are recognizing the value of French-American hybrids as sturdy and reliable blending wines.

A few growers continue to grow native-American hybrids in their vineyards, though their numbers are decreasing in Maryland and Virginia. An occasional Dutchess or Delaware will appear, and it is always interesting to taste how the vintner has handled these wilder tasting grapes.

Finally, let us not forget the place where this discussion started: honest-to-goodness native-American species. In North Carolina, nearly the entire grape industry of the state depends on the cultivation of the vitis rotundifolia, or Muscadine, varieties—the most famous being the Scuppernong. Here, too, researchers at such institutions as North Carolina State University have worked hard at crossing various Muscadines with other Muscadines in order to produce grapes more suitable for winemaking.

With the preceding serving as a brief overview of grapes and viticulture, the following list highlights some of the more important individual varieties being grown in the territory of the mid-Atlantic.

VITIS VINIFERA

Chardonnay

This white vinifera is certainly the darling of today's wine industry. Consumer demand for Chardonnay wines has skyrocketed during the last several years, and for good reason. The grape has proven to be amazingly versatile and succeeds wonderfully in a broad range of climates. Its bright apple and pear fruit flavors have been crafted by vintners into full-blown, ripe, buttery, and oaky versions of Chardonnay, as well as elegant, less assertive, lean versions more suitable for accompanying food. In France, it is the major white variety of Burgundy, and there produces tightly structured wines of significant complexity and depth. In California, pronounced lush and forward fruit is its main strength. In the mid-Atlantic, Chardonnays can exhibit the best of both these regions: a warm growing season ripens lush and intense apple-like fruit while periods of cool, intemperate weather retain high levels of natural acids, lending an attractive leanness and potential for long aging.

Cabernet Sauvignon

The most popular of the red vinifera varieties, Cabernet Sauvignon is the main grape of the Bordeaux region of France. This grape, which is a late ripener and thus requires a long growing season, produces wines of impressive strength and depth as well as subtlety and elegance. Ripe berry, cassis, and black currant fruit flavors are often enhanced by layers of herbs, mint, chocolate, smoke, tar, and vegetal notes. Much like Chardonnay, Cabernet is versatile and produces wines of varying style depending on the growing location. In Bordeaux, wines are often lean and tight, with elegant and complex fruitiness. In California, ripe, full-bodied fruit tends to dominate the impression. Again, the mid-Atlantic shows great promise to become a top Cabernet producer (in terms of quality). Vines in the region are still young and thus have barely begun to approach their potential. However, strong early examples reflect the ripe fullness of the mid-Atlantic's hot summer, yet retain a tight, lower pH/higher acid structure similar to Bordeaux.

Riesling

This is the famous white vinifera variety from Germany, which has been known to produce excellent wines that vary in style from bone dry to exotically sweet. Often lean and austere, the best Rieslings balance acids with some residual sugar and display bright, delicate, floral fruit flavors and aromas reminiscent of peaches, apricots, and citrus. Riesling is a variety that excels in cool climates. In warmer climates, however, the grape seems to suffer. In the mid-Atlantic, results have been extremely variable. More often than not, examples tend to display clumsy, dirty flavors and lack the delicacy of Rieslings from cooler regions. Since the grape cluster is very tight, the variety is susceptible to breakage and rot if late season rains hit the vineyard. Because late season rains often hit the mid-Atlantic, vintners are often forced to pick Riesling before it reaches full ripeness. On occasion, and consistently by certain producers, successful Rieslings are made. Skilled winemakers using the "sweet reserve" method to finish their wines with residual sugar have been able to emphasize the delicate floral and apricot traits of the variety.

Merlot

Merlot, the second most important variety from France's Bordeaux region, is famous the world over for producing wines of the same depth and intensity as Cabernet Sauvignon, yet with a lovely softness that makes the wines approachable in their youth. In California, Merlot is becoming extremely popular for its generous fruit and precocious nature. This popularity has inspired vintners of the mid-Atlantic as well, and many vineyards have had small plots of Merlot planted. However, winegrowers in this part of the country are already learning that this grape is probably unsuitable for the region. It is less winter hardy than the Cabernet Sauvignon and thus often suffers winter kill. If that weren't enough, the Merlot grapes also possess extremely delicate, thin skins which are prone to breakage if late season rains strike. When skins break and sugary juice seeps out, rot is just around the corner. In good years, some wineries have succeeded in producing nice Merlots.

Cabernet Franc

Just as Merlot seems to be fading out, Cabernet Franc seems to be surging in popularity. This Bordeaux red's growing characteristics are much more similar to Cabernet Sauvignon; its loose clusters and thick grape skins allow it to hang in the vineyard through rain, ripen slowly and evenly, and produce wines of richness and depth. Thus far, its role is clearly as a blender with Cabernet Sauvignon. Only one winery has bottled it as a varietal when supplies permit.

Other Vinifera and a Look to the Future

Winegrowers in the mid-Atlantic continue to work with other classic vinifera varieties with mixed results. Cultivars which have succeeded wonderfully on occasion but continue to give growers fits due to their unreliability include Gewurztraminer (which is susceptible to both winter kill and late spring frost damage), Sauvignon Blanc (extremely winter tender), Semillon (a variable producer), and Pinot Noir (very tender and very susceptible to late season rot).

Several winegrowers interviewed for this book speculated on how well other vinifera varieties would grow in the mid-Atlantic. Mentioned more often than any other group, grape varieties of southern Europe were believed by many to be worthy of serious consideration. Individuals such as Ham Mowbray of Montbray Wine Cellars and Shep Rouse of Montdomaine Cellars felt that Italian reds Nebbiolo and Sangiovese might respond well to the warm, Mediterranean-like climate in southern Virginia. Similarly, varieties from the Rhone region of France, such as reds Syrah, Grenache, Mourvedre, and Cinsault, and whites Marsanne and Rousanne, should be tried. For all these grapes, winter hardiness would have to be tested on an experimental basis. But given the warmth of the region, unique wines from these varieties might succeed wonderfully.

FRENCH-AMERICAN HYBRIDS

Seyval

This variety continues to be the most popular white French-American hybrid in the eastern U.S. It consistently produces large crops of ripe, well-balanced, and healthy fruit. Its popularity in the winery seems due to its incredible versatility. Several wineries set out to produce Seyvals in a rich, full-bodied style similar to Chardonnay. By barrel-fermenting the wine, leaving it in contact with its yeast lees, and encouraging the wine to complete malolactic fermentation, complex, oaky, buttery wines with ripe apple components can be produced. Other wineries, however, strive to create more delicate, fruity wines suitable for consumption with food. By fermenting slowly and at cool temperatures in stainless steel, crisp apple and grapefruit flavored wines can be made which often possess a grassy herbaceousness reminiscent of a good Sauvignon Blanc or Muscadet. The public has been slow to appreciate the virtues of Seyval and, in all honesty, when it is not handled well in the winery, the grape produces singularly mediocre wines. However, the name is becoming more commonplace, and Seyval should grow to fill a viable role as an everyday, low-priced varietal. In the mid-Atlantic, where seafood is so abundant and of high quality, Seyval seems an especially appropriate match.

Vidal

If Seyval is the most popular white French-American hybrid, Vidal is not far behind and is quickly gaining ground. Again, it is a consistent bearer of healthy, well-balanced fruit that ripens quite late in the season. It is also a very versatile grape and probably comes closest to mimicking the Riesling in its floral delicacy and citrusy, apricot fruitiness. Most successful versions are fermented slowly at cool temperatures in stainless steel, and then finished with slight residual sugar. Since it can be produced inexpensively, Vidal's future is as a low-priced, versatile aperitif-style wine, ideal for sipping and thirst-quenching on a hot, humid mid-Atlantic summer afternoon.

Chambourcin

Chambourcin is quickly becoming the red French-American hybrid of choice in the mid-Atlantic. A consistent producer, the grape produces wines of deep, almost inky color, medium body, and rich berry fruit with strong smoky, spicy, tarry overtones. It lends itself to aging in American oak very well. One might compare it to something like a Zinfandel, Petite Syrah, or maybe even a Rhone Chateauneuf-du-Pape. Like all hybrids, it is quite low in price and thus fills a natural role as a pasta, pizza, or hamburger wine. Such a description doesn't quite do Chambourcin justice—it is a wine that does well on any occasion demanding a spicy, medium-bodied red.

Foch

Sometimes labeled "Marechal Foch," this variety has confounded winemakers in this region; until very recently, winemakers have not quite known how to handle it! A very early ripener, this deeply colored red can produce intensely herbaceous, unpleasant wines when it is fermented in a traditional manner, in full contact with its skins. Shortening skin contact and lowering fermentation temperatures succeed in emphasizing the grape's cherry/berry fruitiness, creating base wines appropriate for blending. Some wineries have had moderate success eliminating all skin contact to produce rosé wines (the grape's free run juice is simply too dark to produce a "blush"). Perhaps the most promising direction some winemakers have chosen for Foch is to serve a Gamay-like role in producing Nouveau wines. The grape is well suited to the Beaujolais whole-berry fermentation method called "carbonic maceration" and has produced strikingly fresh and fruity quaffers.

Chancellor

Another red that is reliable and yields ample crops, Chancellor ripens mid-season and can produce pleasant if unspectacular wines of bright cherry and berry fruitiness, medium body, and good color. Some wineries bottle Chancellor as a varietal while others use it as a blender.

Other French-American Hybrids

A whole slew of other French-American hybrids is cultivated throughout the mid-Atlantic, some more successfully than others. Some varieties are definitely on the upswing in popularity among growers, such as the lovely and delicate Cayuga White, while others seem destined to fade into obscurity, such as the acidic and uninteresting Aurora. Occupying acreage in many vineyards across Maryland and Virginia can be found varieties such as the difficult-to-grow reds Baco Noir and Cascade, the attractively fruity red Chelois, the intense and herbaceous red DeChaunac, the Foch look- and grow-alike Leon Millot, the fruity but simple white Villard Blanc, its spicy red cousin Villard Noir, and the obscure but often delightful white Rayon d'Or.

Blending Vinifera with French-American Hybrids

As a preview of things to come, it is appropriate here to mention an important new trend in mid-Atlantic winemaking. Let it first be said that some of the most exciting wines currently being produced in this region are also some of the best bargains. Winemakers have discovered that, by blending small but meaningful proportions of vinifera wine into wines made from French-American hybrids, significantly more complex, flavorful wines can be produced. Many wineries have begun to offer wonderfully drinkable, everyday table wines, which are based on French-American hybrids — and are therefore quite inexpensive — enhanced and refined by blending with carefully chosen vinifera wines.

Some of the best examples are delicate white wines made from Vidal blended with Riesling, or crisp and dry Seyvals blended with Chardonnay. Several red hybrids such as Chancellor and Chambourcin are measurably improved when 10-20% Cabernet Sauvignon is added. These wines will be pointed out throughout this touring guide.

NATIVE-AMERICAN SPECIES AND HYBRIDS

Clearly not big players in the wine scenes of Maryland and Virginia, native-American hybrids fill a limited, select role. In a few cases, aromatic white grapes such as the Delaware and Niagara are made into dessert wines. The Dutchess variety, a white possessing the least overt "foxy" grapiness of this group, is made by a few wineries into a dry, fairly complex, high acid table wine. Concord, the most widely planted native hybrid, is used mainly as a table grape variety.

Down in North Carolina, however, the biggest "players" in the state are members of the native species vitis rotundifolia. These unique grapes will be discussed extensively in the section on North Carolina. For now, suffice it to say that white varieties Carlos, Magnolia, and Scuppernong, and the red Noble, are the most widely planted and vinified.

WINE TOURING IN MARYLAND
AN OVERVIEW

Unlike the state of Virginia, which can point to a rich history related to winegrowing (from the early Jamestown settlers to diligent efforts by one of the fathers of our country, Thomas Jefferson), Maryland's evolution as a wine-producing state is really a tale focused on modern history.

Men like Philip Wagner and G. Hamilton "Ham" Mowbray played instrumental roles in nurturing a young, inexperienced industry not only in their home states but up and down the entire eastern seaboard as well. It was Wagner, a war correspondent for the *Baltimore Sun*, who smuggled vine cuttings out of war-torn Europe in the 1940s. Grape hybridizers in France had been hard at work crossing classic vinifera varieties with hardier American cultivars in an effort to create new breeds that could stand up to the harshest of climates. Wagner had a vision that, equipped with these French-American hybrids, Maryland might become successful wine country. His vision and later deeds were to revolutionize the entire eastern winegrowing industry.

Ham Mowbray would also break new ground for the Maryland wine industry. A firm supporter of French-American hybrids, Ham also believed he could cultivate the classic vinifera varieties in the mid-Atlantic. When everyone else thought he was crazy, all Ham did was produce the state's first Chardonnay, Cabernet Sauvignon, and Riesling wines.

Modern Maryland provides the wine tourist with eleven wineries from which to choose. A state for those with adventurous palates, the visitor can encounter wines of all types—viniferas, French-American hybrids, and even fruit wines. In the eastern part of the state, north of Baltimore, a tour can include up to four wineries, including the state's oldest and two of its newest. Along the corridor between Baltimore and Frederick, in the central portion of the state, a convenient concentration of five winegrowers can be found. And further west, two more vintners are producing wine—one high in the Catoctin Mountains, the other on the edge of the historic Antietam Civil War battlefield.

Again, in contrast to their neighbors to the south, Maryland winegrowers have had to forge an industry purely on their initiative. Until very recently, support from the state has been nonexistent. In spite of this disadvantage, strong associations of Maryland wineries and grape growers have created a supportive atmosphere allowing for slow but steady growth.

Today, there are around a hundred acres of grapes being cultivated in Maryland. More than fifty independent growers split their acreage almost evenly between vinifera and French-American hybrid varieties, as seen below.

GRAPE ACREAGE BY VARIETY

Vinifera		French-Amer. Hybrids		Native-Amer. Hybrids	
Chardonnay	18%	Seyval	22%	All types	1%
Cabernet Sau-vignon	16%	Vidal	9%		
		Chambourcin	6%		
Riesling	7%	Chancellor	3%		
Cabernet Franc	6%	Foch	3%		
		Villard Blanc	2%		
Others	2%	Others	5%		
TOTALS	49%		50%		

Maryland is located in the heart of an area that has been called the "Golden Crescent." This large, semicircular region starts in southeastern Pennsylvania, curves in a southwesterly direction to encompass the Catoctin Mountains in western Maryland and the upper reaches of the Blue Ridge Mountains in northern Virginia, and then arcs back toward the sea to include the piedmont of central and eastern Virginia. This mid-Atlantic region has been increasingly singled out by experts as one particularly well suited to the growing of wine grapes and the production of fine wines.

It won't take long for the wine tourist to discover that many of the very finest wines the Golden Crescent has to offer are produced in the state of Maryland.

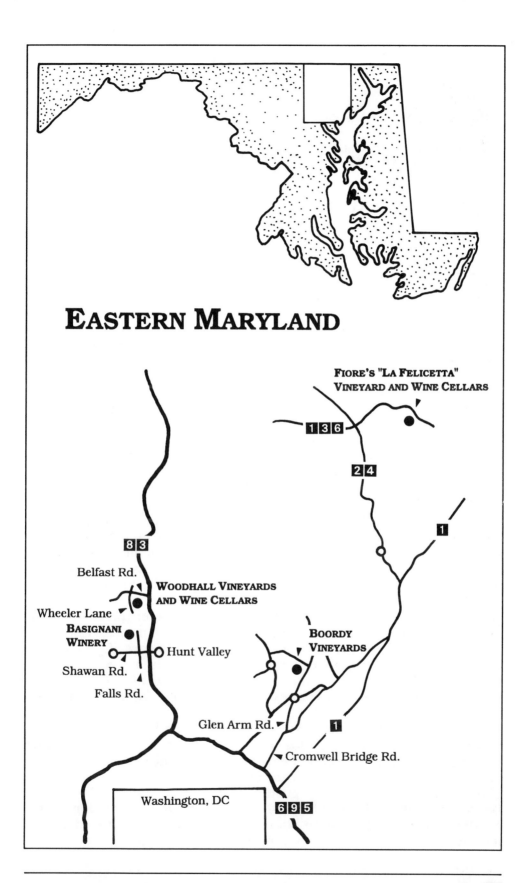

EASTERN MARYLAND

FIORE'S "LA FELICETTA"
VINEYARD AND WINE CELLARS

1 3 6

2 4

1

8 3

Belfast Rd.

WOODHALL VINEYARDS
AND WINE CELLARS

Wheeler Lane

BASIGNANI
WINERY

Hunt Valley

BOORDY
VINEYARDS

Shawan Rd.

Falls Rd.

Glen Arm Rd.

1

Cromwell Bridge Rd.

Washington, DC

6 9 5

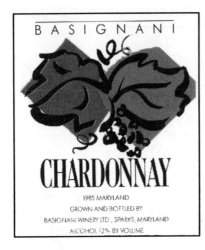

Basignani Winery

ADDRESS: 15722 Falls Road
Sparks, MD 21152
PHONE: (301) 472-4718
OWNERS: Bertero and Marilyn Basignani
WINEMAKER: Bert Basignani
TOTAL ACRES: 8.5
CASES/YR: 1,200
HOURS: Saturday 12-5, Sunday 1-6; please
      call ahead for appointment

In the gorgeous rural landscape north of Baltimore, just a few miles off Interstate 83, is Maryland's newest and from all early signs perhaps one of its best wineries. It is Basignani Winery, named for Bertero "Bert" Basignani, whose hobby of growing grapes and making wine finally got the best of him.

A second generation American of Italian descent, Bert was raised in the Baltimore area in a family who "always had wine on the table." With grandparents who were home winemakers, it was only a matter of time before Bert tried his hand at the noble art. "In 1973, I went to the farmers market in downtown Baltimore and bought several boxes of muscat grapes which were shipped in from the Central Valley of California by rail. I made my first wine and it was truly horrible stuff, but I was definitely hooked," explains Bert.

A rugged, strong individual with a thick, dark beard and a warm, ever-present smile, Bert was not too quick to pursue his newly discovered love. Instead, he joined his father's business — Lawrence Construction Co.—and helped build countless churches and buildings on college campuses such as Johns Hopkins. His father is still very active in directing the business, which has most recently begun building several life-care communities for the elderly.

In his spare time, he planted grapes. An experimental acre in 1975 was followed by a small planting of vinifera. "In their first growing season, the vines grew like crazy. I thought to myself, 'What's everybody so worked up about with vinifera? This is a piece of cake,'" says Bert. The following winter and spring, when nearly every vine was killed or damaged by cold extremes or spring frost, Bert had his answer.

Undaunted, he continued to plant more and more vines, both hardy French-American hybrids and vinifera, while at the same time hanging around with well-known winemaking neighbors like Ham Mowbray of Montbray Vineyards and Marvin Yengst, a retired biochemist who is known as the guru of Maryland amateur winemakers. By the mid-1980s, Bert's vineyard and winery were producing at levels that jeopardized his legal status as "amateur." Encouraged by numerous successes in amateur competitions, he applied for and received a license in October 1986. Suddenly, Basignani Winery was a reality.

THE VINEYARD

Basignani's 8.5 acre vineyard is perched on a gentle slope rising behind his home. An experimenter, Bert has (over the years) planted ten varieties in order to judge which would fare best in a region where only one other vineyard is nearby (see Woodhall Vineyards and Wine Cellars). Today, white vinifera varieties Chardonnay and Riesling share rows next to reds Cabernet Sauvignon and Merlot. The French-American hybrid Seyval receives equal space with Chardonnay at 1.75 acres, followed by smaller amounts of white hybrid Vidal and red hybrids Chambourcin, Chancellor, and Foch.

GRAPE VARIETIES AND ACREAGE

French/Amer. Variety	Vinifera	Hybrids
Chardonnay	1.75	—.—
Seyval	—.—	1.75
Cabernet Sauvignon	1.4	—.—
Chambourcin	—.—	0.75
Chancellor	—.—	0.75
Foch	—.—	0.5
Riesling	0.5	—.—
Merlot	0.3	—.—
Vidal	—.—	0.3
Miscellaneous	—.—	0.5
TOTALS	3.95	4.55

When wandering through the vineyard, visitors might notice some vines growing in a rather unorthodox "bushy" manner rather than the single trunk usually seen in California vineyards. "I learned my lesson my first winter when so many vines were killed. Now, for Cabernet and Merlot, I grow multiple trunks and encourage bud growth low on the canes. In winter, this allows me to bend canes to the ground where I can bury them with insulating earth," explains Bert. So far, the labor-intensive technique is working well.

THE WINES

Basignani's current winery facility is certainly one of the most modest you could find on a mid-Atlantic wine tour. Not much larger than a converted garage, a certain charm exudes from this efficient workplace where practically every square foot of floor space is occupied by 60-gallon American oak barrels.

As a winemaker, Bert has been described by nearby neighbor and friend Robert Parker (writer and publisher of the influential consumer tasting and buying guide *The Wine Advocate*) as a purist and a traditionalist. In an April 1987 *Baltimore Sun* article, Parker was quoted as saying, "I think he's got what the great winemakers have. He knows what great wines are all about . . ."

This translates into classic, minimalist techniques of making wine. For example, all Bert's white wines (with the exception of Riesling) are barrel-fermented in small American oak cooperage, are inoculated for a secondary *malolactic fermentation*, and are allowed extended contact with the fermentation *lees* (the dead yeast cells that settle at the bottom of the barrel). His reds are allowed to rest undisturbed for twenty to twenty-four months in oak. In keeping with his bent towards minimal handling, none of his wines is filtered, and his whites are *fined* just enough to ensure *protein stability*. The result of these techniques is wines of incredible depth, warmth, concentration, and complexity.

Bert's liberal use of oak achieves much more than adding "woody" flavors to wines. As he explains, "What's more important than flavor enhancement is the fact that oak fermentation and aging allows wines to breathe, literally. Water and volatile gases escape through the pores of the wood, leaving cleaner, more concentrated flavors." This breathing simply cannot take place in stainless steel, nor does it have time to take place when finished wines are aged briefly in oak.

Bert's mentor relationship with Ham Mowbray certainly reveals itself when tasting his Seyval and Chardonnay. Basignani's Seyvals mimic Montbray's Seyve-Villard 5276 in style—the wines are wonderfully extracted, deeply fruited, and taste of rich, ripe apples and pears, set off against a measure of grassy herbaceousness, and balanced well with toasty oak.

Even better are the Chardonnays, which blend fruit from both older vines planted in 1978 and younger vines planted in 1983. In vintages like 1988 and 1986, these wines can easily compete not only with the best Chardonnays of the region, but also the best Chardonnays of the world. They are rich, complex, and exactingly clean and varietal. Spicy, toasty, almost butterscotchy oak notes surround fruit flavors of ripe, buttery green apples.

The Riesling is produced dry, with clean, spicy, floral fruit. Only due to the outstanding character of the previous two wines does this wine end up taking a back seat.

Bert's Cabernet Sauvignons (which usually have up to 10% Merlot blended in) and Merlots lend strong support to the argument that the mid-Atlantic can produce world class examples of these Bordeaux varieties. For the '84 through '87 vintages, the Cabernets are big and robust, with spicy cherry, cassis, and berry flavors framed by young, hard tannins and creamy vanillan oak. The Merlots are a bit lighter in body, but offer up pleasingly clean cherry fruit with soft, toasty oak notes. Termed his "versatility grape," Bert says that in years when his delicate Merlot produces an ample crop he will bottle it separately. In rough years, all of it will go into the Cab.

Not to be ignored are Basignani's everyday white and red, called Elena and Marisa (respectively) after his two daughters. The Marisa, especially, is a terrific value and reflects considerable winemaking skill. A blend of red hybrids Foch ("for fruit"), Chancellor ("for flesh"), and Chambourcin ("for complexity"), it has a dense nose of smoke, plums, and prunes. A deep, inky purple, the wine is soft and round, mouthfilling and full-bodied, and displays bright, vibrant cherry fruit rounded off by spicy oak. Like a good Cru Beaujolais, this wine is an inspiring example of how good red hybrid wines can be. The Elena offers considerably less excitement, but is still a nice, everyday white. A blend of the hybrids Villard Blanc and the virtually unknown Burdin, it is straightforward and fruity and is enhanced by buttery oakiness.

INCIDENTALLY . . .

One of the state's smaller wineries, Basignani produced just 1,200 cases in 1986. Future expansion will include a new tasting room at the vineyard and, if he can find suitable property, expanded vineyard plantings. For now, however, Bert's just "taking it slow and steady."

DIRECTIONS

Take Interstate 83 north from Baltimore. Exit at Shawan Road and turn left (west). Proceed to Falls Road and turn right. Drive north for a few miles, and .5 miles past Black Rock Road turn left into Basignani's driveway.

Boordy Vineyards

ADDRESS: 12820 Long Green Pike
Hydes, MD 21082
PHONE: (301) 592-5015
OWNERS: The Deford Family
WINEMAKERS: Rob Deford and Tom Burns
TOTAL ACRES: 16
CASES/YR: 7,500
HOURS: Monday through Saturday 10-5,
       Sunday 1-5, groups call for appointment

To tell the current story behind Boordy Vineyards, located in the beautiful Long Green Valley just north of Baltimore, we must focus on the handsome and energetic Rob Deford, operating owner and winemaker. But to focus only on Rob would do a disservice to Maryland's oldest pioneering vineyard and winery. To complete the story, we first must talk of Philip Wagner.

Philip Wagner can be credited for having started not only the modern wine industry in Maryland, but also for having, to a large degree, influenced much of the development of winegrowing up and down the east coast. Through Boordy Vineyards and Winery, established in 1945, he supplied many an eastern winegrower with his or her first vines and first lessons on how to grow grapes and make wine. Born in 1904 in New Haven, Connecticut, Wagner spent most of his career as a writer, and then editor, for the *Sun* papers of Baltimore. He acquired a taste for and interest in wine at an early age and published his first book on the topic, *American Wines and Winemaking*, in 1933. It was a few years later, as a war correspondent during the late 1930s, that Philip Wagner became acquainted with many of the leading grape hybridizers experimenting in the wine regions of France. By crossing classic vinifera with hardier American varieties, these botanists hoped to create new strains that could both survive harsh climates and produce high quality table wine.

Wagner was encouraged by what he saw and tasted, and intrigued by the idea of growing these French-American hybrids in his home state of Maryland, an area considered at the time to be capable of supporting only the sturdiest native varieties. By literally sneaking vine cuttings out of Europe in his suitcases and in his wife Jocelyn's purse, the Wagners were able to begin cultivating these new French-American hybrids. When it quickly became clear that hybrids could flourish in the mid-Atlantic, a small nursery was established, and Wagner was soon supplying growers all over the east with these breakthrough varieties.

Wagner's paramount interest was always in viticulture; however, a natural byproduct of his interest was lots of grapes! In 1945, a commercial winery license was obtained, and Boordy Vineyards began raising eyebrows throughout the wine world. Wagner's red, white, and rosé table wines were highly praised, and tasters were consistently stunned that wines of such quality could be produced on the east coast.

Over the years, Philip Wagner became a well-known figure across the country. Twice invited by the University of California at Davis to serve as Regents' Lecturer, awarded the *Officier du Merite Agricole* by the French government, Wagner also authored *A Wine Grower's Guide* in 1945 and in 1974, *Grapes Into Wine*, considered the amateur winemaker's bible. Always a champion of French-American hybrids, Wagner's underlying principle was that winegrowers, if they were to succeed, must successfully match the right grape variety with the right location. Living by this rule, Wagner was, in more recent times, known to vocally resist the movement towards vinifera expansion, stating that it violated this principle.

That brings us to the current era of Boordy Vineyards. In 1965, the Deford family of Hydes, Maryland ran a farm, which produced corn, tomatoes, beans, and turkeys. In order to diversify further, the family also planted French-American hybrid grapes, knowing that their friend, Philip Wagner, would happily use their crop for his wine production. Over the years, the Defords' son, Rob, grew up on the farm and among his daily chores were tasks like pruning and spraying vines and harvesting grapes. Later, Rob studied how things other than grapes grew, namely fungi, as he worked towards a degree in Mycology at the College of the Atlantic in Bar Harbor, Maine. "I had lots of fun one summer hunting mushrooms in the Andes Mountains in South America," he explains, "But when it came down to reality, I wasn't too optimistic about my being able to earn a living doing so!"

After several years in Maine, many of which were spent renovating a colonial farm and farmhouse, Rob returned to Maryland in 1978 when his father's health began to deteriorate. "I had only been home for a few months when Philip Wagner, who was eighty years old, contacted us to say he wanted to retire and sell Boordy," explains Rob. Many suitors to the Wagner legacy were interested, including Maryland U.S. Senator Bob Mathias, but it was the Deford family to whom Boordy was sold, with the family to take control before the 1980 crush. To prepare, Rob enrolled in the U.C. Davis enology program and completed one year of the two-year curriculum.

Rob describes the situation: "I came back from Davis in the summer of 1980, with just a couple of months to prepare for harvest. Our farm had to be renovated, equipment needed to be ordered, and to top it off, an unusually warm summer had grapes coming in on August 10th—the earliest harvest on record. It was a wild start!"

Under Rob's direction, the first vintage continued Wagner's practice of releasing three blended wines, a white, a red, and a rosé. Interestingly, recent years have seen Boordy experiment and grow, so that now the winery offers ten different bottlings. In 1986, the winery even produced its first vinifera wines — a Chardonnay and a Cabernet Sauvignon—something that Philip Wagner did not look fondly upon. But no hard feelings were engendered. As Rob explains, "I feel like a second generation winemaker here. Philip is here helping out quite often and takes a great interest in how things are progressing. I'm learning from him all the time. But I also felt I had to experiment. In the past, vinifera were largely out of the realm of possibility. Today, technology allows us to succeed. In the past, people were shocked that the east could even produce a palatable wine. Today, people are coming to expect great wines from this area."

Boordy offers visitors a unique chance to be exposed to the rich heritage of eastern winegrowing's past as well as the pioneering spirit of a young and creative new force. Under the able direction of Rob Deford, Boordy takes a special place in the ranks of mid-Atlantic wineries.

THE VINEYARD

While the Boordy location is striking, in a fertile green valley dotted with lovely rustic farms, it is not necessarily the best site for growing grapes. Vines are planted on a northwest-facing slope, which enjoys neither the benefits of early morning sun nor late afternoon warmth. Winter kill is a common problem. The way Rob sees it, "If we can grow grapes here, we can grow them anywhere! That is why we've relied on hybrids on the farm with just a small plot of vinifera."

As displayed below, 11 of the estate's 16 acres are planted to French- American hybrids (white varieties Seyval and Vidal, and red varieties Chancellor, Chambourcin, and Foch), and a 3-acre experimental plot of Cabernet Sauvignon was added in 1984. The vines have, thus far, fared quite well and produced their first crop in 1986. Additional small plantings are testing out the viability of vinifera varieties like Riesling.

GRAPE VARIETIES AND ACREAGE

Variety	Vinifera	French/Amer. Hybrids
Seyval	—.—	3.0
Vidal	—.—	3.0
Cabernet Sauvignon	3.0	—.—
Chancellor	—.—	2.0
Riesling	1.0	—.—
Chambourcin	—.—	1.0
Foch	—.—	1.0
Chardonnay	2.0	—.—
Miscellaneous	—.—	1.0
TOTALS	6.0	11.0

Because of the small size of Boordy's own vineyard, the winery purchases about 60% of its fruit each year. Primary sources for grapes (in particular, vinifera) have been on the Eastern Shore of Maryland, where more moderate temperatures hold great promise for grape cultivation.

THE WINES

Inside the impressive rustic barn on the Boordy farm lies a well-equipped modern winery, barrel room, and tasting area. Jacketed stainless steel tanks ferment all white wines at cool temperatures to preserve fruitiness and delicacy. American oak barrels are used for aging certain fuller-bodied whites and most reds.

Tasting the wines at Boordy is a wonderfully diverse experience. Although produced in limited quantities, one must start by discussing Boordy's two "wines of the vintage": the red "Nouveau" and white "Nouvelle." Rob Deford and assistant winemaker Tom Burns have perfected the art of creating an utterly terrific Beaujolais-style wine by employing the technique of *carbonic maceration* (in which whole, uncrushed berries are allowed to ferment internally, producing fresh fruity wines of good color and low tannin) with the hybrid varieties Foch, Chancellor, and Chambourcin. Fermented, cold stabilized, filtered, and bottled all in the course of six to eight weeks, the "Nouveau" is released each November with considerable fanfare. With a keen sense of marketing, Deford has unveiled each year's "Nouveau" under special circumstances; one year he arranged a police motorcade to escort him, in a limousine, to a downtown Baltimore French restaurant. Another year saw him organize a fund-raiser for the Chesapeake Bay Foundation. Rob rode into Baltimore's Inner Harbor amid a parade of tugboats and police vessels.

But rest assured, behind all the hype is a real product. Each year, the "Nouveau" has consistently offered a wine possessing a lovely, ruby color with youthful, purple edges (avoiding the ominous, inky purple/black so often seen in nouveaux made from Foch) and enticing, warm carbonic scent of cherries and strawberries. In the mouth, the wine is supple, soft, and engagingly fruity with fresh cherry and strawberry flavors and a slight background of green olive herbaceousness. It really could pass for a first-rate Beaujolais Nouveau!

Beginning in 1987, Boordy began to offer "Nouveau's" sister, "Nouvelle." Actually a cold-fermented Vidal, sweetened to about 2% *residual sugar* (sugar contact at bottling) by adding a *sweet reserve* of unfermented Riesling juice, the Nouvelle is also released each year in November (quite a feat given that Vidal is harvested as late as mid-October). It, too, is pleasing and exuberantly fruity; a lovely companion to its sibling.

The winery's four dry whites offer variety in their own right. The Seyval is fermented to dryness in stainless steel and receives brief aging in oak. The wine has a creamy, slightly herbal nose, and crisp, bone-dry fruit that recalls a nice Italian Pinot Grigio.

Boordy also makes a terrific Seyval "Sur Lie Reserve." Barrel fermented and aged on its fermentation *lees* for five months, the wine rivals the great Seyvals produced by Maryland colleague Ham Mowbray at Montbray Wine Cellars. Successful vintages like 1986 and 1988 found the wine possessing a beautiful, complex nose of wildflowers, herbs, and yeast. In the mouth it is round, full-bodied but never heavy, with rich, slightly grassy and buttery apple and pear flavors touched by toasty vanillan notes. This limited production wine is available only at the winery.

Boordy's Chardonnay is made from 100% Maryland fruit. A lovely rendering in each of its three first vintages, the wine is lean, crisp, and emphasizes lemony, green apple fruit, with a touch of hazelnuts, in a very refreshing style.

Finally, the "Premium White," a blend of hybrids Chardonnay, Vidal, and Seyval, offers dry, pleasant, somewhat earthy flavors.

In the past, Boordy produced only red wines made from blends of hybrid varieties. The lineup was altered and streamlined in 1987 with the release of the winery's first vinifera red—the '86 Petit Cabernet. (The special name was used for this release due to its lighter style and the fact that it was produced from three-year-old vines). From the '87 vintage, a full-fledged Cab was bottled. It has a correct Cabernet nose, and offers tightly knit, somewhat lean ripe cherry and currant flavors.

As the Cabernet's partner, Boordy will continue to produce its Premium Red, a peppery, robust blend of Chancellor, Foch, and Chambourcin. Fermented in contact with the skins for just three days to avert the excess herbaceousness that can sometimes hamper red hybrids, the wine is medium-bodied with clean, chubby berry and cherry flavors.

In the semi-sweet category, Boordy also produces a spicy, floral, crisp Vidal (with 2% residual sugar) and a clean, berryish blanc de noir Blush made from the free run juice of red hybrids Chelois and Villard Noir, with a bit of Vidal (10%) added to accent fruitiness.

INCIDENTALLY . . .

Boordy is the latest entrant in the mid-Atlantic sparkling wine business. While not available in time to taste for this book, Boordy has begun bottling small quantities of méthode champenoise blanc de blanc, made entirely from Chardonnay. Keep a lookout for this exciting new wine.

DIRECTIONS

From the Baltimore Beltway, take Exit 29 (left onto Cromwell Bridge Road) follow to Glen Arm Road. Turn left and proceed three miles to Long Green Pike. Turn left and continue two miles to winery on the left.

Fiore's "La Felicetta" Vineyard and Wine Cellars

ADDRESS: 3026 Whiteford Road, Md. Rt. 136 Pylesville, MD 21132
PHONE: (301) 836-7605/1860
OWNERS: Michael, Rose, and Eric Fiore
WINEMAKER: Michael Fiore
TOTAL ACRES: 5.5
CASES/YR: 2,000
HOURS: Saturday and Sunday 12-6, or by appointment

Within a stone's throw of the Pennsylvania border lies Maryland's northernmost and easternmost winery—Fiore's La Felicetta Vineyard and Wine Cellars near Pylesville in Harford County. Owned by the gregarious Michael Fiore, this operation (bonded in the fall of 1986) takes its name (La Felicetta—Little Happiness) from Mike's exuberant and enthusiastic feelings towards his rebirth as a winegrower.

Mike Fiore's life story is a long and varied one, filled with adventure, joyful triumphs, and tragic setbacks. Born in the Calabria region of southern Italy, Fiore grew up in a family that cultivated 300 acres of grapes for a government-owned winery cooperative. (With a long history of involvement with wine, Mike's mother was actually a descendant of the Mazzei family. Filippo Mazzei originally tried to grow grapes with Thomas Jefferson in colonial Virginia.) Mike recalls fondly this picturesque land where he could look out across the Mediterranean and see Mt. Aetna on the distant shores of Greece. When his father died in the late 1950s, the seventeen-year-old Fiore was left to care for the family's 300 acres. Finding the stress and responsibility nearly overwhelming, he left the operation to his brothers and mother and set out for America.

Over the next several years, Mike lived the life of "a bad boy of the '60s." A self-proclaimed beatnik, he worked odd jobs, hung out, and drank a lot of espresso in Cambridge, Massachusetts and became a part of the Harvard University community. Missing his wine roots, Mike recalls buying a 50-gallon oak barrel and for several years bought hundreds of pounds of California Zinfandel grapes at the Boston farmers market so that he could make wine.

Needing a change in scenery and lifestyle, Mike moved to Baltimore in 1965 where he began working for that city's utility company. He met his wife Rose shortly thereafter and they had two sons, Anthony and Eric. Wanting to raise their family in the country, Mike and Rose found their present home and moved there in 1975 because the rolling rural landscape reminded them of Mike's homeland.

In 1981, their happy life was struck by tragedy when, at the age of sixteen, the Fiores' son Anthony died in an accident. Consumed with grief, it was during the aftermath of Anthony's death that Mike began planting his vineyard. "It was like therapy for me. I was in the field twelve hours a day," he describes. A few years later, when his second son Eric married and his daughter-in-law gave birth to Mike's first grandson, Mike came to the realization that "it was time to stop crying and to begin celebrating." Eric named the child Anthony, after his brother. As Mike reflects philosophically, "If Anthony had not died, I probably wouldn't have ever started my vineyard. Now, my grandchild is here and I've committed myself to building this all for him."

Today, with an attractive new winery building, and a lovely vineyard coming into full maturity, the Fiores are looking forward to a bright future.

THE VINEYARD

Due to the risks associated with growing grapes in this cold northern region of the state, Mike chose to establish his vineyard initially to hardy French- and native-American hybrid varieties. His largest planting is to the white grape Vidal—3 acres. An additional acre of Seyval was recently planted. Rounding out Fiore's 5.5 acres of grapes are red varieties Chambourcin, Chancellor, and Foch and a small plot of the white native hybrid Dutchess.

GRAPE VARIETIES AND ACREAGE

Variety	Vinifera	French/Amer. Hybrids
Vidal	—.—	3.0
Seyval	—.—	1.0
Chambourcin	—.—	0.5
Chancellor	—.—	0.5
Foch	—.—	0.25
Dutchess	—.—	0.25
TOTALS	0.0	5.5

While he draws similarities between the grapes he's chosen to grow and those of his homeland ("Vidal reminds me of Trebbiano and Chancellor of the grapes we'd use for our 'peasant red'"), Mike still plans on adding an 8-acre expansion of vinifera vines. Located on a well-exposed, southern-facing slope, Fiore plans to plant Chardonnay, Cabernet Sauvignon and, as an experiment, Zinfandel and perhaps Malvasia.

"I grew up on Zinfandel! How could I not try it?" he exclaims. To the north in Pennsylvania, Mike's good friend Dick Naylor of Naylor Vineyards has successfully produced a medium-bodied Zinfandel, which Mike feels is a promising start.

THE WINES

At the time of this writing, Fiore bottled four wines: a 100% Vidal Blanc, a small amount of Dutchess, and two proprietary wines called Vino Bianco (100% Vidal fermented with Italian yeast) and Vino Rosso (a blend of Foch, Chambourcin, and Chancellor). As time passes and new vines begin producing, this lineup will probably evolve. Mike hopes to reach a total annual output of 2,000 cases.

Fiore's winemaking emphasizes the production of the cleanest, fruitiest wine possible. He goes to great length to achieve this goal. For each of his wines, he keeps only the *free run juice* of freshly crushed grapes and does not use any of the harsher *press juice*. After chilling the juices at 40°, he adds a polyclear fining material that helps pull any suspended solids to the bottom of the tanks. He then separates the clear juice from the sediment, inoculates it with yeast, and when fermentation is half complete, adds another fining material, bentonite, to clarify the new wines further. All fermentations take place at a cool 55° in order to preserve fruitiness. While such methods of extensive finings are a bit unorthodox, Mike feels they are justified. He hopes to, one day, purchase a centrifuge, which is often used in the high-tech wineries of California in order to clarify fresh grape juice.

Both the Vidal and Vino Bianco reflect their winemaking process. They are delicate and crisp, and while a bit shy on fruit, are clean and pleasant. The Vino Bianco, which is processed in the exact manner as the Vidal except for Mike's use of a rare Italian yeast, is the fruitier of the two. Tasting side by side offers an interesting comparison of the different effects of wine yeasts.

Fiore's Vino Rosso is a rosé produced as described above, in the white wine method. It has a light brick/red color darker than a typical blush, and possesses crisp, straightforward cherry fruit flavors. Light oaky flavors are derived from brief aging in American oak barrels. The wine would go nicely with pasta and barbecue fare.

The Dutchess is a delightful sweet, aperitif-style wine with 3% residual sugar. It has mouth-filling, viscous fruit with mild grapey/*labrusca* flavors.

In future years, Fiore plans to add a Chambourcin, fermented as a full-bodied red aged in French oak. "What the heck, I'm Italian so I can say this: I really want to produce a traditional, hearty, 'Dago Red' like the wines I grew up with. Perhaps the Chambourcin will fill this role," explains Mike.

INCIDENTALLY . . .

Mike Fiore has elaborate plans for enhancing the grounds at the winery. He would like to soon add a pavilion/picnic area in the midst of the vineyard, as well as a field for his guests to play Bocce Ball, an Italian form of lawn bowling.

DIRECTIONS

Take Route 1 north out of Baltimore. Follow the Bel Air bypass to Route 24 and turn left (north). Follow Route 24 until you reach Route 136 and turn right. Winery is .5 miles ahead on right.

Woodhall Chambourcin

Maryland
Red Wine
1985

Dry table wine produced and bottled by
Woodhall Vineyards and Wine Cellars, Inc.
Sparks, Maryland   Alcohol by volume 11.5%

Woodhall Vineyards and Wine Cellars

ADDRESS: 15115 Wheeler Lane
Sparks, MD 21152
PHONE: (301) 771-4664
OWNERS: Albert Copp, Herbert and Rufus Davis,
    Michael and Helle DeSimone, Kent and Carolyn
    Muhly
WINEMAKER: Albert Copp
TOTAL ACRES: 6.5
CASES/YR: 1,800
HOURS: Saturday and Sunday 10-5; please call
    ahead for appointment

Woodhall Vineyards and Wine Cellars is a truly communal project developed through the good-natured cooperation of seven individuals: Al Copp, Mike and Helle DeSimone, Herbert and Rufus Davis, and Kent and Carolyn Muhly. From its beginnings in amateur winemaking, through its early years as a small vineyard supplying other wineries, to its present state as a full-fledged winery (which was bonded in 1983), Woodhall has evolved and now produces five dry table wines from both noble vinifera and French-American hybrid varieties.

The idea of operating a commercial winery emerged slowly amongst the members of this spirited group. Al Copp, president of Baltimore's Inner Harbor Project, began making wine as a hobby in 1967. A member of the Chesapeake Bacchus club, he spent much of his spare time brokering grapes between growers and home winemakers and later managing a small crushing and pressing service for these groups. Al met Mike DeSimone, a realtor in the Baltimore area, in the early 1970s. They became fast friends and made wine together for many years. A fellow realtor and friend of Mike's, Herbert Davis, and his wife Rufus owned a 100-acre farm in the rolling dairy lands north of Baltimore. Lovers of fine wines themselves, the Davises offered part of their property for the growing of vines. The idea of starting a "commercial" winery occurred to them, and they announced the idea widely to their friends, neighbors, and amateur winemaking acquaintances. While nineteen individuals found "all sorts of reasons not join the group," says Al, Kent Muhly and his wife Carolyn thought it was a great idea. The first vines were planted in 1976, with additional acreage added each year until 1983. A license was received in that year, and the winery has produced approximately 1,800 cases of wine each year since.

The current setting for Woodhall is gorgeous. A large farmhouse dating to 1790 sits adjacent to a wonderful old barn, which functioned for decades as home for dairy cattle. It now is filled with stainless steel dairy tanks (converted for fermenting wine) and rows of American oak barrels. A gentle slope falls away from the barn to the southeast and at the bottom, on a facing slope, sits a long, rectangular 6.5 acre vineyard.

Duties and responsibilities are divided up fairly among the group: Al directs all winemaking while Mike takes the lead in vineyard management and spraying. Rufus, Herbert, Kent, Carolyn, and Helle pitch in at harvest, bottling, and racking, and also take shared responsibility for selling and distributing the product. Since all are involved with busy careers, Woodhall is really a weekend operation. Each Saturday's and Sunday's work is usually highlighted by a sumptuous potluck lunch of dishes each partner brings. At harvest time, this event is magnified ten-fold as the group brings friends and volunteers from all over to help pick grapes in the morning and feast on a huge Bacchanalian picnic in the afternoon.

THE VINEYARD

Woodhall's 6.5 acres are devoted primarily to seven varieties — four whites and three reds. Leading the way is the white French-American hybrid Seyval with two acres. Three other hybrids — the white Vidal and reds Foch and Chambourcin — each have one acre devoted to them. Vinifera varieties, being less winter hardy and thus riskier in this relatively untested region of the state, are planted sparingly. One-half acre each is planted to white varieties Riesling and Chardonnay and the red Cabernet Sauvignon. Rounding out the vineyard are single experimental rows of red hybrids Chancellor and Chelois and the white hybrid Vignoles, which is rarely planted in the mid-Atlantic but enjoys widespread success in the Finger Lakes region of New York.

GRAPE VARIETIES AND ACREAGE

Variety	Vinifera	French/Amer. Hybrids
Seyval	—.—	2.0
Chambourcin	—.—	1.0
Foch	—.—	1.0
Vidal	—.—	1.0
Chardonnay	0.5	—.—
Riesling	0.5	—.—
Cabernet Sauvignon	0.5	—.—
TOTALS	1.5	5.0

To supplement its own crop, Woodhall purchases about two-thirds of its fruit each year from other Maryland growers with whom they have long-standing relationships. A normal source of Vidal, Foch, and Chambourcin, for example, is neighbor Bert Basignani.

THE WINES

Currently six wines are produced at Woodhall; each quite different in style, ensuring that nearly everyone can find something to their liking at the winery.

In the serious white table wine category, Woodhall's Seyval fits nicely. After settling and inoculation with yeast while in stainless steel tanks, the wine is transferred to 60-gallon American oak barrels for fermentation. The wine is then encouraged to complete a secondary *malolactic fermentation* (a process which converts sharper malic acid into softer lactic acid, lending complexity and buttery qualities, sometimes at the expense of overt fruitiness). Woodhall's Seyval is clean and crisp on the palate with evident oak running throughout its appley, slightly herbal fruit.

Woodhall's Vidal, instead of being produced in a slightly sweet, Riesling style as is most common, is instead processed much like the Seyval. It is fermented dry in stainless steel, aged in American oak, and malolactic in this case is inhibited in order to highlight the Vidal grape's fresh fruitiness. Often blended with as much as 10% Riesling, the wine is light, crisp, and citrusy, again with evident oak throughout the nose and flavors. Woodhall's Riesling is produced in extremely small supplies and is 100% *estate bottled*; that is, made only with grapes grown on the estate.

Two reds are produced, each in a distinctly different style. In a lighter, Beaujolais framework is the Chambourcin. Blended with 15% Chancellor, the wine is fermented for just two days on the skins in order to pick up color and light tannins. However, by shortening skin contact, Al avoids the sometimes unpleasant herbaceousness that can be characteristic of red hybrids. The wine is softened by malolactic fermentation and spends seven to eight months in oak. The wine has an inky, vibrant young purple color, and possesses broad, fleshy, perky fruit redolent of black cherries and raspberries.

Woodhall's Cabernet is a fuller-bodied, gutsier wine. The grapes are fermented for a full two weeks in contact with the skins and the wine spends two years aging in American oak barrels. Early versions of the wine, produced from very young vines, have possessed a lighter style not unlike the Chambourcin—young, grapey, with light tannins and a subtle, appropriate touch of oak. Look for future Woodhall Cabs to be bigger, more classic wines.

Finally, Woodhall's Garnet is a rosé wine made from 100% Foch grapes. For this wine, Al crushes Foch and immediately presses the juice from the skins. This method, which produces completely colorless wine from such grapes as Pinot Noir, produces with the notoriously inky Foch a wine darker than the average blush. The wine is inhibited from undergoing malolactic fermentation, and spends three to four months in oak. A rich, red-pink color, the wine is refreshingly fruity, has faint highlights of oak, and has enough natural acidity to go well with picnic or barbecue fare.

DIRECTIONS

Take Interstate 83 north out of Baltimore. Proceed to Exit 24 (Belfast Road) and turn left (west). At Wheeler Lane, turn left again and proceed to winery on left.

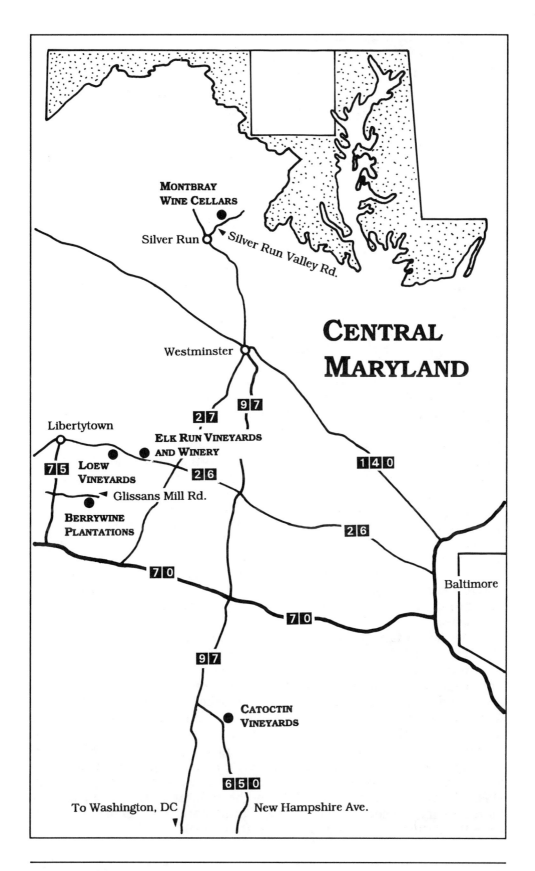

MONTBRAY
WINE CELLARS

Silver Run

Silver Run Valley Rd.

CENTRAL
MARYLAND

Westminster

27 97

Libertytown

ELK RUN VINEYARDS
AND WINERY

140

75 LOEW
VINEYARDS

26

Glissans Mill Rd.

BERRYWINE
PLANTATIONS

26

70

Baltimore

70

97

CATOCTIN
VINEYARDS

650

To Washington, DC

New Hampshire Ave.

Linganore Winecellars

Estate   Bottled

Linganore
Cayuga
1986

Grown, Fermented And Bottled By
Linganore Winecellars
Mt. Airy, Md.
MD-W-26

Alcohol 8 Percent By Volume

Berrywine Plantations (Linganore Winecellars)

ADDRESS: 13601 Glissans Mill Road
Mt. Airy, MD 21771
PHONE: (301) 662-8687
OWNERS: Jack and Lucille Aellen
WINEMAKERS: Jack and Anthony Aellen
TOTAL ACRES: 40
CASES/YR: 4,000
HOURS: Monday through Friday 10-5,
     Saturday 10-6, Sunday 12-6

A trip to Berrywine Plantations (a.k.a. Linganore Winecellars) will certainly open your eyes. On a "normal" day, visitors will enter the winery's tasting room and be faced with a staggering array of dry table wines, sweet fruit wines, a couple of honey meads, and even some flavored wines. If you happen upon the winery on one of its "special" days, you might be greeted by an authentic ninth century Viking vessel afloat on the farm's pond, or perhaps by a band of Scottish bagpipe players.

"We've always felt that the best way to promote ourselves and our wine is through festivals which combine food, history, wine, and fun!" explains Jack Aellen who, along with his wife Lucille and son Anthony, owns and operates the farm winery.

To be sure, these festivals are no small affair. Each year, the winery hosts numerous events such as the "Scottish Highlands Fling Festival" (which features, along with the bagpipes, Scottish-Irish arts and crafts, sheep herding demonstrations with a Border Collie Dog, and traditional foods like sausage rolls, Cornish pasties, scones, and Scotch and Cream Codies balls), the "Razz Jazz Cajun Festival" (featuring a wide array of Cajun and Creole delicacies along with live Dixieland jazz), and the (most unusual) "Great Medieval Lammastide Fair." This final event concentrates on historical/educational aspects of the medieval period—replicas of early Anglo-Saxon thatched dwellings are erected amid jousters, roaming entertainers, beggars, lords, and peasants.

The Aellen family moved to central Maryland, north of the town of Mt. Airy, in 1972. After a long career in the military service and private industry, which kept them moving among spots such as Oakland, California, Spokane, Washington, and San Antonio, Texas, the family settled on their large farm while Jack worked as a chemical engineer with the National Bureau of Standards. Both Jack's parents (who were German-Swiss) and Lucille's (Italian) had made wine for family consumption while their families were growing up. Inspired by this heritage, the Aellens began immediately cultivating grapes on the farm and, over the following decade, developed a full 40 acres of producing vines. Upon Jack's retirement from the federal government, a commercial winery license was pursued. Linganore Winecellars at Berrywine Plantations was bonded in August of 1976.

THE VINEYARD

The fifteen-year period following the family's move to Maryland and preceding the receipt of their license afforded the Aellens valuable time to hone their viticultural skills and experiment with a wide range of grape varieties. The family has chosen to grow only French-American hybrids and native-American hybrids in its vineyard due to the harshness of winters in their region.

"For the past three years," says Jack, "we've had temperatures drop to -14°, -20°, and -14° F. We just never felt we could consistently grow vinifera here."

The different grape varieties grown at Berrywine number at least ten. "To be honest," admits Jack, "there are so many varieties out there, it's hard to specifically divide up the acreage. Let's just say two-thirds are whites and one-third are reds!" White varieties include the French-American hybrids Aurora, Seyval, and Vidal, and the American hybrid Cayuga. An experimental white called Melody is also grown. Red French-American hybrids such as Cascade, Chancellor, and Chelois are grown along with the native-American hybrids Concord and Niagara. Grapes the Aellens are less fond of, such as Cascade, are slowly being replaced with plantings of more Chancellor and Vidal.

During the first few years of operation, younger vines did not produce enough grapes to supply the winery's needs. In the late '70s, there were also very few vineyard sources from which to purchase grapes. So the family began buying fruit such as apples, strawberries, and peaches to enhance their offerings. The response to this move was so positive that Berrywine has continued to make fruit wines a central part of its production.

THE WINES

One look at the wine lineup at Berrywine and you can see that experimentation and a whimsical, "anything goes" attitude have pervaded the winemaking philosophies of Jack and Anthony Aellen. Dry to medium-sweet table wine, sweet fruit wines, and grape wines flavored with natural extracts can all be found.

All wines are fermented cool (50-60° F) in stainless steel tanks, some of which are temperature controlled. One of the tenets of winemaking at Berrywine is that hybrid table wines should be produced at lower alcohol levels (8 to 10%) and should thus be harvested earlier (at 17-18° *Brix*). A controversial opinion, to be sure. Oak is seldom used to age wines.

The winery bottles a 100% varietal Cayuga—the only such wine in the state—which is dry, crisp, and slightly earthy. The Vidal, finished with 2% residual sugar, is light and floral. An attractive Chelois Blush is made from the *free run juice* of this red variety. It is medium-sweet and possesses candyish cherry flavors. Other varietal grape wines include a dry, grassy Seyval, a Foch, and a spicy, fruity Chancellor. Blended grape wines include a proprietary white called "Skipjack" and "Mountain Pink," made from native-American hybrids.

The Aellens produce five unusual flavored wines—"White Sangria," "Almond House Red" and "White," "Holiday Red," and "Spiced Apple." The first uses Aurora as a base to which is added citrus fruit juices to produce a bizarre but somewhat pleasing citrusy quaffer. The latter four have almond extract or other spices added, creating wines more suitable for warming up and sipping by the fire on a snowy day than for consumption with food.

Two honey meads are produced. (Mead is a traditional medieval wine made from fermented honey and water. Different recipes blend this concoction with spices and grape juice or other fruit juices during fermentation.) Their regular "Mead" was served to Prince Charles and Princess Diana of England at their visit to Washington, DC in 1984. "Tej," a drier, saba honey wine made in the Ethiopian style, is made to supply a DC restaurant.

Finally, a whole string of fruit wines is offered. All are approximately 6% residual sugar (with the exception of the tart, dry apple wine) and thus are suitable for dessert or to finish off a nice picnic. (The winery literally recommends pouring these wines over seasonal fruit or vanilla ice cream!) Of them all (Peach, Cherry, Raspberry, Blackberry, Damson Plum, Strawberry, and Elderberry), I liked the Raspberry, the flavors of which seemed truest to the natural fruit. (The Elderberry offers a challenge to only the most adventurous of palates!)

The Aellens produce their wines under three labels: The "Linganore Winecellars" label appears on vintage-dated, *estate bottled* table wines. The "Plantation" label is seen on flavored, sweeter wines. Finally, the "Berrywine Plantations" label is used to identify all fruit wines.

INCIDENTALLY . . .

Jack Aellen led the crusade with the United States Bureau of Alcohol, Tobacco and Firearms for the establishment of the Linganore Viticultural Area (which also contains Elk Run Vineyards and Loew Vineyards). Viticultural Area designations officially recognize the unique climatological and topographical characteristics of the growing area.

DIRECTIONS

From Baltimore, take Interstate 70 west to the Libertytown Exit (Number 62). Follow Route 75 north for 4.5 miles to Glissans Mill Road. Turn right and proceed 3.7 miles to winery.

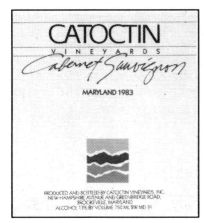

Catoctin Vineyards

ADDRESS: 20901 New Hampshire Avenue
Brookville, MD 20833
PHONE: (301) 774-2310
OWNERS: Robert Lyon, Shahin Bagheri,
    Ann, Jerry, and Molly Milne
WINEMAKER: Robert Lyon
TOTAL ACRES: 32
CASES/YR: 4,200
HOURS: Saturday and Sunday 12-5,
    weekdays by appointment

Located just 14 miles outside of the Capitol Beltway on Maryland Route 650 (New Hampshire Avenue), Catoctin Vineyards enjoys the distinction of being located closer to Washington, DC than any other winery in this guide. But visitors will also quickly realize, upon tasting the wines, that Catoctin also enjoys the distinction of being one of the showcase producers of wines in the mid-Atlantic.

Bob Lyon, winemaker and co-owner of Catoctin Vineyards, moved east in 1979 with the goal of helping to pioneer quality winemaking in the mid-Atlantic region. After studying biochemistry at the University of Oklahoma, Bob attended what is universally considered the leading "wine school" in this country, the University of California at Davis, to earn degrees in enology and viticulture. While at school, he worked summers as a "cellar rat" in such well-known Napa and Sonoma wineries as Inglenook, Sebastiani, and the sparkling wine house, Domaine Chandon. Bob's most valuable experience, however, occurred after graduation during his year-long apprenticeship at Napa Valley's Chateau Montelena. "It was there that I learned how to artfully apply the classroom theories I had learned," explains Bob, "to the actual production of fine wine."

Believing that his chances of owning and operating his own winery were better outside of California, Bob moved east and landed his first job as winemaker at Byrd Vineyards in Myersville, Maryland. Between 1979 and 1982, Bob was responsible for producing the fine, award-winning Cabernets and Chardonnays that earned Byrd its initial national acclaim. While such recognition was rewarding, Lyon still desired an operation of his own.

In late summer of 1983 Catoctin Vineyards was born. After developing a strong friendship with grape growers Ann and Jerry Milne, the three, along with close friend Shahin Bagheri, pooled their resources and leased the old Provinza Winery in Brookville, Maryland. For a frantic two-week period, the group set up the winery in the nick of time, just hours before grapes from the first September crush came in.

THE VINEYARD

Catoctin's vineyards are perched high in the Catoctin Mountains of Frederick County. Jerry and Ann Milne have developed what has to be one of the premier vineyards in the mid-Atlantic. "The vineyard location is ideal. The climate is moderated by a temperature inversion—when it is hot in the lowlands and DC, it's cool in the mountains; and when it is frigid at the lower elevations, it's usually several degrees warmer in the hills." A benefit not enjoyed by most vineyards in the mid-Atlantic, grapes grown in the mountains ripen slower and more evenly over a longer growing season. The fact that this location experiences milder temperatures, lower humidity, and less damaging frost allows Catoctin to grow classic vinifera grapes.

As seen in the table below, 90% of the total 32 acres is devoted to vinifera varieties. The vast bulk of the planting is to Chardonnay and Cabernet Sauvignon (more than 22 acres) with lesser amounts set aside for Riesling and Cabernet Franc. White French-American hybrids Seyval and Vidal share one 3-acre plot, while a few rows of red hybrids Chambourcin and Chancellor fill out the vineyard.

GRAPE VARIETIES AND ACREAGE

Variety	Vinifera	French/Amer. Hybrids
Chardonnay	11.2	—.—
Cabernet Sauvignon	11.2	—.—
Cabernet Franc	3.2	—.—
Riesling	3.2	—.—
Seyval	—.—	2.5
Vidal	—.—	0.7
TOTALS	28.8	3.2

THE WINES

Bob Lyon's California heritage shows itself clearly in the wines at Catoctin. The Chardonnays are made in a big, ripe, lush style, while the Cabernet is also deep, densely fruity, with strong, assertive tannins. Of all the wines produced in the mid-Atlantic, Catoctin's are clearly the most Californian in style and impression.

When vintages permit, two Chardonnays are produced. One is fermented to dryness in temperature-controlled stainless steel tanks and then aged in French Limousin oak. The other is completely barrel fermented in the French wood and is allowed to remain in contact with the fermentation *lees* for an extended period. Both wines are outstanding. In 1983 and 1986, Oak Fermented Chardonnays were produced. The '83 was especially noteworthy, with ripe appley fruit, lush butter and vanillan highlights, and a deft dose of creamy oak throughout. Year in and year out, Catoctin's regular Chardonnay has possessed an impressive level of ripe apple and pear fruit, with more restrained oakiness, framed nicely with lively citrine acidity.

Cabernet Sauvignon at Catoctin is actually a cuvée with significant portions of Cabernet Franc blended in for complexity. The wine is fermented with an extended *maceration* (contact with the skins) in order to extract deep fruit elements and soften the tannic impression.

The wine spends up to two years aging in French Nevers oak. In special vintages, like 1983, both a regular Cabernet and a "Reserve" are produced. While the regular bottling is consistently impressive in its own right, with its bright cherry and berry fruit, it is the winery's "Reserve" that is a complete knockout. The '83 version has a deep, deep ruby color, massively fruity cassis and blackberry layers, and is highlighted with notes of tar, black pepper, and anise. A dense barrage of tannins and ample structure have allowed this wine to age slowly and gracefully. The '83 "Reserve" is a true standard-bearer for the mid-Atlantic.

As impressive as these varietals are, one cannot overlook Catoctin's Riesling, in its own right one of the best examples in the mid-Atlantic of wine made from this grape. Fermented in stainless steel at very low temperatures to preserve fruitiness, the wine is finished with less than 1% residual sugar. It is lush, delicately floral in aroma, and possesses clean apricot and peach fruitiness.

Finally, Catoctin also produces a Seyval—dry, clean and refreshing as a food wine (which is actually blended with varying proportions of another French-American hybrid, Vidal); and a delightful blush wine, which also scores points for its clever name: "Eye of the Oriole." Actually 95% Seyval and 5% Chambourcin (for color), the wine is finished with 2.5% residual sugar, has a subtle salmon/pink color, and has clean, crisp fruit flavors.

Besides a climate that can be harsh (all of 1985's Chardonnay crop was lost when temperatures throughout the area dropped to -10° F with 50 mph winds), Bob sees Catoctin's biggest obstacle as trying to crack the Maryland and Washington, DC wine market. "People don't think of Maryland when discussing world class wines," he says with frustration. "The Washington market is huge, yet tends to be very biased toward Europe, and especially France. We would just like everyone to know that great wine is also being produced in their back yard!"

INCIDENTALLY . . .

Look, in future vintages, for a 100% varietal Cabernet Franc. Helping to lead a groundswell of support for this grape, which grows particularly well in the variable climate of the mid-Atlantic, Catoctin's vineyard is now producing ample amounts of this variety to serve as both a blender for the Cabernet Sauvignon and to bottle on its own.

DIRECTIONS

From Washington, DC, take Route 650 (New Hampshire Avenue) north approximately 14 miles beyond the Capitol Beltway to winery on right side of road. From Baltimore, follow Interstate 70 west to Route 97. Go south on Route 97 (Georgia Avenue) to Route 650 and turn left. Proceed to winery on left.

Elk Run Vineyards and Winery

ADDRESS: 15113 Liberty Road
Mount Airy, MD 21771
PHONE: (301) 775-2513
OWNERS: Fred and Carol Wilson
WINEMAKER: Fred Wilson
TOTAL ACRES: 4
CASES/YR: 2,600
HOURS: Saturday 10-5, Sunday 1-5,
    weekdays by appointment

One of the more easily accessible wineries in the state of Maryland is the tiny, charming, and extremely quality-conscious Elk Run Vineyards and Winery. Located on Route 26 midway between Baltimore and Frederick and just 40 miles north of Washington, DC in the rural heart of the state is the farm of owners Fred and Carol Wilson.

The Wilsons are, like many other winegrowers in the mid-Atlantic, hobbyists turned professionals. Both extremely busy with demanding careers (Fred as an engineer with the Naval Science Assistance Program; Carol as a teacher of dance) and raising their children, the two somehow found the time to cultivate a fascination with wine. While touring the Finger Lakes of New York in 1974, the couple became acquainted with the late Dr. Konstantin Frank, the legendary Russian émigré who had pioneered the growing of vinifera grapes in that cold, harsh growing region. Frank, a colorful and headstrong man (whose hatred of French-American hybrids led him once to claim that drinking them caused birth defects!), had grown vinifera grapes in the northern reaches of his homeland. When he arrived in New York, he saw a region steeped in the growing of Concord and other *vitis labrusca* varieties and, struggling against ethnic and language barriers, fought for years an inflexible industry unwilling to accept the risk of vinifera production. Finally, at the age of sixty-five, he was able to start his own winery (which is now successfully operated by his son Willi) and, over the years, played a huge role in the shaping of the eastern wine industry.

Naturally, the Wilsons felt they could learn a lot from Frank and traveled for the next five years to the Finger Lakes to assist him at harvest time. Over that period, the Wilsons made wine from purchased vinifera fruit and, as a side business, started grafting vinifera *scion wood* onto American *certified virus-free rootstock* to sell to eastern vineyard growers.

Encouraged by Fred's numerous successes in amateur wine competitions and bolstered by their third income from the grafting business, the Wilsons decided to take the plunge themselves in 1980. They had recently purchased their present property, which had not only a 4-acre pasture suitable for vines, but also a grand old brick house

---

dating back to the 1750s. Vines were planted and, by 1983, a license was received just in time for their first harvest.

Seven years later with the vineyards flourishing, a self-constructed winery building perched behind the house, and a rustic tasting room in the house's "summer kitchen," Elk Run Vineyards has succeeded nicely and has earned considerable praise from numerous wine critics. Even as established as they have become, the Wilsons say, without hesitation, that marketing locally-produced wine presents their biggest challenge. "The state of Maryland has been a bit slow in developing its support of the industry," says Carol. "We've worked hard in Annapolis to pass legislation establishing the Maryland Winegrowers Advisory Board. This new organization could really move us all forward."

The Wilsons continue to spend "what seems like half our lives" on the road, distributing and marketing their wines to shops and restaurants through the state. In fact, today the winery custom-bottles a significant amount of its wine for restaurants in Baltimore and Washington, DC to serve as their premium "house wines."

THE VINEYARD

Elk Run's vineyard currently supports 4 acres of vinifera grapes. As seen in the table below, 2.5 are planted to Chardonnay, 1 to Cabernet Sauvignon, .5 to Riesling, with a few rows of Gewurztraminer to round things out.

GRAPE VARIETIES AND ACREAGE

Variety	Vinifera	French/Amer. Hybrids
Chardonnay	2.5	—.—
Cabernet Sauvignon	1.0	—.—
Riesling	0.5	—.—
TOTALS	4.0	0.0

The relatively small size of this vineyard has presented Elk Run with a basic economic problem—demand for its wine far exceeds the output produced by their 4 acres. There is also an insufficient number of grape growers in the state of Maryland from whom to purchase vinifera grapes. While they are actively searching out additional property on which to plant, the Wilsons have coped with their dilemma through an effective although not totally uncontroversial strategy — they've gone outside of Maryland state borders to purchase nearly two-thirds of their fruit. This practice is becoming quite common in California where fruit from Oregon and Washington state is sometimes imported for vinification.

Since there is an extreme shortage of vinifera fruit grown for sale in Maryland (and Virginia, for that matter), the Wilsons opted instead to seek grapes from other eastern states well known for their quality growing conditions. Well acquainted with New York viticulture, Elk Run established close contractual ties with growers of Riesling in the

Finger Lakes and growers of Chardonnay and Cabernet Sauvignon on Long Island (another burgeoning eastern winegrowing region).

But while the grapes may come from another state, you can be sure that the wines produced are 100% Elk Run. Fred Wilson, from first step to last, produces the wines from the fresh fruit shipped from New York. Under careful arrangements that dictate picking on pH, sugar, and acid parameters, Elk Run's growers will harvest their fruit and, the same day, load up the fruit in refrigerated trucks, and drive to Maryland. The system works wonderfully well, says Carol, except for one aspect. "Since the grapes are picked beginning in the early morning, and then loaded up and driven south during the same day and evening, we end up receiving the fruit in the middle of the night," she explains. "Having 10 tons of Chardonnay dumped in your lap at midnight can be quite an experience!"

When visiting the winery, take time to look at Elk Run's vineyard and notice its unusual trellis system. Called a catenary system, the trellis is designed similarly to a suspension bridge, with long, drooping wires suspended from widely spaced 12-foot locust trunk posts. While it looks downright sloppy compared to more typical, neatly manicured vineyards, Fred (an engineer, remember?) says it is vastly superior in its ability to shift its support based on the uneven growing characteristics of vinifera vineyards from year to year.

THE WINES

While some Maryland winegrowers are fearful of the consumer confusion that might result from a Maryland winery selling wine made from out-of-state grapes, I find the Elk Run approach represents a reasonable and an effective solution to an economic reality while also offering the taster a fascinating tasting experience.

Elk Run produces 2,600 cases of wine each year. One-third is *estate bottled* and appears under the "Liberty Tavern" label. Two-thirds of the wine is labeled with the "American" designation (as required by the U.S. Bureau of Alcohol, Tobacco and Firearms) because it is produced from the out-of-state fruit. But since all of the wines are produced by Elk Run, both lines bear the imprint of the considerable winemaking skills of Fred Wilson.

The Liberty Tavern Chardonnay and Cabernet Sauvignon clearly represent some of the finer wines being produced in Maryland. The Chardonnay, which is fermented in stainless steel, inhibited from undergoing a secondary *malolactic fermentation*, and aged for four months in French Limousin oak, is consistently a gorgeous, ripe, fruity yet elegant wine. Full flavors of apples enhanced by vanillan oak are balanced wonderfully by firm acids. Recent offerings from the '86 and '88 vintage stand out. While always in short supply, it is a wine well worth seeking out.

The Cabernet Sauvignon is, as well, a real star. I tasted, side by side, the Cabs from '83, '84, and '85, and the progression and positive development exhibited from the vineyard's first-ever harvest to its third were remarkable in both degree and rapidity. While the '83 was simple and pleasantly straightforward, the '84 and then '85 each displayed noticeably improved depth, complexity, and nuance. Fermented in traditional Bordeaux methods and aged for two years in both American and French Limousin oak, the '85 is rich in berry and cassis fruit, enveloped in warm, toasty, and spicy oak, and has the structure to age well for several years.

Under the Elk Run "American" label, a broader, less expensive line of wines is offered including: another Chardonnay and another Cabernet, a Riesling (which includes Elk Run's .5 acre worth of grapes), a Seyval, a blush wine called "Annapolis Sunset," and a dessert Cabernet called "Sweet Katherine" after one of the couple's daughters. All are very pleasant, well-made wines, offering the taster a nice opportunity to sample the varying characteristics of some of the east's premier growing regions.

The American Chardonnay is fuller bodied and more buttery than the Estate version, reflecting the milder growing season of Long Island, yet lacks the finesse and complexity of its partner. Similarly, the Cabernet is a fleshy, fruity, soft, and ripe wine with more pronounced herbal overtones than the estate Cab—quite nice and a real value. The Riesling from the Finger Lakes (which is, in many people's opinion, the best Riesling region in this country) displays a distinct floral, blossomy nose, and a texture a bit more lush and ripe than most from this very Germanic region. It's a refreshing sipper with 1.1% residual sugar. The "Annapolis Sunset," 95% Seyval and 5% Cabernet, is drier than most blushes with just .8% residual sugar and is a pleasant, fruity quaffer. The "Sweet Katherine" may not appeal to everyone's tastes. Brought up to 8% residual sugar by adding sugar back to a portion of the Long Island Cabernet, it is rich and fruity but a bit flat and sticky, even for dessert.

INCIDENTALLY . . .

At one point in its history, the circa 1750 house in which the Wilsons live had been called the Liberty Tavern, a resting stop for weary colonial travelers. Today, the Wilsons use that moniker to designate wine bottled from their estate vineyard, and a sketch of the house appears on the Elk Run labels.

DIRECTIONS

From Baltimore, the winery is 26 miles due east on Route 26. From Frederick, drive 17 miles due west on Route 26. From Washington, DC, take Georgia Avenue (Route 97) north about 40 miles to the junction of Route 26. Turn left and proceed 7 miles to winery on right.

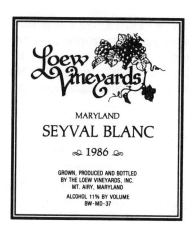

Loew Vineyards

ADDRESS: 14001 Liberty Road (Rt. 26)
Mt. Airy, MD 21771
PHONE: (301) 460-5728
OWNERS: Bill and Lois Loew
WINEMAKER: Bill Loew
TOTAL ACRES: 4
CASES/YR: 500
HOURS: Saturday 12-5, Sunday 1-5

Upon meeting Bill Loew, you can't help but be drawn to his soft voice with its warm Austrian accent. After a short time of hearing him speak of his vineyard, the listener quickly realizes that here is a man with a profound respect for nature, the land, and grapevines. "What has impressed me about winegrowing in the east," says Bill, "is that vines have an incredible will to live, regardless of climate."

Born in Austria, Bill Loew was raised by parents who were in the wine business. In this country, while raising a family with his wife Lois (a psychologist practicing in the Rockville area), Bill has pursued a career as an electrical engineer. However, "My heart was always with wine," he says.

One year, after several years of purchasing juice and grapes for his home winemaking hobby, Bill couldn't find any fruit for sale of an acceptable quality. It was at that point that he decided it made more sense to grow his own. In 1982, the family bought 37 acres near Libertytown in Frederick County and planted one acre to several grape varieties—viniferas Chardonnay and Riesling, and French-American hybrids Foch, Leon Millot, Chancellor, and Seyval.

"It was a fascinating learning experience," says Bill, "seeing what would grow and getting to know the personalities of the different varieties." By joining the Maryland Grape Growers Association and consulting with the University of Maryland Agriculture Department, he was able to learn a great deal from the experiences of others about viticulture and spray programs.

By 1985, fully caught up in the excitement of a growing state wine movement, the Loews decided to obtain a commercial license and share their product with the public. "We will remain a small, family-oriented winery, though," he says. Loving their avocation-turned-vocation so much, not doing everything themselves just wouldn't seem right.

THE VINEYARD

After the initial experimental planting in 1982, the Loews have added more vines each year to grow to a total of 4 producing acres. In 1983, a full acre of Seyval was planted, as well as an additional row of Riesling. In 1984 came .25 acre of Cabernet Sauvignon, and in 1985 an acre of Chardonnay. A few rows of Cabernet Franc were planted in 1986 for blending with the Cabernet Sauvignon.

The Loews had originally planted a half acre to two varieties of table grapes, Venus and Reliance, to help with cash flow and to attract the fruit-picking market. After finding the practice more distracting than beneficial, they decided on two experimental solutions. In 1988, Bill field-grafted Cabernet Sauvignon onto the Venus root stock. In 1989, the Loews made a semi-sweet wine from the Reliance based on successful attempts made by researchers at the University of Arkansas.

GRAPE VARIETIES AND ACREAGE

Variety	Vinifera	French/Amer. Hybrids
Chardonnay	1.2	—.—
Seyval	—.—	1.2
Cabernet Sauvignon (w/ some Cab Franc)	0.5	—.—
Chancellor	—.—	0.2
Foch	—.—	0.2
Leon Millot	—.—	0.2
Riesling	0.2	—.—
Reliance	—.—	0.3
TOTALS	1.9	2.1

Lois and Bill have experimented with new and different trellising systems each year of expansion. Today, red hybrids grow on a six-arm Kniffin trellis while vinifera and the Seyval can be seen growing on a neat bilateral cordon system.

THE WINES

"I honestly believe that Californians have it too easy!" says Bill. "Don't get me wrong, they make some great wines. But every year has good weather. Vinifera thrive there. Straightforward winemaking produces fine wine. The east really pushes a winemaker to his or her limits. We have to be creative, flexible. We have to invent things. Every bit of winemaking skill I have is used to create a drinkable wine."

Strong opinions? Clearly. But also words adequately supported by actions. Rarely does one find in such a small operation the widely varying approaches to winemaking found at Loew. Almost constant experimentation creates an ever-changing lineup of wines.

"Red hybrids were the first challenge," he explains. "I've learned that with Foch, Millot, and Chancellor, you must avoid skin contact at all costs." Fermenting these reds in a traditional method, in contact with the skins, can produce wines of intensely herbaceous character. For his "Light Red" then, Bill ferments the lightly pressed juice of Foch grapes, inhibits a secondary *malolactic fermentation*, gives the wine no contact with oak, and bottles fresh and young.

For more complexity, Loew produces a wine called "Classic Red" through the whole-berry fermentation technique called *carbonic maceration*. This traditional method of Beaujolais shuns the usual crushing and pressing of grapes prior to fermentation. Instead, uncrushed clusters are placed in a tank under a protective layer of carbon dioxide and are allowed to ferment internally. Inside the unbroken grape skins, wine is created as sugar is converted to alcohol, and from the skins color but little tannin is extracted. After an extended period of fermentation, the grapes are gently pressed and the wine/juice is then treated much like any other wine. Foch and Leon Millot are combined in Loew's "Classic Red" to produce a wine with characteristic carbonic style—an intense yet delicate nose and fresh cherry fruit flavors. The "Classic Red" also touches no oak and offers a pleasant nouveau-type wine for sipping or for consumption with pasta and pizza.

The Loew "Harvest Red" is a pleasant 80% Chancellor, 20% Cabernet Sauvignon blend offering a more full-bodied, robust character. Aged in American oak, the wine is spicy, fruity, and clean; perfect as an everyday table wine. At the time of this writing, Loew had yet to release its first Cabernet Sauvignon.

Bill Loew emphasizes the critical importance of cold fermentation for his white wines. "To capture freshness and delicacy, and to avoid heavier, earthier impressions, I ferment in stainless steel at 45-50°," he explains. Seyval is a particular favorite. "I like it better than Sauvignon Blanc—it has a similar crisp fruitiness but less overt grassiness," he adds. When bottled on its own, Loew's Seyvals are crisp and clean, with attractive spiced apple flavors, and possess a nice roundness acquired from brief aging in American oak. In recent vintages, Loew has taken to blending Seyval with both Chardonnay (to produce the proprietary "Harvest Gold") and Riesling (to create "Twilight").

Chardonnay and Riesling are both fermented at the same cool temperatures, with the Chardonnay receiving brief aging time in American oak and the Riesling being produced in both a dry style ('86) and semi-sweet ('87 and '88).

It's hard to imagine that all these wines, produced by such varying methods, are made in a winery not much bigger than a large garage. Clearly, though, it is an illustration of the intensity and dedication with which the Loews pursue their enological passions.

INCIDENTALLY . . .

Loew Vineyards is located within just a few miles of both Elk Run Vineyards and Berrywine Plantations. In a single, convenient outing, this proximity offers visitors perhaps the most varied and diverse one-day wine experience available in the mid-Atlantic region.

DIRECTIONS

From the Washington, DC area, go north on Georgia Avenue (Route 97) to Route 26, and turn left (west). From Baltimore, just drive directly west on Route 26. In both cases, proceed approximately 5 miles past the intersection of Routes 26 and 27 to winery on the left.

Produced and Bottled by
MONTBRAY
WINE CELLARS

SeyveVillard WHITE TABLE WINE
SILVER RUN VALLEY, WESTMINSTER, MD., ALCOHOL BY VOL. 12%

Montbray Wine Cellars

ADDRESS: 818 Silver Run Valley Road
Westminster, MD 21157
PHONE: (301) 346-7878
OWNERS: G. Hamilton and Phyllis
Mowbray
WINEMAKER: G. Hamilton Mowbray
TOTAL ACRES: 30
CASES/YR: 2,200
HOURS: Monday through Saturday 10-
6, Sunday 1-6

Another man who might be considered a patriarch of the Eastern wine industry is G. Hamilton Mowbray. He can be credited for putting the French-American hybrid Seyval on the winegrowing map, for producing the first commercial vinifera wines in Maryland, and for providing untold advice, inspiration, and leadership to generations of winegrowers in the mid-Atlantic.

In the 1950s, Ham went to England to pursue graduate studies. He and his wife, Phyllis, were able to spend their time between terms traveling throughout Europe. In France, they developed a special love for the wines of Bordeaux and Burgundy. After receiving his degree, he was hired by Johns Hopkins University in Baltimore as a research psychologist. Unable to find or afford the wines he had become accustomed to drinking, the thought struck him that, perhaps, he could create his own. He began visiting men like Philip Wagner at Boordy Vineyards, and neighbors closer to his Westminster home like Emile Lucier and Charles Singleton, both pioneer grape growers. Soon Ham was convinced that he, too, could successfully grow grapes and make wine. In 1964, the first vines of what was to become Montbray Wine Cellars were put into the ground.

That year can be thought of as the beginning of a long love affair Ham was to develop for a grape variety that was actually unnamed at the time. Several years earlier, the French hybridizer Bertille Seyve had, by crossing a vinifera clone with a native-American grape, created a hybrid variety labeled Seyve-Villard 5276. A vine promising both to produce high quality wine and to vigorously withstand the cold eastern winters, Seyve-Villard 5276 was planted extensively by Mowbray. Today, known by the more popular name Seyval Blanc, this wine has become the mainstay of Montbray's production and represents, arguably, the finest example produced in the world.

THE VINEYARD

Montbray's vineyard is planted on schistous slate soil on a gently sloping, south-facing hillside in Maryland's Silver Run Valley. Located just a few miles south of the Pennsylvania border, the valley runs almost due east-west, and is situated in the heart of what has been called the "Golden Crescent." A label coined by a man named George Reisling (really!) while he was working for Mowbray, the crescent encompasses what many feel to be the prime grape-growing region in the eastern United States.

It took men like Ham Mowbray to demonstrate that premium wine grapes could be grown in the region. Painstaking experiments with a large number of varieties enabled Mowbray to isolate those grapes that develop most favorably.

"Of course, Seyve-Villard is my favorite," says Mowbray. "I've learned a great deal over the years. Of the varieties I've grown, I've eliminated Pinot Noir as too prone to rot, Merlot and Sauvignon Blanc as too winter-tender, and Gewurztraminer as a beautiful variety which, unfortunately, experiences winter-kill two or three years out of every five," he explains. Besides Seyve-Villard, Mowbray's favorite French-American hybrid is the red Marechal Foch. "Vidal is OK," he continues, "but why grow it if you can grow Riesling?"

"Obviously, what this industry needs to do is identify the best grapes for the best micro-climates," says Mowbray. A man of strong opinions, Ham feels that many growers, especially in Virginia, are making big mistakes in their selection of varieties. "Why try to grow Riesling in heavy red loam soil in a southern climate which experiences Mediterranean-style summers? Why try to grow Merlot in frost-prone lowlands?" he asks. While such questions may offend some, one must conclude that perhaps no other man in the mid-Atlantic is more entitled to his beliefs.

"In the warmer regions, besides Chardonnay, Cabernet Sauvignon, and Cabernet Franc, people should be trying many of the Rhone varieties like Syrah, Mourvedre, Marsanne, Cinsault, and Carignane. Maybe even the Italian Nebbiolo would do well. Merlot really has no hope except out on the Eastern Shore where the climate is milder. Even there, the sandy soil will probably prevent it from ever offering much depth or complexity."

Today, Montbray's vineyard has been fine-tuned to reflect his years of experimental learning. Two-thirds of the acreage is planted to Seyve-Villard, while the remaining 10 acres are divided between good-sized plots of Cabernet Sauvignon and Cabernet Franc, and small parcels of Chardonnay and Riesling.

GRAPE VARIETIES AND ACREAGE

Variety	Vinifera	French/Amer. Hybrids
Seyval Blanc	—.—	20.0
Cabernet Sauvignon	6.0	—.—
Cabernet Franc	3.0	—.—
Chardonnay	0.5	—.—
Riesling	0.5	—.—
TOTALS	10.0	20.0

THE WINES

Not surprisingly, Mowbray subscribes devoutly to the French notions of how to make wine. In his efforts to produce wines like the ones he grew to love in France, he follows pure Burgundian methods with his whites (except Riesling) and for Cabernet, anything Emile Peynaud says is OK by Ham. "His word is gospel when it comes to how to make Bordeaux-styled wines," says Mowbray. He is referring to the world famous Bordeaux winemaker, scholar, and consultant to many of the region's finest chateaux.

For both the Seyve-Villard and Chardonnay, the freshly crushed and pressed juice is chilled and settled overnight in stainless steel tanks. Next, the clarified juice is put in American oak barrels and inoculated with yeast and allowed to ferment to dryness in oak. The wines are left quietly alone to age on the yeast *lees* and are allowed to complete a secondary *malolactic fermentation*. This extended yeast contact, coupled with the malolactic fermentation, serves to add a roundness and richness to the wines' texture, as well as a buttery, yeasty complexity to the wines' flavor.

The Seyve-Villard produced at Montbray is truly breathtaking. In the nose, rich honey, peach, and cinnamon scents billow from the glass. These impressions are echoed in the wine's flavors, but are accented further by touches of butterscotch and spicy oak. The palate feels lush and viscous, and the finish is long and fruity. The wine is as complex and weighty as a top-flight French Burgundy, yet is sold for about $5. It is fascinating to consider that this wine is made from the very same variety that is also so successfully made in a light, crisp, fruity style by most mid-Atlantic wineries. (Please remember that while all other wineries will label this wine "Seyval," Mowbray sticks to the traditional title, "Seyve-Villard.")

Montbray's Chardonnay is made in very small amounts and at the time of this writing, none was available for tasting.

The Cabernet Sauvignon and Cabernet Franc varieties grow "beautifully in this valley," according to Mowbray. "The spring and summer are warm enough and long enough to ripen the fruit adequately, and the vines are vigorous enough to tolerate the winter quite well. Different from California Cabs, I think that mid-Atlantic Cabernets can be made in a style which closely resembles Bordeaux," he adds.

Mowbray ferments these varieties in open-topped vats in contact with their skins until proper color and tannins are extracted, usually for seven to ten days. He then presses the juice away from its skins and allows it to complete its fermentation in American oak. The two varieties are usually blended during the February after the vintage and then rest for two full years in barrels. The wine's only treatment is a light *fining* with egg whites before bottling to remove some of the harsher tannins.

Not enough praise can be heaped upon Montbray's Cabernet Sauvignon. Both of the 1985 and 1986 versions are classically proportioned, with rich, soft fruit yet firm, tight acids. They possess a deep ruby color and a creamy nose redolent of cassis, black currants, berries, and chocolate. In the mouth, the wines are invitingly soft, round, and silky. Richly fruited, the wines' powerful berry and cassis flavors are framed by just the right measure of soft tannin and creamy, smoky oak. (As a footnote, the author placed this wine in a blind tasting against such heavyweights as a 1982 Chateau L'Evangile from Pomerol and a Napa Valley Sequoia Grove from the renowned 1984 vintage. Some may be surprised to know that, amongst an experienced tasting panel, albeit not professional, the Montbray won hands down!)

Each year, a varying proportion of Cabernet Franc is blended with the Cabernet Sauvignon. In 1985, it was 18% Cabernet Franc; in '86, 9%. Whatever is left over is usually bottled as a 100% varietal and is both tasted and sold only at the annual Maryland Wine Festival. Both the '86 and '85 Cabernet Franc showed good extraction, a spicy cherry fruitiness, and similar soft/firm textures and tannins. Of the two, the '85 showed slightly deeper, more extracted intensity. While obviously not a wine easily found, the reader is advised to seek it out at the next Maryland Wine Festival.

The Riesling is fermented entirely in stainless steel tanks, is allowed to finish completely dry, in the Alsatian style, and is bottled fresh and crisp. (The only time this regimen was altered was in 1974 when an early freeze hit the area. The Riesling froze on the vine, was quickly picked and pressed, and a 3% residual sugar "Ice Wine" was produced—the first in America.) Again, made in very small amounts, the Riesling was not available for tasting at the time of this writing.

Finally, Montbray also produces a pleasant rosé wine called "Garnet." Made from 100% Foch, the juice from this red grape is pressed from its skins after only three to four hours of skin contact, is transferred to barrels for fermentation, and is bottled young and fruity. The wine is a deep, rosy-red color ("garnet" suits it well), and is fine for everyday drinking with pasta, at picnics, and with lighter meats.

INCIDENTALLY . . .

One last plug for the Seyve-Villard: In a 1982 article for the *American Wine Society Journal* entitled "Can You Have a Crush on a Grape?", Mowbray wrote, "For the last 25 years, barring hail, it has never let me down: grand crops, excellent balance between sugars and acids and, treated with loving care, a wine that approaches the best the noblest vinifera grapes can do—including that king of all white grapes, the Chardonnay." All I can say is keep an open mind and give it a try. (I just know you'll like it!)

DIRECTIONS

From Westminster, take Route 97 north (toward Gettysburg) 7 miles to Silver Run Valley Road. Turn right. Proceed 2 miles and stop at winery on left side of road.

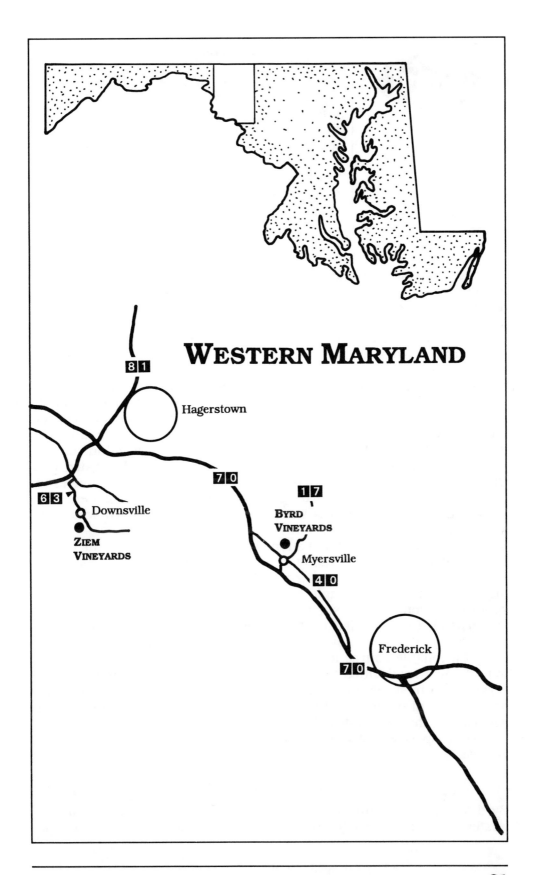

WESTERN MARYLAND

81

Hagerstown

70

17

63

Downsville

BYRD
VINEYARDS

ZIEM
VINEYARDS

Myersville

40

Frederick

70

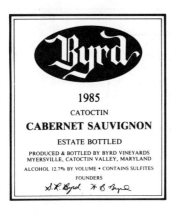

1985

CATOCTIN

CABERNET SAUVIGNON

ESTATE BOTTLED

PRODUCED & BOTTLED BY BYRD VINEYARDS
MYERSVILLE, CATOCTIN VALLEY, MARYLAND

ALCOHOL 12.7% BY VOLUME • CONTAINS SULFITES

FOUNDERS

Byrd Vineyards

ADDRESS: Church Hill Road
Myersville, MD 21773
PHONE: (301) 293-1110
OWNERS: William and Sharon Byrd
WINEMAKER: William Byrd and Curt Sherrer
   (consultant)
TOTAL ACRES: 30.5
CASES/YR: 10,000
HOURS: Saturday and Sunday 1-5 (1-6 during
   Daylight Savings Time)

Plain and simple, William "Bret" Byrd deserves a great deal of credit for putting Maryland wines on the modern enological map. While predecessors like Philip Wagner and Ham Mowbray paved the way for many a Maryland winemaker (not to mention many a winemaker up and down the entire east coast), it was the stunning Cabernet Sauvignons from Byrd Vineyards in the early '80s that grabbed the attention of critics and connoisseurs alike.

In an event that might be compared to the famous "Paris Tasting" in the late 1970s, in which several California Cabernets gained international recognition by soundly beating their Bordeaux counterparts, the wines of Maryland gained worldwide respect in a wine tasting that took place in 1982. Hosted by the *Baltimore Sun*, the "blind" tasting pitted such heavyweights as Chateau Latour, Chateau Margaux, and Chateau Petrus against each other. To make the competition especially interesting, a 1980 Byrd Cabernet Sauvignon was also entered. Well, you guessed it. Judges were shocked when the Byrd wine beat all comers!

This achievement fulfilled a long sought after dream for the Byrds. Bret, a pharmacist by training, and his wife Sharon, a teacher, had purchased their 48-acre property in 1972 with plans to build a housing development. The couple quickly fell too deeply in love with the spot to ever contemplate such a move.

Instead, they decided to grow grapes and build their own home and winery. Wanting only to plant the noblest varieties, the couple sought a reliable source for virus-free vinifera planting stock. Unable to find one, they decided to graft their own plants and soon had a successful side business in place. Besides supplying themselves with 30 acres worth of plants, the Byrds ended up supplying vinifera vines to wineries in thirteen states. By 1976, Bret and Sharon received their license to operate just in time to crush 3,000 gallons from their first vintage.

THE VINEYARD

Byrd Vineyards occupies a lovely spot in the Catoctin Mountains of western Maryland. Perched on a hill 880 feet above sea level, the vineyard faces south towards the little town of Myersville. Row upon row of vines crisscross the 25° slope, sending roots down through rich, red soils.

All but four of Byrd's acres are devoted to vinifera varieties. The relatively high elevation allows these tender vines to enjoy the effects of a temperature inversion whereby summer days are slightly cooler and winter days are somewhat warmer than experienced at lower elevations. In addition, the steep grade allows cold air to spill down the hillside so that damaging frost cannot take hold of the vines.

The largest plot in the vineyard is planted to Chardonnay, 12.5 acres. Four acres are devoted to Sauvignon Blanc, a variety seldom grown in the east due to its winter-tenderness. Smaller plots are planted to other white varieties including Riesling, Gewurztraminer, and the French-American hybrid Seyval. For the reds, Bordeaux varieties Cabernet Sauvignon (4 acres), Merlot (1 acre), and Cabernet Franc (.5 acre) are grown. In addition, a new 2-acre section of the vineyard has been planted to the red French-American hybrid Chambourcin.

GRAPE VARIETIES AND ACREAGE

Variety	Vinifera	French/Amer. Hybrids
Chardonnay	12.5	—.—
Cabernet Sauvignon	4.0	—.—
Sauvignon Blanc	4.0	—.—
Riesling	3.0	—.—
Seyval	—.—	2.0
Chambourcin	—.—	2.0
Gewurztraminer	1.5	—.—
Merlot	1.0	—.—
Cabernet Franc	0.5	—.—
TOTALS	26.5	4.0

THE WINES

From the beginning, Bret Byrd knew that if he were to create world-class wines, he would need to employ world-class winemakers. He has found two of them over the history of the winery, both of whom received training at this country's premier enology program: the University of California at Davis.

For the 1979 through 1982 vintages, Byrd engaged the services of Bob Lyons, who had worked his way through school by apprenticing at such prestigious Napa Valley wineries as Domaine Chandon and Chateau Montelena. It was Bob's 1980 Cab that beat the Bordelais. In early 1983, Lyons and Byrd parted company. Later Bob became part owner and winemaker at Catoctin Vineyards.

Beginning in 1983, Byrd hired Curt Sherrer. Sherrer continued taking the excellent Catoctin Mountain fruit and converting it into award-winning wines. While now pursuing full-time winemaking in

Virginia, most recently at Piedmont Vineyards, Sherrer continues to provide consultation to Byrd once a week.

Byrd Vineyards is certainly one of the most well-equipped wineries in the state. Besides operating several temperature-controlled stainless steel tanks and maintaining an impressive number of both French and American oak barrels, the winery boasts a centrifuge. The centrifuge is used to clarify freshly picked juice as well as to assist in stopping the fermentation of wines Byrd wishes to finish with residual sugar.

Typically, Byrd's white wines are clarified with the centrifuge and then are cool-fermented in stainless steel. Chardonnay spends approximately six months in French oak, while Sauvignon Blanc is allowed to age for three months in American oak. For the reds, fermentation takes place in open vats. Lots are allowed to remain in contact with the skins for fourteen to twenty days, and are then aged in French and American oak for seventeen to twenty-one months. Before bottling, the Cabernet is lightly fined with egg whites and goes through a light filtration.

Byrd Chardonnays have shown consistently high, if not spectacular, quality. Both the '86 and '87 versions show very pretty scents of apples, citrus blossoms, and smoky oak. In the mouth, the wines possess a silky texture gained from having gone through a partial *malolactic fermentation*. Flavors of rich, buttery apples and toasty, yeasty notes are bolstered by firm citrine acidity. Byrd Chardonnays are tight and lean in their youth, yet develop nicely for several years.

Byrd's Sauvignon Blancs are typically very assertive in their varietal character. Strong grassy and smoky themes tend to dominate the fruit. While somewhat of an acquired taste, the wines are well-made and solid.

Byrd's Gewurztraminer can be a very impressive wine which, in successful vintages like 1987, could fool anyone into believing he was drinking a fine Alsatian wine. Gorgeous rose petal and perfume scents blossom up from the glass. In the mouth, velvety, long-lasting flavors of wildflowers, apricots, and cloves persist assertively. Finished with just a touch of residual sugar (under 1%), the wine is one of the best examples of this varietal in the east.

Though the Cabernets are always in short supply, wine fans should each year seek out a few bottles of Byrd's now-famous Cabernet Sauvignons. Containing varying proportions of Merlot and Cabernet Franc, the 1984, 1985, and 1986 editions were tasted in preparation for this book. All three were consistent and amazing. Tasting notes for the wines are strikingly similar: intense, dark, and inky in color with strong, concentrated noses of cassis, cedar, tar, smoke, and slight vegetal notes. In the mouth, the wines are again concentrated and muscular, with lush berry and cassis fruit, and enticing hints of chocolate, mint, herbs, and anise. Each wine also finishes with a barrage of mouth-puckering tannins which convince that they are built for long aging. What more can be said except that the wines are certainly among the best the mid-Atlantic has to offer and, just as certainly, can compete with any Cabernets made in California or France.

Note that in 1986, for the first time, a large enough crop of Merlot was harvested to bottle that wine as a varietal. While none was tasted in preparing this book, the wine received critical praise from the wine press.

INCIDENTALLY . . .

In recent years, controversy has reared its ugly head surrounding one move by Bret Byrd. Beginning in 1986, after successive years when crops were severely diminished by winter kill and spring frost, Byrd began importing bulk wine from California and other states. Acting in the French tradition as a *négociant*, this wine is bought just after fermentation, and is cellared, blended, clarified, and bottled by Byrd in his winery. One hundred percent varietal Napa Valley Chardonnay and Cabernet are bottled under the William Byrd label, while blended red, white, and blush wines are bottled under the Byrd Cellars label.

Some critics feel strongly that such a practice undermines the movement to build a strong Maryland wine industry. Suffice it to say that, without the négociant wines, the state would probably have lost one of its most talented winegrowers and some of its most reputable wines. Remember folks, this is a tough and cruel business. It doesn't take too many bad breaks from Mother Nature to drive someone into bankruptcy. The négociant bottlings, some of which represent nice quality wine at a very reasonable price, have literally kept the Byrds in business.

For the wine tourist, I simply recommend exercising a bit of careful consumerism. Estate bottled Byrd Vineyards wines are clearly distinguishable from the négociant bottlings. By a simple reading of the label, you can readily tell which wines are from Maryland and which are not.

DIRECTIONS

Myersville is located approximately 10 miles west of Frederick. From Interstate 70, take exit 42. Head north, through the town of Myersville, for about 1 mile to Church Hill Road. Turn right and proceed for another mile to winery entrance on the left.

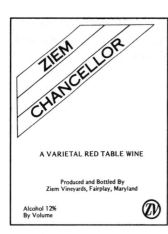

A VARIETAL RED TABLE WINE

Produced and Bottled By
Ziem Vineyards, Fairplay, Maryland

Alcohol 12%
By Volume

Ziem Vineyards

ADDRESS: Route 1
Fairplay, MD 21733
PHONE: (301) 223-8352
OWNERS: Robert and Ruth Ziem
WINEMAKER: Robert Ziem
TOTAL ACRES: 8
CASES/YR: 1,050
HOURS: Thursday through Sunday 1-6, others by
      appointment

Robert Ziem is a man with a mission based on some very strong opinions on what winegrowing in the eastern United States should be about.

While browsing through this book, readers will encounter persons who will grow only the European vinifera varieties, stating they are the most "noble." They will meet families with a broader view, taking the risk of planting the delicate vinifera grapes while "hedging their bets" by growing winter-hardy French-American hybrids as well, stating all the while that both are capable of making fine wine. Still others covered within these pages follow a less traveled path by making wine from fruits. Robert Ziem, however, is a strict devotee of French-American hybrids and is convinced that the future of eastern winemaking lies in the cultivation of these types of grapes.

"First of all," Ziem explains, "I don't believe vinifera grapes were meant to be grown in this region. Grape vines respond strikingly to climate and soil, and we are not in Bordeaux or the Napa Valley. Vinifera vines, I believe, don't produce the same fine wines of these regions here in the east. And besides, the world is already awash in vinifera wines, so why should we strive so hard to copy others?" Ziem goes so far as to say that vinifera growers are actually doing a disservice to the eastern wine industry. "Genetic engineering will one day permit us to create wines in the east which are the match of the great wines of the world. Those who believe otherwise are rejecting the great role that genetics has played in all other branches of agriculture."

The Ziems, Robert and his wife Ruth, purchased their 55-acre farm with its impressive 200-year-old stone house in 1971. They immediately began planting grapes and by 1977 had 8 acres under vines and their commercial license in hand. Bob, a chemist whose long and diverse federal career included eleven years of work with NASA as a "rocketeer" specializing in solid propulsion systems, recently retired to devote his full energies to the winery. The Ziems have very definite goals in mind for the eastern wine industry. "I think we have something unique to offer here. French-American hybrids thrive in this climate and can produce excellent wines. Many are reminiscent of their European parentage, but possess their own individual characteristics and tastes. We feel that, in not too many years, these wines will have their own independent reputation and will be eagerly sought out on their own behalf," says the ever-optimistic Bob.

The Ziems are well aware of the monumental obstacles standing in the way of achieving this bold objective. From a marketing standpoint, vinifera wines like Chardonnay have name-recognition, while hybrid counterparts like Chancellor and DeChaunac are practically unheard of. Further, the quality of eastern wines was, in the past, not very high. Consumers often assume incorrectly that eastern wine, especially from non-vinifera varieties, must be sickly sweet, *labrusca*-styled wine such as Concord.

One taste of Ziem Vineyards wine will quickly dispel this latter misconception and convincingly lend credence to Bob's views on the vinifera vs. hybrid debate! Surely vintners will continue to argue over the goals and objectives of eastern winegrowing, but the high quality of Ziem wines will at least assure that there is a well-deserved place for French-American and other hybrids amid the sea of high quality wine being produced in the mid-Atlantic.

THE VINEYARD

Ziem Vineyards is currently the only winery located in the Cumberland Valley Viticultural Area. (Quarry Hill and Blue Ridge Vineyards, which shared the region with Ziem, have recently closed.) The viticultural area occupies an 80 mile-long valley that bends in a northeasterly direction from the Potomac River in Washington County, Maryland to the Susquehanna River in Cumberland County, Pennsylvania.

Eight acres of vines are planted in the limestone soils of the Ziem estate. Typical of the arable land in the Cumberland Valley Viticultural Area, the vineyard is planted on level ground at a low elevation, 300 to 400 feet above sea level. Due to its proximity to the Allegheny Mountains to the northwest and the prevailing southwesterly winds, the region is slightly cooler and wetter than the Shenandoah Valley Viticultural Area in Virginia to the southwest.

GRAPE VARIETIES AND ACREAGE

Variety	Vinifera	French/Amer. Hybrids
Chancellor	—.—	2.0
Dutchess	—.—	2.0
Vidal	—.—	1.0
Chambourcin	—.—	0.5
Foch	—.—	0.5
Seyval	—.—	0.5
Aurora	—.—	0.25
Chelois	—.—	0.25
DeChaunac	—.—	0.25
Delaware	—.—	0.25
Landot Noir	—.—	0.25
Leon Millot	—.—	0.25
TOTALS	0.0	8.0

Ziem's vineyard, as seen in the table above, is planted to a staggering number of varieties (sixteen), all French- and native-American hybrids, divided evenly between red and white grapes. The largest plantings are to the red Chancellor and the white Dutchess, each receiving two acres. Other reds include Foch, Chambourcin, Landot Noir (the only planting of its type in the mid-Atlantic), DeChaunac, Leon Millot, and Chelois. The whites joining Dutchess in the vineyard are Vidal, Seyval, Aurora, and the native white Delaware. Tiny amounts of other hybrids (Verdelet, Baco Noir, Cascade, and Vignoles) are also grown on an experimental basis.

THE WINES

As if Bob Ziem hasn't already taken on a large enough task with his crusade to promote French-American hybrids, he has also defied the popular trends by specializing in producing red wines from hybrid grapes. Of all the hybrids, only the white varieties Seyval and Vidal have, arguably, begun to successfully crack the vinifera barrier and make a name for themselves. Most red French-American hybrid varieties have, to date, enjoyed a much less respected reputation. As discussed in the overview of this book, early efforts at winemaking with red hybrids resulted in soft, intensely herbaceous, often medicinal tasting wines with few redeeming characteristics. With time, however, winemakers have begun to learn more about the individual grapes and how best to handle them in the vineyard and in the winery.

"I watch pH levels very carefully," explains Bob, "and actually time my harvest based on pH more than sugar and acid levels in the grape." Ziem never lets his grapes' pH rise above 3.3 to ensure both color and biological stability.

Other special techniques required by red hybrids include carefully controlling skin contact. Unlike vinification of traditional Bordeaux varieties like Cabernet Sauvignon, which are often fermented on the skins for up to three weeks, skin contact with hybrids is now often kept to an absolute minimum. Foch, for example, is left on the skins for only six hours to minimize herbaceousness, while other varieties like Chancellor are fermented in contact with the skins for just three to four days. All wines are bottled as 100% varietals at Ziem to emphasize each grape's individual character. All wines are fermented to dryness in stainless steel dairy tanks located in the Ziems' barn (which was converted into a winery). Reds are then aged in small Missouri Oak cooperage for whatever period Bob believes necessary for the best balance between fruit and oak flavors. *Racking* is the only cellar treatment for Ziem red wines and ordinarily they are bottled both *unfiltered* and *unfined*. For this reason, reds may throw a sediment in the bottle during aging—this is to be expected and in no way detracts from wine quality if the wine is carefully decanted from the precipitate.

Of the red wines, Bob feels his Chancellor has been consistently the best, year after year. The wine possesses a rich purple/ruby color and a light intensity nose of berries. Its flavors are full and fruity and are enhanced by a light touch of smoky oak. The wine is reminiscent of a good, hearty Cru Beaujolais, a Morgon perhaps. The DeChaunac is similar in style, with a more forward nose of raspberries and cherries and slightly rounder, riper fruit flavors. A bigger wine, the DeChaunac tastes as if it spent more time in oak, displaying an evident layer of smoky notes. The Landot Noir is a particular favorite of Bob's. While a bit tart, the wine shows bright, candied cherry flavors contrasted with heavier vegetal, earthy, almost Burgundian "goute de terroir" characteristics. Other reds include a very nice Foch (tart acidity balanced by bright cherry fruit), a pleasant Chambourcin, and a Leon Millot.

The white wines made at Ziem all display an austere, crisp style, reflecting the high natural acids characteristic of the grape varieties. The Aurora is light and tart, with citrusy lemon fruitiness. The Dutchess (the only one produced in Maryland), made by most eastern wineries in a sweet style, is here bone dry. Like the Aurora, this wine is crisp and citrusy, and shows only the faintest hints of the labrusca or "foxy" flavors usually associated with native-American hybrid grapes. This wine is Ziem's most popular white.

Production at Ziem Vineyards is just over 1,000 cases annually. All wines are *estate bottled*.

INCIDENTALLY . . .

When visiting Ziem Vineyards, be sure to look at the 200-year-old spring house sitting near the Ziem home. This structure, built over the natural spring that supplies cool, fresh water to the family, provided early settlers with a primitive refrigerator and a pool in which to bathe. By storing, underwater, containers of milk and other perishables, colonial families could preserve freshness. Also, the historic Antietam Civil War battlefield is just a few miles away from the winery.

DIRECTIONS

From Baltimore (Interstate 70) or Washington, DC (Interstate 270/70), travel west toward Hagerstown. Follow Interstate 81 south and exit onto Route 63. Follow Route 63 south for four miles to winery on right. Winery is just south of the town of Downsville.

WINE TOURING IN VIRGINIA
AN OVERVIEW

An event that symbolized wonderfully the striking progress being made by today's wine industry in the mid-Atlantic occurred in August 1988. At Monticello, the historic home of Thomas Jefferson, the first grape crop was harvested by groundskeepers from a new, experimental .25-acre vineyard planted to the original twenty-three varieties Jefferson attempted to grow himself back in 1807.

Besides being this country's third president and one of its most revered historical leaders, Thomas Jefferson was also an avid wine enthusiast. A fan of Bordeaux red wine in particular, Jefferson had had high hopes of making the colony of Virginia a premium wine producer, but his efforts failed as early vineyards succumbed to the ravages of harsh weather, disease, and insects.

Today, under the direction of head groundskeeper Peter Hatch, and with the consulting advice of leading Virginia viticulturist Gabriele Rausse, the Northeast Vineyard was planted in 1984 based on notes and sketches from Jefferson's own Garden Book. Benefiting from advanced viticultural know-how and modern fungicidal and insecticidal sprays, nineteen terraces of vinifera grapes—some familiar, some obscure—can now thrive just as Jefferson would have dreamed.

Virginia today offers the wine tourist a selection of forty-two wineries from which to choose, all of which are no older than fifteen years or so. Finding much of the state to possess extremely hospitable climes and soil, vineyards and wineries dot the landscape from north to south and east to west. A significant concentration can be conveniently found just an hour or so west of Washington, DC in the rolling hunt country around the towns of Middleburg and Leesburg. Further to the south, the state's largest official viticulture area occupies the foothills of the Blue Ridge Mountains surrounding Charlottesville, where a total of ten wineries may be visited. Halfway between Washington and Charlottesville, in and around the town of Culpeper, another cluster of winegrowers exists, as does a diverse handful of wineries up and down the picturesque Shenandoah River Valley just west of the Blue Ridge. An especially promising new region is being developed along the eastern stretches of the state in the Northern

Neck between the Potomac and Rappahannock Rivers, in the lowlands around colonial Williamsburg, and out on the lovely, mild Eastern Shore. Finally, the southern reaches of the state offer exciting variety—from a winery located on the top of a mountain along the famous Skyline Drive, to a colorful group of pioneers making wine on the Appomattox Plateau east of Lynchburg.

Since 1980, the rapid growth of the Virginia industry has been stimulated by the striking support offered by the state itself. That year, the Virginia Farm Winery Law was passed, progressive legislation that made it easier for growers to attain licensure to produce and sell their own wine. In 1984, significant state general revenue was earmarked to establish the Virginia Wine Marketing Program in the state's Department of Agriculture. Further monies were set aside to create the Wine Growers Advisory Board. Under these auspices, the state hired an enologist, Bruce Zoecklein, and a viticulturist, Tony Wolf, to work full-time in support of winegrowers and makers throughout the state. A series of events, which has been repeatedly credited with improving the quality of Virginia wine, as well as the market visibility of Virginia wine products, state support of the wine industry has catapulted Virginia to the position of the seventh largest wine producer in America.

In all, 1,400 acres are currently cultivated in grapes. This acreage supports a wine production level nearing the 360,000 gallon mark. (That's 150,000 cases!). Nearly 150 independent growers (including wineries with vineyards) devote 65% of their acreage to vinifera varieties, 28% to French-American hybrids, and 7% to native-American hybrids, as seen below.

GRAPE ACREAGE BY VARIETY

Vinifera		French-Amer. Hybrids		Native-Amer. Hybrids	
Chardonnay	29%	Seyval	6%	Concord	4%
Riesling	14%	Vidal	5%		
Cabernet Sauvignon	11%	Villard Blanc	2%		
Merlot	3%	Chancellor	2%		
Pinot Noir	2%	Chambourcin	2%		
Gewurztraminer	1%	Foch	2%		
Other	5%	Other	9%	Other	3%
TOTALS	65%		28%		7%

Thomas Jefferson would have been proud of the persistence and dedication of Virginia's modern winegrowing pioneers. Today, we can all benefit from their efforts and enjoy the fruits of their labors while touring the many wine roads of the Old Dominion.

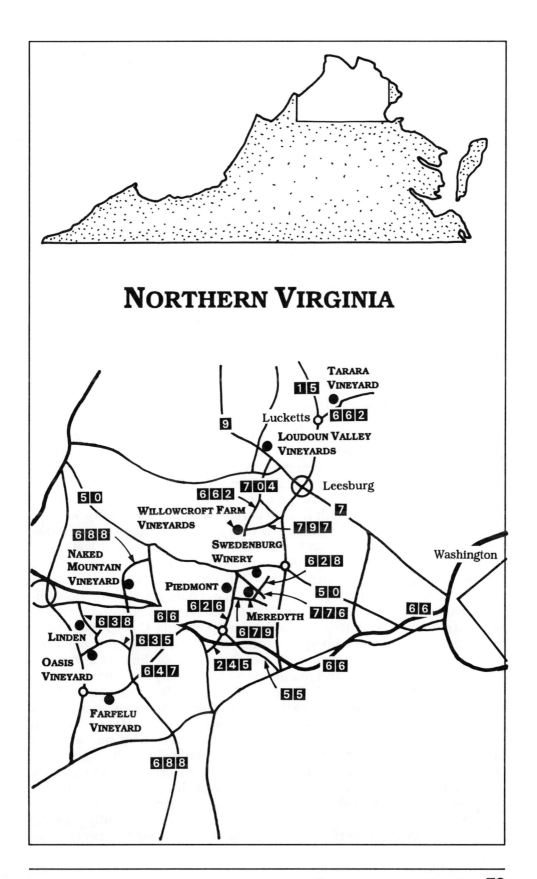

NORTHERN VIRGINIA

TARARA VINEYARD

15

Lucketts

662

9

LOUDOUN VALLEY VINEYARDS

704

Leesburg

50

662

7

WILLOWCROFT FARM VINEYARDS

797

688

SWEDENBURG WINERY

Washington

NAKED MOUNTAIN VINEYARD

628

PIEDMONT

50

626

MEREDYTH

776

66

638

66

LINDEN

635

679

OASIS VINEYARD

647

245

66

FARFELU VINEYARD

55

688

PRODUCED AND BOTTLED BY FARFELU VINEYARD HERE IN RAPPAHANNOCK COUNTY FLINT HILL, VIRGINIA ALCOHOL 11% BY VOLUME

Farfelu Vineyard

ADDRESS: Highway 647
Flint Hill, VA 22627
PHONE: (703) 364-2930
OWNER: Charles J. Raney
WINEMAKER: Charles J. Raney
TOTAL ACRES: 7
CASES/YR: Variable
HOURS: By appointment

Charles "C.J." Raney is an excited man. Since 1988, he has finally been able to devote his full energies to something he's been doing in Virginia, on a part-time basis, as long as anyone. Upon his retirement in January 1988 from a demanding career as an airline pilot, he could finally call himself a full-time vintner.

C.J. Raney's interest in wine began while working in the Mediterranean, as a pilot for the U.S. Navy. While stationed in and around Italy, he fondly recalls seeing old towns "literally immersed in vines and wine. At that point, the bug bit me and there was no question I would have to try it someday myself," explains C.J. Years later, while flying for the airlines and living on Long Island, he set down his first roots by planting eight vines by the side of his garage.

It was not until 1966 that C.J. could get a bit more serious about grape growing. A transfer brought him to northern Virginia where he had a home built in Rappahannock County near Flint Hill. The following spring (1967), C.J. began planting his real vineyard. At the time, grape growing in Virginia was practically unheard of and few people had any real experience with it. One person who did was Philip Wagner of Maryland's Boordy Vineyards — a true pioneer of eastern winegrowing — who provided C.J. with valuable advice on the cultivation of French-American hybrids. Another person who did was one Dr. George Oberle of Virginia Tech with whom C.J. consulted. Dr. Oberle gave him thirty-two vines, all different, so that C.J. could learn about how different varieties grew in this relatively untested region. "That move sort of symbolized the next fifteen years for me," explains C.J. "From those thirty-two different vines I began planting anything and everything. I became too diversified, too divided." Over the course of the next few years, 13 acres were developed and planted to a broad array of varieties.

By August of 1974, C.J. Raney had applied for and received his commercial winery license, making him (by only a week or so ahead of Meredyth Vineyards) the first bonded farm winery in the state. (C.J. and Archie Smith engage in good-natured haggling over who was actually first and today, for whatever it's worth, essentially share the claim.) He chose to name the winery "Farfelu"—a French word meaning strange or peculiar—for it seemed to accurately reflect the entire endeavor.

Over the next several years, however, all was far from smooth sailing. Explains C.J., "The '70s and early '80s saw me constantly juggling my career with the winery. I never had enough time or any permanent help." Logistically speaking, the inconsistent schedule of an airline pilot presented huge difficulty in trying to keep to a good spray program, to prune his 13 acres, to oversee fermentation, racking and bottling of wine, and perhaps most important, to schedule harvesting. "A few years ago, I was expecting my first vinifera harvest. I was really excited about it. Then I got called off on a couple of flights. When I returned, I found that my cows had harvested for me! The Chardonnay must have been nice—there was none left!" Over the years, Farfelu managed a steady but small production of Seyval and a "Dry Red Table Wine" blended from red French-American hybrid grapes Chancellor and DeChaunac.

In the last few years, however, Raney has been gearing up in anticipation of his retirement from flying. Richard Vine, a professor of viticulture and enology from Mississippi State University and author of *Commercial Winemaking*, was consulted. Based on some of his advice, Farfelu's vineyard was streamlined and vinifera plantings were increased. Renovation was also begun on the farm's 125-year-old barn. "I'm really excited and am looking forward to this little renaissance of Farfelu," exclaims Raney. While production will remain small —around 2,000 cases annually—the winemaker's renewed energy and commitment should reap dividends for both owner and consumer.

THE VINEYARD

Based on both a realization of his own physical limits and the advice of consultant Richard Vine, C.J. Raney has decreased the acreage of his vineyard from 13 to 7. Additionally, he has increased his plantings of vinifera based on his own growth as a viticulturist and advances in technology that make their cultivation today more feasible.

Remaining from early plantings are 1 acre each of the red French-American hybrids Chancellor and DeChaunac, 1 acre of the white hybrid Cayuga, and 1 of Chardonnay. More recently added are a second acre of Chardonnay, and 1 each of Merlot and Cabernet Sauvignon, bringing total vineyard size to 7 acres.

GRAPE VARIETIES AND ACREAGE

Variety	Vinifera	French/Amer. Hybrids
Chardonnay	2.0	—.—
Cabernet Sauvignon	1.0	—.—
Cayuga	—.—	1.0
Chancellor	—.—	1.0
DeChaunac	—.—	1.0
Merlot	1.0	—.—
TOTALS	4.0	3.0

THE WINES

Again, in an attempt to streamline production and focus energy, C.J. Raney now produces just four wines at Farfelu, with Chardonnay and

Cabernet Sauvignon taking the lead. For everyday drinking, a couple of "picnic" wines will be made as well — a "White" from the vineyard's Cayuga and a "Red" continuing the blend of Chancellor and DeChaunac. Merlot will be added to this lineup in future years when these young vines begin producing.

Whites are fermented in stainless steel while reds ferment in traditional open vats. To date, Raney has used American oak barrels to age his reds, but looks forward to experimenting with French oak in coming years for both Chardonnay and Cabernet.

At the time of this writing, only a bit of 1985 "Dry Red" was available for tasting. If this wine is an indication of things to come, we may all have something to look forward to in the rebirth of Farfelu. The wine showed deep extract, a generous nose of berries, oak, and caramel, and full-bodied flavors of raspberries and cherries.

DIRECTIONS

From Washington, DC, travel west on Interstate 66. Take Exit 6 and travel on Route 647 for 12.5 miles to winery on left.

Linden Vineyards

ADDRESS: Route 1, Box 96
Linden, VA 22642
PHONE: (703) 364-1997
OWNERS: Jim and Peggy Law, Nancy, Richard,
    and Robert Law
WINEMAKERS: Jim and Peggy Law
TOTAL ACRES: 11.5
CASES/YR: 1,400
HOURS: Wednesday through Sunday 11-5,
    March-December; weekends only, January
    and February

Jim and Peggy Law, an engaging young couple with seemingly bound-less energy, probably did as much serious planning for their new Linden Vineyards as any winery in the area. The two spent more than two years just looking for the land on which to plant their vineyard and build a winery. Three criteria had to be met before Jim and Peggy would take the plunge: 1) The site had to be optimal for growing vinifera varieties; 2) the site had to be easily accessible to consumers in order to attract a good flow of customers; and 3) the couple had to love it for, after all, they would have to spend their lives there!

While looking at Linden's breathtaking setting, it doesn't take too long to see that all three requirements were successfully achieved. First off, the location is simply beautiful—who wouldn't want to settle down in this lovely 76-acre mountain estate on the eastern slope of the Blue Ridge? Second, the winery is just two miles south of Interstate 66, very near the Skyline Drive, and just an hour or so west of Washington, DC, so marketability shouldn't be a problem. Finally, and most important, at 1,320 feet above sea level, the vineyard, which occupies an amphitheater-like bowl on an even but not too steep eastern-facing slope, should enjoy a wonderful growing season.

As Jim explains, "We're high enough to benefit from a temperature inversion effect. The summers will be cooler than down in the valley and the winters should be several degrees warmer since cold air sinks and forces the warm air up." This critical advantage Jim and Peggy learned from nearby neighbors Bob and Phoebe Harper of Naked Mountain Vineyard, whose plants have fared much better than many growers in the state. "We also preferred an eastern-facing slope," adds Peggy. "Morning sun helps dry out dew and moisture early in the day, before any rot begins. Also, our vines won't be exposed to the blistering heat of the late afternoon sun, since they're not on a southern slope, thereby lengthening our growing season."

The couple, coming from very different backgrounds, were brought together by grapes and wine. Jim had received a Bachelor's degree in liberal arts from the University of Miami, Ohio and then worked for two years in Zaire as a Peace Corps volunteer to teach modern agricultural methods. Upon returning to the United States, he wished to learn more about winegrowing and apprenticed at Chalet Debonne Vineyards near the shores of Lake Erie in Ohio. He came to Virginia in 1981 to further his learning. Peggy, originally from Connecticut, studied English and biology in school and worked for several years with the Bird Division of the National Zoo. She then transferred to the Smithsonian Conservation and Research Center near Front Royal. In rural Virginia, Peggy's interest in agriculture grew to where she picked up part-time jobs at Oasis Vineyard and Willow Run Vineyards. It was in 1981 that Jim and Peggy first met while each was working at Tri-Mountain Vineyards in nearby Middletown. Well, romance ensued followed by marriage, and soon they were dreaming of their own winery. Within a few short years they were on their way. Today, the winery, which was licensed in the summer of 1987 and opened its doors for the first time in April 1988, appears to face a very rosy future indeed.

THE VINEYARD

Linden's vineyard was first planted in the spring of 1985. Feeling strongly that both vinifera and French-American hybrids play significant and legitimate roles in mid-Atlantic winegrowing, the Laws carefully chose five varieties based on their own unique distinctions. For the vinifera, Chardonnay and Cabernet Sauvignon were each planted in 1.25 acre plots. Once again, learning from the experiences of other growers, they planted a third of an acre of Cabernet Franc for blending with the Cabernet Sauvignon. (Merlot, which occasionally produces fine wines in Virginia as witnessed at Montdomaine Cellars in Charlottesville, is both extremely winter-tender and, due to its delicate, thin skin, susceptible to late season rot. Many persons, like Ham Mowbray in Maryland, see the sturdier Cabernet Franc playing a much larger future role.) In addition, 3.5 acres of French-American hybrids were planted; one to Seyval and 2.5 to Vidal.

The estate vineyard has been slowly expanded each year, bringing total acreage to 11.5. Of special note, the Laws planted .5 acre to Petite Verdot in 1990. This represents the only commercial acreage of this seldom-seen Bordeaux varietal in the mid-Atlantic.

GRAPE VARIETIES AND ACREAGE

Variety	Vinifera	French/Amer. Hybrids
Vidal	—.—	2.0
Chardonnay	3.5	—.—
Cabernet Sauvignon	2.5	—.—
Seyval	—.—	2.0
Cabernet Franc	1.0	—.—
Petite Verdot	0.5	—.—
TOTALS	7.5	4.0

Jim, who on the side teaches viticulture seminars at the Virginia Tech-Northern Virginia Graduate Center, has kept on top of the latest research in pH management in the vineyard. Because of the rich soil in Virginia, grapevines are often excessively vigorous and produce large amounts of foliage. If this foliage is left unchecked, too many leaves are shaded by one another, and pH levels in the grapes rise. High pH grapes lead to many problems later, in the cellar, where new wine experiences increased susceptibility to spoilage.

To avoid these problems, the Laws have employed a trellis system in which vines are pruned to bilateral cordons and extra wires at the top of the trellis allow for dividing the leaf canopy. By positioning shoots and canes along the divided canopy, more leaves are exposed to sunlight and pH levels are kept safely low.

To supplement their own crop, Jim and Peggy have entered into a long-term lease/management agreement with the owners of nearby Flint Hill Vineyards. The Laws are extremely impressed by the quality of the Chardonnay (2.5 acres), Riesling (2.0 acres), and Sauvignon Blanc (1.0 acre) they have been able to produce from this property.

THE WINES

The winery at Linden Vineyards is beautifully designed. Modern yet rustic, it sits at the top of the hill and commands impressive views of row upon row of vines on the slopes below. With a production area cut into the hillside on the first floor, and a spacious tasting area on the second, the winery also boasts a third floor conference room. Jim and Peggy hope to use this space for formal tastings, receptions and seminars, and also for businesses wishing to hold one-day executive retreats.

The Laws knew from day one that an extra investment in state-of-the-art equipment would improve their chances of making high quality wines. Therefore, they bought and put into use in 1987 the state's first dejuicing tank. On the outside, it looks much like any other stainless steel fermenter. But on the inside, it contains a long vertical cylinder perforated like a sieve. Fresh, chilled, and crushed grapes are pumped into the tank where they can either be held for long periods in a temperature-controlled, oxygen-free environment if skin contact is desired, or the juice can be allowed to flow out through the sieve. Under its own weight, 80% of the juice can be separated from skins and seeds in this gentle manner before skins are ever pressed. What results is a cleaner juice with very low solids content. Skins can then be pressed efficiently in the Laws' pneumatic bladder press.

All white wines are fermented cool in jacketed, temperature-controlled stainless steel tanks. Small French Allier oak cooperage is used for aging Chardonnay, and toasted American oak barrels from Missouri are used for aging the Cabernet Sauvignon.

Fruit for Linden's Chardonnay is left in contact with the skins for six hours in the dejuicing tank to pick up extra varietal character. It is then fermented in stainless steel, allowed to remain in contact with its *lees* for three months, and aged in French oak for four months. Jim does not allow his Chardonnay to go through *malolactic fermentation* in order to preserve fresh fruitiness and lower pH levels. Both the initial '87 release and the subsequent '88 Chardonnay are lovely, delicate wines. Clean citrus and apple fruit shows well in both aromas and flavors. Very subtle, enhancing oak frames the overall impression.

Beginning with the 1988 vintage, Linden released a 100% varietal Sauvignon Blanc. Made from grapes grown in the leased Flint Hill Vineyard, the wine possesses outstanding varietal character, an intense grassy/citrus nose, lively melon flavors touched with herbs, and a terrifically long finish. The wine is fermented cool and receives very brief aging in French oak. This wine is especially impressive given the difficulty mid-Atlantic growers often experience with this grape.

Linden's Seyval is a terrific example of the heights this hybrid variety can achieve in the hands of a skilled winemaker. Cool-fermented in stainless steel, the Seyval is bone dry and receives no oak aging. Wonderful grassy, herbal aromas reminiscent of a light-intensity Sauvignon Blanc jump out of the glass. In the mouth the wine is crisp, clean, and refreshing, with grassy fruit flavors of apples and pears. This wine is an ideal one to pair with a wide range of mid-Atlantic seafood recipes.

A delightful Riesling/Vidal wine is also produced. The blend of roughly two-thirds Riesling and one-third Vidal is cold-fermented to preserve delicate aromatics and is sweetened to 2% residual sugar by adding a *sweet reserve* of unfermented Riesling juice. Jim and Peggy are both huge fans of Vidal and feel it is a perfect match for Riesling. Says Jim, "Riesling does not always ripen well in Virginia, but even at low sugar levels it is delicate and aromatic. Vidal, on the other hand, can hang well and ripen to 22° *Brix* consistently. We blend the two; Vidal provides the backbone and Riesling provides the floral delicacy." The wine certainly lives up to this plan. Pretty scents of spring blossoms dominate the nose. On the palate it is silky and viscous, clean and crisp, and boasts well-defined fruit of apricots and citrus.

Linden's inaugural Cabernet Sauvignon from the 1987 vintage is blended with 16% Cabernet Franc. Jim Law ferments the Cabernet Sauvignon grapes in contact with the skins for seven days, while keeping the clusters of Cabernet Franc intact, in whole berry form, to lend extra fruitiness. Yet another promising release from this most-promising Virginia winery, the wine offers vibrant, youthful fruit and mouth-filling texture.

DIRECTIONS

From Washington, DC, travel west on Interstate 66. Take exit 3 at Linden and turn left. Turn left again on Route 55 and drive for one mile. At Route 638, turn right and drive 2 miles to winery on right.

Loudoun Valley Vineyards

ADDRESS: RD 1, Box 340
Waterford, VA 22190
PHONE: (703) 882-3375
OWNERS: Hubert Tucker and Charles
    Ellis
WINEMAKER: Hubert Tucker
TOTAL ACRES: 22
CASES/YR: 5,000 capacity
HOURS: Saturday and Sunday 11-5

Located just a short drive west of the lovely historic town of Leesburg lies Loudoun Valley Vineyards. The winery, which opened in the spring of 1989, is perched on a gentle knoll and overlooks 22 acres of vine-covered rolling hills. Co-owned and managed by Hubert Tucker, Loudoun Valley promises to become one of Virginia's "cutting edge" operations due to its scientific focus on the ultimate source of fine wine: the vineyard.

Hubert Tucker is also the co-owner and founder of Schloss Tucker-Ellis Nursery, the only nursery in the east that is state-certified as producing virus-free, bench grafted vinifera grapevines. For the last several years, Tucker has been supplying vineyards all over the east with vines. As one tours vineyards and wineries of the mid-Atlantic, chances are many of the vines encountered began their lives at Schloss Tucker-Ellis. It is through careful experimentation in his own vineyard, however, that Hubert is trying to shed new light on the question of which grapes grow best in the state of Virginia.

Hubert Tucker is a second generation American of German extraction. He and his father tended 60 acres of vines in the Finger Lakes of New York back in the 1960s, under contract with the Taylor Wine Company. While in the area, Hubert studied, along with his formal degrees in physics and chemistry, viticulture and enology at Cornell University in Ithaca. When his father retired, the family sold its New York property and Hubert moved to Virginia and began working as an aeronautical engineer with the Federal Aviation Administration. In 1978, he and his wife Dolores bought their current property, a lovely farm with rolling pastures, near Waterford.

Drawing on his past experiences in grape growing, Hubert assessed the industry in Virginia and witnessed what he felt to be a shortage of both vinifera vineyards and reliable sources of vinifera vines for planting. To help fill this gap, he began his nursery.

The grafting process is a complex one. As discussed in the introduction, vinifera vines cannot grow on their own roots due to their lack of resistance to the ever-present root louse, phylloxera. Therefore, vinifera cuttings must be grafted onto heartier, phylloxera-resistant American vine rootstock. The process begins when pruned cuttings from Tucker's 2 acres of "rootstock" vines are gathered, sorted, and clipped into 6"-10" pieces. Buds are left intact on these. The rootstock cuttings and vinifera cuttings are then joined like pieces in a puzzle by a special machine, which cuts an omega-shaped union between the two. To secure the union, the graft is dipped in wax. Then the grafted vines are placed in "callousing" boxes, packed row-upon-row with peat moss, and placed for twenty-three days in a special room heated to 90° F and 100% humidity. After this time, roots have sprouted from the rootstock and buds have emerged from the vinifera stock. The vines are then planted in a nursery and allowed to grow for one season. When winter arrives, the vines are allowed to go dormant, and are pruned, uprooted, bundled (by variety), and stored under re-frigeration for the rest of the winter. The following spring, they are purchased and planted by Tucker's customers. To date, Schloss Tucker-Ellis has supplied vineyards in twenty states.

THE VINEYARD

Wanting to get into the act himself, Hubert kept close track of the temperature ranges and frost conditions of his own property, which sits at 700 feet above sea level. Deeming his site suitable, he planted 4 acres of his own to Chardonnay, Riesling, and Cabernet Sauvignon in 1983.

His next-door neighbor, Charles Ellis, watched what Tucker was up to with great interest. Ellis, a retired chief financial officer with RCA, approached Tucker with the idea of expanding the vineyard and starting a winery. A corporation was formed and expansion was begun in 1985.

Today, 22 acres of vines grace the property of these two families. The largest planting, by far, is to Chardonnay—11 acres. As seen in the table below, another 7 acres are devoted to vinifera varieties Cabernet Sauvignon, Riesling, Merlot, and Cabernet Franc.

GRAPE VARIETIES AND ACREAGE

Variety	Vinifera	French/Amer. Hybrids
Chardonnay	11.0	—.—
Cabernet Sauvignon	4.5	—.—
Riesling	1.0	—.—
Merlot	1.0	—.—
Cabernet Franc	0.5	—.—
Rootstock	—.—	2.0
Miscellaneous	—.—	2.0
TOTALS	18.0	4.0

Beyond these 22 acres, Loudoun Valley Vineyards becomes a veritable experimental station of just about every variety imaginable.

First, 2 acres are planted to rootstock varieties to supply the nursery. Two additional acres are planted to fifteen different French-American hybrids, mainly to supply the nursery operation (although grapes will be harvested from these each year as well). Finally, a test plot, carefully maintained and monitored, contains such varieties as Chenin Blanc, Grignolino, Ruby Cabernet, Sangiovese, French Colombard, Pinot Noir, Semillon, Muller-Thurgau, Malbec, Charbono, Muscat Canelli, Muscat Ottonel, Zinfandel, Barbera, Malvasia, Pinot Blanc, Pinot Gris, Gamay, Norton, and so on. Most important, Hubert is watching the development of three clones of Nebbiolo (the classic Italian red variety, which produces that country's fine Barolo wines) and nine different clones of Riesling.

Explains Hubert, "I firmly believe that Nebbiolo will do extremely well in Virginia, especially the cooler sections of the state; and Riesling is clearly the toughest grape in Virginia to match correctly with micro-climates. From this test plot, I expect to learn a great deal about which varieties are best suited to Virginia's different regions. I'd like to help Virginia's industry advance into the next decade by contributing my data. The key to future expansion, I feel, will be in matching the correct varieties to the most appropriate micro-climate."

THE WINES

The winery at Loudoun Valley Vineyards is equipped with state-of-the-art tools such as a dejuicing tank (like the one used at Linden Vineyards), jacketed, temperature-controlled stainless steel fermenters, and small French oak cooperage.

Hubert Tucker regularly produces six wines at Loudoun Valley: two Chardonnays (a regular bottling and a special Reserve from the vintage's best lots), a Riesling, a Cabernet Sauvignon, and non-vintage white and red estate-bottled "everyday" table wines.

His Chardonnays are made to achieve as much complexity as possible. Before fermentation, crushed grapes are placed in the dejuicing tank and left in contact with their skins for twelve to sixteen hours to extract additional varietal character. After pressing, part of the wine is then fermented in French Limousin and Nevers oak and is allowed to complete a secondary *malolactic fermentation*. The rest is fermented cool in stainless steel tanks. Both the inaugural release '88 Chardonnay and the '89 version (both regular bottlings) displayed lean but flavorful apple and pear fruitiness. The overall crisp impression was nicely played against warm, toasty oak notes.

Tucker's Cabernet Sauvignon, which contains small percentages of both Merlot and Cabernet Franc, is fermented in contact with the skins for three to four weeks. During fermentation, 10% of the grapes are left uncrushed, in whole-berry form, in order to enhance aromatic fruitiness. It is *fined* lightly after spending a year in American oak, but is not filtered in order to maintain its full-bodied texture. At the time of this writing, no Loudoun Valley Cabernet had yet been released.

The winery's Riesling is produced in a slightly sweet style, with 1.5 to 2.0% residual sugar. Cool fermented in stainless steel, the wine shows a terrific floral/apricot bouquet and lively, delicate fruit flavors.

The Estate Vinifera White offers extremely nice everyday drinking. A blend of 50% Chardonnay and 50% Riesling, the wine shows clean apple, peach, and floral character in both nose and flavors. At this writing, no Estate Red had been released.

Loudoun Valley will also bottle a limited volume of library selections: red and white wines made from the vinifera varieties grown in the experimental plot. Visitors to the winery will be able to taste, judge, and provide Hubert feedback on the characteristics of these wines for future planning and plantings. To date, the only library release was a surprisingly impressive Zinfandel from the 1988 vintage. Displaying nice scents of violets and berries, the wine offers rich, medium-bodied raspberry and plum flavors. While lighter than California Zins, to be sure, the wine is certainly true to its varietal character and creates anticipation for further library releases. (The reader should keep an eye peeled: due for release in the winter of 1990-91, the first Loudoun Valley Sangiovese, a 100% varietal from the Tuscan grape that is used to create Italian Chianti!)

A man of endless ideas and energy, Tucker is also working with growers in the states of Oregon and Washington who have been making plum wine. So enamored of these fruit wines is Hubert that he planted a small orchard in 1988. As an aperitif style wine, he hopes to turn plums into wine in a few years.

INCIDENTALLY . . .

The label for Loudoun Valley Vineyards was designed by Rowan Lacompte, the artist who designed the stained glass windows for the Washington National Cathedral in the District of Columbia.

DIRECTIONS

Follow Route 7 west, past Leesburg. Turn right on Route 9 and proceed 4.5 miles to the winery on the right.

Meredyth Vineyards

ADDRESS: P.O. Box 347
Middleburg, VA 22117
PHONE: (703) 687-6277
OWNERS: The Smith Family
WINEMAKER: Archie Smith III
TOTAL ACRES: 55
CASES/YR: 15,000
HOURS: Seven days a week 10-5

Middleburg, Virginia, a quaint, historic town located just an hour's drive from Washington, DC, is an area best known for its horse farms, fox hunting, and lavish country manners of the well-to-do. Thanks, in part, to Meredyth Vineyards, it is also becoming recognized as one of the centers of the burgeoning Virginia wine industry.

In the early 1970s, Archie Smith, Jr. and his wife Dody, farmers for years in northern Virginia, were thinking of diversification. Their traditional agricultural crops such as corn, as well as their herds of cattle, were thriving. Unfortunately, they were no longer earning a margin of profit that made their continuance sensible. After extensive study of alternatives and thorough consultation with experts, Archie Jr. decided that grapes might be the way to go. In the spring of 1972, the first vines were planted on the Smiths' Stirling Farm and the family hasn't looked back since.

The state of Virginia had practically no track record for grape growing when the Smiths began their "experiment." Proceeding slowly and utilizing the collective knowledge on viticulture gathered on journeys up and down the east coast, Archie Jr. took the strategy of planting many varieties in small individual plots to see which succeeded best in this part of the state. Learning a little more each year, the vineyard was expanded by about 5 acres annually and now measures a total of 55 acres.

The winery received its license in the summer of 1975, becoming one of the first farm wineries in the state.

From the beginning, Archie Jr. was assisted by his son Archie III. Early on, this help was lent during the summers, when Archie III was on vacation from his job teaching philosophy at Oxford University in England. In 1977, he joined his parents on a full-time basis and currently is responsible for both winemaking and vineyard management. "I loved teaching philosophy, but I love this even more," explains Archie III.

THE VINEYARD

At this time, Meredyth's diverse 55 acres are planted to a full sixteen varieties: 65% to French-American hybrids, 33% to vinifera *cultivars*, and 2% to the native-American hybrid Delaware.

As can be seen below, the largest plantings of vinifera are to Chardonnay, Riesling, and Cabernet Sauvignon, with small amounts of Sauvignon Blanc and Merlot. The largest hybrid planting is for the white grape Seyval followed by the red Marechal Foch. Other French-American hybrids include the whites Villard Blanc, Aurora, Vidal Blanc, and Rayon D'or, and the reds Rougeon, Villard Noir, DeChaunac, and Leon Millot.

Estate vineyards supply the vast majority of grapes for Meredyth wines, but the winery also purchases small lots of both Chardonnay and Cabernet Sauvignon to supplement its supply. A common source for these grapes is often Burnley Vineyards in Barboursville.

GRAPE VARIETIES AND ACREAGE

Variety	Vinifera	French/Amer. Hybrids
Seyval	—.—	9.3
Foch	—.—	6.0
Chardonnay	5.9	—.—
Riesling	5.9	—.—
Rougeon	—.—	5.1
Villard Blanc	—.—	4.3
Cabernet Sauvignon	4.0	—.—
Villard Noir	—.—	3.5
DeChaunac	—.—	3.2
Leon Millot	—.—	2.5
Sauvignon Blanc	1.4	—.—
Aurora	—.—	1.1
Delaware	—.—	1.0
Vidal Blanc	—.—	0.7
Rayon D'or	—.—	0.6
Merlot	0.5	—.—
TOTALS	17.7	37.3

THE WINES

Meredyth offers a staggering array of wines sure to please a wide range of palates. From their extensive and diverse vineyard, the winery bottles upwards of twelve varietal-designated wines, four blended wines, and on occasion, special commemorative blends. There is even a non-alcoholic sparkling grape juice for kids, teetotalers, or anyone wishing to try a festive sipping or picnic beverage.

Generally speaking, Archie Smith III ferments his wines at cool temperatures in jacketed stainless steel tanks. All skins-fermented red wines and fuller bodied whites receive aging in oak (French Nevers for vinifera varieties and American oak for all others), while other wines are bottled young to preserve fresh fruitiness.

In the vinifera category, Meredyth's Chardonnay, Cabernet Sauvignon, and Sauvignon Blanc are especially noteworthy. The style of the winery's Chardonnay reflects the warm growing season in the Middleburg area; it is a fairly full-bodied wine, possessing soft appley fruit, a bit of earthy complexity, and an assertive dose of oak. The Meredyth Cabernet can be an impressive wine. The 1985 Cab shows good promise with a deep garnet color and aromas and flavors redolent of black raspberries and cassis. Meredyth's Sauvignon Blanc displays good varietal grassiness in the nose and tart grapefruit and citrus flavors. Other vinifera offerings include Riesling (finished with about 1% residual sugar), Merlot (the '85, a medium-bodied effort with lots of young, straightforward fruitiness), and a 100% varietal Gewurztraminer.

For those who have never tasted wine made from French-American hybrid grapes, Meredyth is a great place to gain a thorough introduction. Archie Smith III is a strong supporter of hybrid grapes. "I think they will continue to serve an important function in the eastern industry. They can be made into great wines, and they are always dependable in this often unkind climate," he explains.

White hybrid grapes can produce, at their best, wines that rival their more prestigious vinifera parents. Grapes such as Seyval are very flexible and can be vinified in a full-bodied style resembling Chardonnay. If fermented at cool temperatures in stainless steel and bottled young with no oak aging, Seyvals can also be produced in a lighter, fresher style resembling a dry, crisp Muscadet. The increasingly popular Vidal, often made in a slightly sweet style, can come awfully close in aroma and flavor to a good Riesling.

Red hybrid grapes have posed more of a challenge to winemakers, however. Vinified in traditional methods (hot fermentation temperatures with extended skin contact), they can yield intensely herbaceous, astringent wines with an unusual salty flavor and medicinal odors. Winemakers with the skill and patience of Archie Smith III, however, have over time modified techniques to optimize the hybrid grape's unique character. "Cooler fermentations allow the wines to retain their more delicate fruitiness, and since red hybrid grapes tend to yield the color from their skins so readily, we don't need to skins-ferment for more than a day or two, if at all. This way, we decrease the tannins and herbaceousness," explains Archie.

Archie has also relied on the fermentation technique of the Beaujolais region—*carbonic maceration*—to produce fresh nouveau-styled wines from hybrid grapes. With this process, whole, uncrushed berry clusters are allowed to ferment under a blanket of carbon dioxide, internally extracting pigment and flavor while leaving tannins behind.

Finally, Archie has mastered the art of blending in order to highlight the best qualities of numerous hybrid grapes.

Among the red hybrids, both the Leon Millot and the Villard Noir provide pleasant drinking. Both are hearty and full-bodied with round, soft berry flavors, very light tannins, and an ample measure of spicy, almost bourbon-like oak. Other red varieties include the more assertive DeChaunac and the more herbal, vegetal Foch. This latter grape also serves as the base for Meredyth's "Nouveau" (the wine made by carbonic maceration), which is abundantly grapey and both smells and tastes like freshly crushed berries. Blended red wines include

"Harvest Red" and, at the time of this writing, a special "Bicentennial Red," celebrating the 200 year anniversary of Middleburg. While an acquired taste to be sure, red hybrids can produce nicely fruity, pleasant wines. Given their low cost, they also fill a critical niche in the affordable, everyday wine category. (On average, these wines sell for about $5 per bottle.)

Meredyth's Seyval Blancs can be quite impressive wines—full and round on the palate with slightly grassy, herbal fruit, sort of a poor man's cross between a Chardonnay and a Sauvignon Blanc. The winery's Villard Blanc is a lighter, crisper wine with much less evident oak, and grapefruit and citrus fruitiness. Meredyth's only dessert-style wine is its Delaware, made from a native-American grape variety, finished with 5% residual sugar and possessing forward *labrusca* grapiness.

The winery also offers its "everyday" table wines, called simply "Premium White," "Red," and "Blush." Each is a blend of numerous, mainly hybrid varieties and offers clean, fruity drinkability at a very modest price. The "Blush" is especially nice, with a floral, perfumed nose derived from Riesling and a soft berry fruitiness from the *free run juice* of the Villard Noir grape. It is finished slightly sweet with 1% residual sugar.

INCIDENTALLY . . .

Looking for a more colorful name than Smith, and not able to name the winery after the family property called Stirling Farm due to the existence of Sterling Vineyards in California, Archie Smith Jr. chose to call his winery Meredyth, his maternal grandmother's maiden name.

DIRECTIONS

From Washington, DC, follow Route 50 west to Middleburg. At the blinking light in town, turn left on Route 776 and drive for 2.5 miles. At Route 628, turn right and proceed to winery on right. Or, from Interstate 66, take exit 8 and travel north on Route 245 to The Plains. Turn right on Route 55 and then quickly left on Route 626. Proceed 4 miles to Route 679 and turn right. Proceed one mile to winery on left.

Naked Mountain Vineyard

ADDRESS: P.O. Box 131
Markham, VA 22643
PHONE: (703) 364-1609
OWNERS: Robert and Phoebe Harper
WINEMAKER: Bob Harper
TOTAL ACRES: 5
CASES/YR: 2,300
HOURS: March through December,
　　　Wednesday through Sunday 11-5

Arguably the most picturesque setting of any winery in the mid-Atlantic, Naked Mountain Vineyard is nestled in a narrow, south-facing hollow along the eastern slope of the Blue Ridge. A rustic, chalet-style winery, whose fabulous tasting room with floors, walls, and ceiling beams finished in split, rough-hewn white pine, sits amid the estate's 5 acres of vineyards. Looming above and behind the winery is the mountain whose flat, treeless top inspired the name "Naked Mountain."

Bob Harper, who along with his wife Phoebe owns and operates the winery, claims that his site is a perfect one for growing premium grapes. "With our elevation above 1,000 feet," says Bob, "we enjoy a marvelous thermal inversion. In January, when temperatures dipped to -10° F in nearby Markham, our temperature was +6° F. Similarly, in the summer when the lowlands toward Washington, DC are sweltering, we're usually several degrees cooler."

Such conditions are necessary in order to grow the grapes Bob and Phoebe grow. "I'm a very stubborn, biased person," continues Bob. "I will only grow vinifera varieties. They can't be grown everywhere, but under the right conditions, I believe they can be made into the best wine."

Reaching their current situation took a great deal of hard work and planning, however. Bob and Phoebe, having both grown up in northern Virginia suburbs of Washington, took up winemaking as a hobby in the 1960s. Finding good grapes a scarce commodity, Bob decided he'd grow his own. His first vineyard planted along the Rappahannock River was a miserable failure, however. "It was a frost pocket. I lost my entire crop every year!" he says. Taking time out from their busy careers (Bob as a salesman for Texaco and Phoebe as a federal employee), they searched high and low for a better vineyard site. As Bob explains, "I learned that the best barometer for successful grape growing was successful peach growing. Peaches bud at about the same time as many vinifera varieties, so I knew that if I could find a thriving peach orchard, one in which spring frosts did not damage the year's crop, I could also find a site suitable for my vineyard."

The Harpers found their spot just 60 miles west of Washington in the foothills of the Blue Ridge in 1972. They built their house in 1975 and put their first vines in the ground (just .25 acre) in 1976. By the summer of 1981, they had 5 acres in production but no license. "We were bonded, finally, at the end of August in 1981 and literally began picking grapes the next day," says Bob.

Bob has since quit his job with Texaco to devote his full energies to winegrowing while Phoebe divides her "too few" hours between her federal career and the operations of the winery.

THE VINEYARD

Naked Mountain's 5 acres are divided among six varieties. The largest planting, 3.25 acres, is devoted to Chardonnay, the classic white grape of Burgundy and the same grape the California wine industry has built itself around. As Bob puts it, "In the east, Chardonnay is risky. It buds early and thus is more susceptible to damage from late cold snaps or frosts."

One acre is planted to Riesling. The same grape that produces delicate, floral, crisp wines in cool climates like Germany and the Finger Lakes of New York can produce much less elegant, heavy-nanded wines in hotter climates like Virginia. But Bob Harper attributes the success of Naked Mountain's Riesling, which is amazingly Germanic, to his vineyard location (with its cooler, longer growing season) and to the clone of the grape he has planted. "There are over 400 clones of Riesling," he explains. "I have planted clone #239 exclusively. This one, while a shy bearer of fruit, has been identified by Geisenheim University in Germany as the one possessing the most intense flavor."

One-half acre is planted to Sauvignon Blanc. This white grape of Bordeaux is not often cultivated in the east, and for good reason. "I may end up grafting it over to Chardonnay. It is a very difficult grape to grow, and produces so much foliage that it is practically impossible to pick," Harper muses.

The last quarter acre at Naked Mountain is planted to Cabernet Sauvignon, with a few plants devoted to Cabernet Franc and Merlot. While the former two are doing quite well, Merlot has proved very difficult to grow. "It is so vigorous that it does not store enough carbohydrates to make it through the winter. Merlot fruit is also very thin-skinned and if it rains around harvest, the grapes burst and rot sets in," says Bob. At this point, the Merlot vines have faded slowly so that now only two remain.

GRAPE VARIETIES AND ACREAGE

Variety	Vinifera	French/Amer. Hybrids
Chardonnay	3.25	—.—
Riesling	1.0	—.—
Sauvignon Blanc	0.5	—.—
Cabernet Sauvignon	0.25	—.—
TOTALS	5.0	0.0

THE WINES

Always the perfectionist, Bob Harper follows the traditional, labor-intensive winemaking methods of Europe with each of his wines.

For his Chardonnay, for example, he settles his fresh juice in stainless steel tanks at 35° F. The cold temperature encourages any solid matter to drop to the bottom of the tank, leaving the Chardonnay juice clearer and purer. Just after getting the fermentation started, he *racks* the *must* into French oak barrels to complete fermentation. Using a combination of Limousin, Nevers, and Allier oak, barrel-fermentation imparts complexity and depth to the Chardonnay. For four months, the freshly fermented wine is left to age *sur lie* (on the yeast sediment that settles at the bottom of the barrels), and Bob stirs the yeast in each barrel every three to four days. Yeast also adds its own toasty, creamy flavors and layers to the finished wine. After racking the wine back into stainless steel for *cold stabilization* and *fining* (two processes that clarify and stabilize the wine), he puts the wine back into barrels for an additional three months of aging. The only point at which Bob departs from the methods of Burgundy is by not letting his Chardonnay complete *malolactic fermentation* — a secondary fermentation that converts harsher malic acid into milder lactic acid.

All of these steps are reflected in the aromas and flavors of Naked Mountain Chardonnays. Vintage in and vintage out, the wines display complex scents of vanillan oak, full, ripe apple and tropical fruit, and delicate yeasty notes. On the palate, they are full and lush with well-defined Chardonnay flavors enhanced by rich, smoky oak. Several examples from recent vintages (namely, 1984, '85, '86, and '88) are fabulous wines that could compete with the best that California or France has to offer.

Bob Harper's versatility as a winemaker is evidenced by his lovely Rieslings. Naked Mountain Rieslings never see oak and instead are fermented at very low temperatures (45-50° F) in stainless steel. Low temperatures allow for a very slow fermentation, which preserves all the fresh, delicate fruit this grape has to offer. Bob Harper halts his Riesling's fermentation by chilling the wine to 28° when there is 2% residual sugar left in the juice. After settling and fining, he sterile-filters out any yeast cells and bottles the wine young. The '89 Riesling has all the characteristics you would expect from a classic German wine—blossomy, perfumed aromas, rich grapefruit and apricot flavors. Finished medium sweet, it is well balanced by vibrant acidity.

When vintages permit, Harper will produce very limited amounts of Sauvignon Blanc. He fashions this wine in a similar manner as his Chardonnays, relying on barrel fermentation for added complexity. In successful vintages like '86, the wine has a precise varietal nose of herbs, grass, and bell pepper and has round, mouth-filling flavors of melony, fig-like fruit and a long, lively finish buoyed by nice acids.

The only red at Naked Mountain is called Claret. Predominantly Cabernet Sauvignon (90%+) with a bit of Cabernet Franc and Merlot blended in, the wine is fermented in an open container in contact with the grape skins for seven days. Fined only with egg whites, the wine spends one and a half years in French oak. Both the '84 and '85 Clarets were pretty wines, medium-bodied with a precise nose of berries and cassis. Warm, mouth-filling flavors, while young and fruity at the time of this writing, promise to broaden in both texture and complexity with additional aging.

Finally, Naked Mountain also offers a low-priced, everyday white called Catamount Hollow. A wine produced from purchased vinifera fruit, it is made in the same manner as the Riesling and is finished slightly sweet.

INCIDENTALLY . . .

At this time, Naked Mountain sells out every year its entire production of approximately 2,000 cases, mostly at the winery. In an effort to expand production and meet the rising public demand, Bob and Phoebe hope to obtain additional land on which to plant vines, but have had trouble finding sites suitable for producing the high quality fruit to which they have become accustomed.

DIRECTIONS

From Washington, DC, follow Interstate 66 west to Markham, Exit 4. Turn right (north) on Route 688 and proceed 1.5 miles to winery on the right.

Oasis Vineyard

ADDRESS: Route 1, Highway 635
Hume, VA 22639
PHONE: (703) 635-7627
OWNERS: Dirgham and Corinne Salahi
WINEMAKER: Dirgham Salahi
TOTAL ACRES: 70
CASES/YR: 10,000
HOURS: Seven days a week 10-4

Located just 7 or so miles south of Interstate 66 near the tiny town of Hume lies Oasis Vineyard, owned and operated by Dirgham and Corinne Salahi. Backed up against the eastern slope of the Blue Ridge Mountains, the vineyard and winery are nestled in a beautiful, rolling valley which is not always cooperative when it comes to winegrowing.

Explains the wiry, effervescent Dirgham, "Winter kill and frost are our biggest problems. The cold air comes out of the mountains and sits in certain pockets of the vineyard. We lose about 30% of our crop each year due to winter kill and bud damage." But such realities are part of the life of mid-Atlantic wine pioneers.

In spite of the hardships, Oasis still produces enough fruit to bottle more than 10,000 cases of wine each year, one of the largest outputs in the state. "We've enjoyed some very nice success and we're here to stay," adds Dirgham.

Dirgham Salahi, born in Jerusalem, moved to the United States in 1955 to study at Louisiana State University. After receiving a Master's degree in geology from George Washington University in Washington, DC, he worked for approximately twenty years for the American Geological Institute in that city and following that, worked as a consultant for several more years.

Yearning for a more agrarian lifestyle, the Salahis began looking for property in the rural Virginia landscape in the mid-1970s. At least partially due to its soil make-up, the geologist chose the family's present farm near Hume. It seemed a promising location for the cultivation of a few acres of grapes—a new hobby of Dirgham's. They built a Mediterranean-style home, reminiscent of what one might see in Dirgham's homeland, in 1977 and also planted 15 acres of French-American hybrid vines. A year later, 25 more acres were added in vinifera varieties.

Before long, the acreage began producing and something had to be done. Encouraged by his successes in amateur competitions, the wine hobbyist turned pro in 1980 when he quit his geological consulting work and received his commercial winery license. Large-scale production still did not occur for a few years—the Salahis sold the bulk of their produce to other wineries at first.

When the basement of their lovely new home began to fill with equipment, the smells of fermenting wine, and the inevitable swarm of fruit flies, Corinne put her foot down and the couple decided to build a separate winery. Completed in 1982, the building boasts a large tasting room and a cellar dug below ground, which has the capacity to process 50,000 cases annually. The concrete, epoxy-lined tanks, unique in Virginia, were imported from Italy and are embossed with the Oasis logo.

Dirgham Salahi, in his pleasing, soft accent, speaks with passion and pride of his vineyard and wines. "I consider my vines my family and my wines the children they give birth to. I raise my family and children with great, loving care," he says. A visit to Oasis provides a wonderful opportunity to sample the fruits of Dirgham's labor.

THE VINEYARD

An ambitious schedule of planting, designed both to increase supply to meet growing consumer demand and to mitigate the ill effects of winter damage, will keep Oasis vineyard one of the largest in the state. For the 1987 crush, 40 acres were producing. But in the spring of 1987, an additional 30 acres were added, bringing total vineyard size to 70 acres.

Oasis' vineyard is currently divided among thirteen varieties. Since the original planting of French-American hybrids, all expansion of the vineyard has been in vinifera varieties. As seen in the table below, 12 acres each have been devoted to Chardonnay and Cabernet Sauvignon and 10 acres each to Riesling and the white hybrid Seyval. Smaller amounts of Gewurztraminer, Sauvignon Blanc, Merlot, Cabernet Franc, and Semillon round out the vinifera. (Both Semillon and Sauvignon Blanc are seldom grown in the mid-Atlantic, due to their particular growing characteristics and tenderness. However, given the large size of his vineyard, Dirgham is willing to take a chance each year on these outstanding wine varieties.) Red hybrid varieties Foch, Chelois, and Chancellor, as well as the relatively obscure white Rayon D'or, join Seyval in the hybrid plots.

GRAPE VARIETIES AND ACREAGE

Variety	Vinifera	French/Amer. Hybrids
Chardonnay	12.0	—.—
Cabernet Sauvignon	12.0	—.—
Riesling	10.0	—.—
Seyval	—.—	10.0
Cabernet Franc	5.0	—.—
Gewurztraminer	5.0	—.—
Merlot	5.0	—.—
Sauvignon Blanc	5.0	—.—
Chancellor	—.—	1.5
Chelois	—.—	1.5
Foch	—.—	1.0
Semillon	1.0	—.—
Rayon D'or	—.—	1.0
TOTALS	55.0	15.0

THE WINES

A self-taught winemaker, Dirgham produced wine as an amateur for more than thirty years before starting Oasis. "I honestly believe that amateurs make some of the best wines. They can give all their love and attention to small lots, and they don't have to worry about commercial concerns such as excess filtering and guarding against wines throwing any sediment or *tartrates* after bottling," he says. Always keeping these values in the back of his mind, Dirgham tries to keep the "handling" of his wines to a minimum in his cellar.

However, one wine which, by its very nature, must be handled a great deal is Oasis' Champagne. The production of sparkling wine is small in the mid-Atlantic, with only Oasis, Piedmont, and Ingleside Plantation in Virginia, Boordy in Maryland, and Biltmore Estate, Duplin, and Southland Estate in North Carolina devoting their efforts to it on a serious scale. It is the expensive, painstaking, and labor-intensive "méthode champenoise" by which all great sparkling wines are made which explains this fact.

To produce Champagne, grapes (usually Chardonnay and Pinot Noir) are picked slightly underripe (at 17-19° *Brix*) so that natural acidity levels will be high. A totally dry wine is then fermented from the juice of these grapes. To the *still* wine is added additional sugar and active yeast. The mixture is then bottled in heavy glass champagne bottles and capped so that, while the yeast is refermenting the sugar, all of the carbon dioxide produced as a byproduct of the fermentation will be absorbed into the wine. Refermentation takes place slowly over the course of several months, and the wine is allowed to rest on the yeast sediment that forms for up to three years. This aging adds a toasty complexity to the wine. Then the slow process of *riddling* begins whereby the bottles are tilted, rotated, and jostled gently each day, by hand, in order to collect the yeast in the neck of the bottle. When the yeast are well compacted in the now upside-down bottles, the necks are frozen in a glycol solution and, again by hand, have their caps removed. The extreme carbon dioxide pressure creates an explosion that blows the frozen sediment cap out of the bottle, a process called *degourgement*. Before much carbon dioxide escapes as bubbles, the winemaker must quickly replace any lost fluid by adding a *dosage* of either still wine (for dry, Brut champagnes) or brandy (for slightly sweeter, Extra Dry champagnes). After the dosage, a cork is immediately inserted and secured by a wire hood.

As can be seen, it is a difficult and exacting process that few wineries undertake. Oasis, however, has risen to the challenge to produce about 1,600 cases each year of a very respectable sparkling wine. A *cuvée* of 80% Chardonnay and 20% Pinot Noir, the wine has a nice golden straw color and possesses lively if somewhat large and short-lived bubbles. A lean and slightly austere champagne, Oasis has produced a wine with a clean, restrained core of fruit, which hints ever-so-faintly at strawberries and cherries, due to the Pinot content.

Beyond the Champagne, which is well worth seeking out, the red wines at Oasis grab the most attention. The Cabernet Sauvignon which is blended with 20% Merlot) can be a clean, generously fruity (wine with medium body, tight young tannins, and faint vegetal overtones. It spends one year in French Nevers oak. The 1985 bottling stands out as an especially nice rendering. When vintages cooperate, a Merlot is sometimes bottled separately as well.

A surprisingly attractive wine (and a good bargain) is the Oasis Chelois (which occasionally is bottled under the moniker "Proprietor's Select" or "Virginia Red"). Actually a blend of 80% Chelois and varying amounts of Cabernet, Chancellor, and Foch, it is a nice choice for everyday drinking—soft, round, and supple with full, spicy blackberry and cherry fruit framed by slightly bourbony oak.

A long string of whites is produced at Oasis including Chardonnay, Riesling, Gewurztraminer, Seyval, Sauvignon Blanc, and a blended Rayon D'or/Seyval/Chardonnay wine called "Chablis." A rosé is also produced from Chancellor. Dirgham uses a heat exchanger to cool his whites during fermentation, a device not unlike a large radiator through which the fermenting wine is pumped. Of the wines mentioned, the Chardonnay and Sauvignon Blanc are both barrel-fermented in French Nevers oak, and the Riesling and Gewurztraminer are finished slightly sweet with 1% residual sugar. The latter has offered the cleanest, fruitiest white from recent vintages, with a pleasing floral/spicy character. The Sauvignon Blanc (blended with 5% Semillon) is produced in minute quantities but consistently wins awards so . . . happy hunting!

DIRECTIONS

From Washington, DC, take Interstate 66 to the second Marshall exit. Take Route 647 south, then turn right onto Route 688, then right onto Route 635. Proceed about 10 miles to winery on the left.

PIEDMONT VINEYARDS

Artist Series   Lloyd Kelly, American   (1946-)

1989
Virginia Semillon

Piedmont Vineyards and Winery

ADDRESS: P.O. Box 286
Middleburg, VA 22117
PHONE: (703) 687-5528
OWNER: Elizabeth H. Worrall
WINEMAKER: Eric Brevart
TOTAL ACRES: 34
CASES/YR: 5,000
HOURS: April-December, 7 days a week 10-5; January-March, Wednesday through Sunday 10-4

The late Elizabeth Furness might truly be called the matriarch of the Virginia wine industry. A grand woman who spent her childhood years prior to World War I growing up in France and Germany, and who later helped oversee the family's lumber fortunes in Minnesota and Washington state, she actually planted Virginia's first vinifera vineyard after she entered her seventh decade. An avid equestrienne, Mrs. Furness had come to Virginia's hunt country and the charming town of Middleburg to shop for horses in 1942. She drove past a stately Greek Revival mansion and was struck with the idea of settling in this lovely part of the country.

In 1973 Mrs. Furness decided to venture into the realm of grape growing. An aficionado of white Burgundies and Bordeaux and not much of a fan of red wines or wines made from French-American hybrids, Furness decided to plant her favorite varieties — Chardonnay and Semillon (each in 5-acre plots). Because the region was completely untested for vinifera at the time, she was also persuaded by more experienced eastern growers to add 5 acres of the white hybrid Seyval. While it was a struggle, the vines did survive and mature. The old dairy barn was converted into a winery, and in 1977 the first Piedmont wines were produced. That year, although in minuscule amounts, Piedmont sold the first bottles of Virginia vinifera wine. In 1985, Mrs. Furness died having realized her goal of developing a successful Virginia winery and vineyard.

The operation is now directed by Mrs. Furness' daughter, Elizabeth Worrall. Mrs. Worrall has carefully cultivated Piedmont's reputation as an ultra-premium, boutique winery. Producing just 5,000 cases per year, the winery has been oriented toward quality rather than quantity. This image of refined excellence fits in well with the stately surrounding hunt country of Middleburg.

To maintain a genuine standard of quality, it was critical that Piedmont hire a top-notch winemaker. Curt Sherrer served in that capacity originally, followed by Eric Brevart since 1989.

Educated at the University of California at Davis, this country's premier institution for enology and viticulture, Sherrer developed a wine program at Piedmont that earned the winery national recognition.

His big, full-bodied Chardonnays in particular received the highest praises of critics like Robert Parker of the *Wine Advocate*. For several years, Sherrer's influence was felt broadly across the mid-Atlantic.

But even this arrangement did not last long. In 1989, Sherrer left Piedmont to pursue other interests. The significant task of filling his shoes was passed on to Eric Brevart, a Frenchman with previous experience making wine at Virginia's Misty Mountain Vineyard, Fetzer Vineyards in California, and Naylor Winery in Pennsylvania. Several of his wines have proved medal-winners.

THE VINEYARD

One of Piedmont's major tasks in recent years has been to retool the vineyard. Over the years, total Chardonnay acreage had reached 20, while Semillon and Seyval acreage stood at 5 acres each. But parts of the Chardonnay plot were not faring as well as others due to excessive dampness. And the Seyval stand was giving Mrs. Worrall fits. A usually vigorous and hardy variety, Piedmont's Seyval appeared to be suffering from a virus infection and was slowly dying back each year and producing smaller and smaller crops.

The revamping effort, while painful, represents a concerted investment in the future. Curt Sherrer persuaded Mrs. Worrall that the Seyval had to go and, after the '87 harvest, he began pulling the 5 acres of fifteen-year-old vines. He also removed 4 of Piedmont's 20 acres of Chardonnay. In their place, 5 acres of Chardonnay were planted on a site deemed more suitable for success. Another 4 acres of Cabernet Sauvignon and 1 acre of Cabernet Franc were added. The previous spring, Piedmont had begun its foray into the production of red wine by planting 2.5 acres of Cabernet Sauvignon and .5 acres of Cabernet Franc. While Mrs. Furness may have objected in principle, Curt and Mrs. Worrall agree that a premium vinifera red is needed to fill out Piedmont's lineup.

Today, including the newly planted vines, Piedmont's total acreage stands at 34. As seen below, 21 of these are devoted to Chardonnay, 5 to Semillon, 6.5 to Cabernet Sauvignon, and 1.5 to Cabernet Franc.

GRAPE VARIETIES AND ACREAGE

Variety	Vinifera	French/Amer. Hybrids
Chardonnay	21.0	—.—
Cabernet Sauvignon	6.5	—.—
Semillon	5.0	—.—
Cabernet Franc	1.5	—.—
TOTALS	34.0	0.0

As accurately implied by the winery's name, this Middleburg operation is located on the rolling piedmont plain fronting the eastern edge of the Blue Ridge Mountains and running the entire north-south length of the state. Situated at less than 1,000 feet above sea level, the site has worked relatively well for the cultivation of vinifera grapes. Winter cold and spring frost have caused their share of damage over the years, and drought conditions prevail surprisingly often in the Little River Valley in which they sit. Fortunately, consistent westerly breezes help move the humid air during the summer months, sparing Piedmont much of the rot problems Virginia growers usually face.

Piedmont is the only winery in the mid-Atlantic that grows the Semillon grape in commercial quantities. What started out as the preferential whim of the original owner has ended up placing Piedmont in a unique position in the eastern market. But cultivating Semillon does not come easily. A winter-tender variety, the Semillon crop at Piedmont tends to be quite small given the vineyard acreage.

THE WINES

In its neat, well-designed, renovated barn, Piedmont produces a wide array of white wines. (Newly planted red varieties will not be producing for several years.) The winery produces two Chardonnays, two Semillons, and three Seyvals from purchased fruit.

For their Chardonnays, Piedmont likes to barrel ferment as much of the wine as barrel capacity permits. After chilling and settling, fermentation is started in stainless steel tanks. When the sugar level has dropped to about 16° *Brix*, the wine is moved into oak to complete fermentation. To add complexity, a secondary *malolactic fermentation* is induced. While the process tends to rob a wine of some of its overt fruitiness, it adds a buttery, viscous complexity to wines like Chardonnay. For the last several vintages, Piedmont has produced both regular and reserve Chardonnays. The wines consistently possess lovely lemon, apple, and vanillan fruit rounded out with soft and subtle toasted oak. The 1986 Winemaker's Reserve really placed Piedmont on the Chardonnay map. Intense buttery richness surrounds fruit flavors that taste like spiced apples. Silky, viscous, and long finishing, the wine will hold as a true standard bearer.

Piedmont produces both a regular bottling of Semillon and an Artists Series, reserve-style bottling. Both are fermented in stainless steel and receive three months of oak aging; the regular in American and the Artists Series in French oak. A large berry, low intensity grape with a high pulp-to-skin ratio, Semillon benefits by being left on the skins for several hours prior to fermentation in order to extract as much varietal intensity as possible. The Artists Series bottlings consistently possess light but clean, crisp, citrusy fruit flavors of grapefruit framed by toasty oak. The regular Semillon is similarly fruity but less intense, displaying the spicier, bourbony flavors characteristic of American oak. Both Semillons are much leaner in style than their French, California, or Washington state counterparts.

Seyvals at Piedmont are offered in three different styles. The 100% varietal Seyval is fermented to dryness in stainless steel and is then aged for six months in American oak. It is a fine, grassy, well-oaked Sauvignon Blanc-like wine, which would go wonderfully with mid-Atlantic seafood. The "Hunt Country White" is also a dry version of Seyval with 10% Chardonnay added to the blend. Oaky, crisp, and fruity, it offers a good value for everyday drinking. Finally, the "Little River White" is a 100% Seyval finished with 2% residual sugar. Rounder and silkier due to the sugar, the wine is pleasant if unexciting and works well as an aperitif.

INCIDENTALLY . . .

In keeping with her goal of hiring young, talented forward thinkers, Mrs. Worrall brought Ernest "Bud" Hufnagel onto the Piedmont staff several years ago. Now in charge of marketing and promotion, Bud has taken a leading role in organizing numerous grand events at the winery, including the annual Middleburg Wine Festival, horse shows, and elegant catered tastings and dinners held by candlelight in the winery, amid barrels and tanks.

Also, beginning in 1988, Piedmont offered its first sparkling wine, a *méthode champenoise* blanc de blanc made from 100% Chardonnay. This wine will only be made in selected years depending on harvest conditions.

DIRECTIONS

From Washington, DC, follow Route 50 west to Middleburg. At Route 626, turn left (south) and proceed 3 miles to winery on right. Or, from Interstate 66, take exit 8 and proceed north to The Plains. Turn right on Route 55 and then quickly left on Route 626. Proceed approximately 5 miles to winery on left.

Swedenburg Winery

ADDRESS: Route 50
Middleburg, VA 22117
PHONE: (703) 687-5219
OWNERS: Wayne and Juanita
    Swedenburg
WINEMAKER: Wayne Swedenburg
TOTAL ACRES: 15
CASES/YR: 2,300
HOURS: Seven days a week 10-4

You would be hard pressed to find a more charming, likeable vintner in the mid-Atlantic than Juanita Swedenburg. Juanita, along with her husband Wayne, owns and operates Middleburg's newest winery — Swedenburg Winery. A vital, engaging, and energetic figure, she and her husband have embraced what started out as a retirement sideline and transformed it into a progressive, promising wine showcase.

Located just a mile or so east of the historic, quaint town of Middleburg, the first thing you notice about Swedenburg Winery is that it doesn't look anything like a winery! With sensitivity to fitting in with the surrounding estates and bucolic environs, the couple decided to construct their winery in the style of a small country house. Inside, the tasting room as well reflects much more the elegance and fine taste of a hunt country parlor than a winery visitor center. Recessed lighting, polished hardwood floors, brass chandeliers, and a magnificent antique dining table that serves as a pouring/tasting site all welcome the visitor with warmth and refinement. Pass through an adjoining door to the winery, however, and the business side of this endeavor becomes immediately apparent. From a convenient observation deck, visitors can gaze down upon sparkling white walls, a neat row of gleaming stainless steel tanks and, behind a tilted pane of glass, a spacious, well-equipped laboratory.

Both Wayne and Juanita Swedenburg retired from careers in the Foreign Service to their present farm in Middleburg. After spending many years working and raising a family in such overseas locations as Africa, Saudi Arabia, and Saigon, the two wished to settle down and stay put. Says Juanita, "Most retirees spend a lot of their time traveling. Well, we did that for thirty years! Our idea of a change of pace was to live in one place and call it home."

Juanita, who grew up in the Midwest, knew that in order to keep a farm from falling into disarray, it had to be worked. Not only did the Swedenburgs begin to raise cattle, they planted 15 acres of grapes in 1982, because they perceived that grapes offered one of the better agricultural cash crops in the state.

For a few years, the two sold grapes commercially quite successfully. Juanita became involved with the Board of the Virginia Wine Growers Association. And, for fun, they also made wine themselves in small lots with a portion of their crop.

On starting a winery, Juanita explains, "Things would get pretty quiet in the winter. We were busy with tending grapes and cattle all summer and began to think up things we could do in the cold, when the vines were dormant." The winemaker's busiest time, when fermentation, racking, fining, filtering, test-blending, and bottling take place, is the cold months from October through April.

Things began to take shape, and in 1987 the couple built their winery and received their license. Now guaranteed to have their hands full twelve months a year, Juanita's and Wayne's Swedenburg Winery opened its doors in April 1988.

THE VINEYARD

For the Swedenburgs, division of labor provides Juanita with responsibility for vineyard management. A knowledgeable farmer, she studied the grape-growing characteristics of northern Virginia and planted her vineyard accordingly. "Unlike many locations in Europe, Virginia has rich, fertile soil—almost too rich for grapes," she explains. Because of this, vines tend to grow too vigorously and produce too much foliage, which can restrict air flow and promote rot. Excessive foliage can also result in too many leaves being shaded, which leads to fruit maturing with unfavorably high pH levels. Vigorous vines also grow well into the fall months and thus do not store ample nutrients to withstand the long winter nor leave themselves enough time to harden-off before cold weather hits.

Explains Juanita, "Conventional wisdom was to plant 500 to 600 vines per acre. To force the vines to compete with each other and thereby reduce vigor, I planted 1,000 vines per acre." While her close, 5-foot spacing requires more frequent clipping and hedging of leaves and canes during the summer, Juanita finds that this system produces high quality fruit. Today, this method of planting is becoming widespread across the mid-Atlantic.

The Swedenburgs planted their first vines in 1982 and added more acreage between 1983 and 1985. Today, total acreage stands at 15, with the white vinifera variety Riesling leading the way with 6 acres. White French-American hybrid Seyval has been planted across 4 acres, with 3 acres devoted to Chardonnay and 2 to Cabernet Sauvignon.

GRAPE VARIETIES AND ACREAGE

Variety	Vinifera	French/Amer. Hybrids
Riesling	6.0	—.—
Seyval	—.—	4.0
Chardonnay	3.0	—.—
Cabernet Sauvignon	2.0	—.—
TOTALS	11.0	4.0

To date, the site in Middleburg has worked quite well for the grapes. In their individual micro-climate, frequent steady winds during summer months have helped to inhibit rot and counter the ill effects of humidity. Only occasional bitter winter cold has caused damage to the Chardonnay.

THE WINES

Like so many vintners in the mid-Atlantic, the Swedenburgs are self-taught and began making wine by experimenting with some of the crop they had been producing for sale. Wayne takes the lead in the cellar, at least in part due to his physical strength. Juanita states, "People can talk about the art of winemaking all they want . . . but when you're actually working with the tons of grapes and all the equipment, it's just plain hard labor!"

All six wines are *estate bottled* at Swedenburg. Fermentation of all white wines takes place in temperature-controlled stainless steel tanks at 45-48° F. Such cool temperatures allow for a slow, long fermentation that tends to preserve the delicate fruitiness and aromatics of varieties like Riesling and Chardonnay.

Both the Chardonnay and Seyval spend a brief period aging in American oak. The early releases of the winery's Chardonnay have been light-bodied, crisp, and refreshing wines with pronounced citrus fruitiness. The Seyval is similarly styled — refreshing with a palate-cleansing herbaceousness.

The Riesling, which is finished at 1-2% residual sugar, exhibits crisp citrus and apricot flavors and aromas. The Blush, which is 80% Riesling, 19% Seyval, and 1% Cabernet Sauvignon, displays very similar characteristics. "Chantilly," a 100% Seyval wine produced from the regular crop, is sweetened to 1.5% residual sugar by adding a *sweet reserve* of unfermented Seyval juice from grapes that are left to hang on the vine to be harvested late, at 22° *Brix*. It's a clean, well-balanced wine with lively, grassy herbaceousness.

The winery had not, at the time of this writing, released its first bottling of Cabernet Sauvignon.

DIRECTIONS

From Washington, DC, travel west on Route 50 towards Middleburg. One mile east of town, enter winery on left.

Charval
Virginia
•
DRY WHITE TABLE WINE
TARARA

PRODUCED AND BOTTLED BY TARARA   LEESBURG, VA 22075
BW VA 75 CONTAINS SULFITES

Tarara Vineyard

ADDRESS: Route 4, Box 229
Leesburg, VA 22075
PHONE: (703) 771-7100
OWNERS: R.J. and Michael Hubert
WINEMAKER: Debbi Dellinger
TOTAL ACRES: 23.5
CASES/YR: 2,000
HOURS: Thursday through Monday 11-5

From one perspective, Tarara Vineyards might be called a "Mom and Pop" operation. To be sure, proprietors R.J. (he prefers "Whitie") and Margaret Hubert conceived of Tarara as a nice retirement sideline and are intimately involved in the day-to-day business. But if "Mom and Pop" conjures up images of a tiny, fermented-in-the-basement wine hobby, forget it. Tarara Vineyards, which opened its doors in June 1990, has quietly burst upon the Virginia wine scene as one of the most ambitious and promising undertakings witnessed in recent years.

Tarara sits on a spectacular 475-acre property that fronts on the Potomac River just a few miles north of Leesburg. With nearly 25 acres already under cultivation, Tarara possesses sufficient additional plantable acreage to allow the vineyard to be expanded four-fold. To supply the farm with adequate water, three bulldozers spent a summer clearing a 75-foot deep ravine and building a clay dam over 100 feet high, allowing for the creation of a 10-acre manmade lake. Wine is currently fermented and stored in a 3,000 square foot cave that was blasted out of a prominent rocky knoll. Already outgrowing this space, plans call for construction of a three-tiered winery facility perched overlooking the vineyard. (The cave would then be used exclusively for barrel aging.) The Huberts have also developed a 45-acre ornamental nursery, a state-certified, virus-free rootstock vineyard (which will allow them to graft their own vinifera vines), and several other acres are farmed for crops ranging from peaches to thornless blackberries to asparagus.

The only thing that makes this story even more amazing is that the Huberts have accomplished all this in just a few years. The Tarara farm was purchased by the couple in the summer of 1985.

Obviously, it takes very special people to achieve such feats. And Whitie and Margaret Hubert are very special. The two exude energy and vitality that a twenty year old would be envious of. Whitie grew up in Ohio where his father grew grapes for the Welch's grape juice and jam empire. With this upbringing, you might say he had winegrowing in his blood. But Hubert pursued other ambitions. He built a successful construction business in the Washington, DC area and ran it for more than thirty years. Upon retirement, the couple sought a piece of property that would allow them to enjoy a more peaceful, bucolic lifestyle. Well, as the preceding description points out, they got bucolic. But peaceful?

To oversee the development of their wine operation, the Huberts needed someone with talents and energies to match their own. Consultation with well-known eastern viticulturist Lucie Morton Garrett put them in touch with Debbi Dellinger. Debbi had been working with eastern wineries over the previous twelve years. She had learned the basics as an assistant at Shenandoah Vineyards. She had spent her summer vacations in the far reaches of Michigan and upstate New York, learning all she could about cool-climate winegrowing. Coursework at Penn State and Mississippi State had prepared her for her first winemaker position in, of all places, South Carolina.

"Truluck Vineyards was an amazing experience for me," says Dellinger, a vibrant and exuberant young woman. "I was able to manage over 80 acres of grapes ranging from vitis vinifera to vitis rotundifolia. My first gold medal was for a Muscadine wine made from Carlos. I could barely drink the wine, myself!" she says with a laugh.

But her most valuable experience was that leading up to her hiring at Tarara. "I spent six years assisting Jacques Recht at Ingleside Plantation Vineyard. The amount I learned from that man is unmeasurable," she explains. Under the tutelage of one of the most influential vintners in the east, Debbi honed the skills that would allow her to be given the responsibility of her own operation.

Debbi and husband Steve Parsons, whom she met in South Carolina, now have their hands full keeping pace with the Huberts. "This is so exciting," says Parsons. "As long as we don't keel over from trying to keep up with Whitie, we should have quite a time over the next few years."

THE VINEYARD

The vineyard at Tarara was planted over three years, from 1988 through 1990. Thus far, the site seems especially well suited to grape growing. "We have almost constant breezes throughout the year," explains Debbi. "The air flowing east, down from the Catoctin Mountains, keeps rot in check and allows the vines to dry quickly after rains." This benefit allows Dellinger to spray fungicides and pesticides much less often than most growers.

Being located farther north than any other grower in the state, Tarara actually has more in common with growers in western Maryland than with most other Virginia growers. "We have rich, heavy clay soils like the vineyards of Byrd and Catoctin. That's why I'm especially hopeful that our Cabernet will perform like theirs," says Dellinger.

Tarara has made a large commitment to red vinifera varieties Cabernet Sauvignon and Cabernet Franc, planting 5 acres of each. Chardonnay occupies the single largest plot with 6 acres. Two and one-half acres have been planted to Pinot Noir, a move many in the wine community regard as risky. But Dellinger has a different view. "The way I see it, in good years we'll make red wine from the Pinot. In bad years, we'll pick it young and use it to produce sparkling wine," she explains. The entire vineyard is equipped with a drip irrigation system.

GRAPE VARIETIES AND ACREAGE

Variety	Vinifera	French/Amer. Hybrids
Cabernet Franc	5.0	—.—
Cabernet Sauvignon	5.0	—.—
Chambourcin	—.—	2.0
Chardonnay	6.0	—.—
Pinot Noir	2.5	—.—
Seyval	—.—	1.0
Vidal	—.—	2.0
TOTALS	18.5	5.0

As the vineyard grows in future years, Dellinger wants to experiment with new grape varieties. "I am going to try Sangiovese," says Debbi, referring to the classic Tuscan variety that forms the foundation for Italy's Chianti. "I also want to plant Chasselas d'Ore, a sturdy white variety widely planted in Switzerland. Virginia needs to find a good crisp, fruity white to keep Chardonnay company. I'm not too pleased with how Riesling grows in Virginia and maybe something like Chasselas will do better."

THE WINES

For Tarara's inaugural vintage, 1989, all wines were made from purchased grapes. In future years, expect to see all wines *estate bottled*. Tarara's winery/cave is very well equipped. All fermentations are conducted in temperature-controlled stainless steel tanks. All aging takes place in French Nevers and American oak.

Typically, five wines will be produced each year. With her Chardonnay, Dellinger strives to create an elegant, fruity wine rather than a full-blown oaky rendition. The '89 Chardonnay was fermented entirely in stainless steel. Half of the wine was then aged briefly in barrels. What results is a lean, crisp, slightly herbal wine with beautiful, albeit subtle, apple and pear fruitiness. A careful dose of vanillan oak softens the overall impression of this lovely Chardonnay.

Tarara next offers a delightful vinifera/French-American hybrid blend called "Charval." A mix of 60% Seyval and 40% Chardonnay, the wine offers a splendid alternative to the often neutral Seyval. The hefty proportion of Chardonnay has improved the wine's nose, flavor, and body, creating a wine that almost recalls a crisp Sauvignon Blanc. The wine is fermented to dryness in stainless steel and receives no oak aging. It is very clean and refreshing, with bright green apple fruit framed with attractive grassy herbaceousness.

Two sweetened wines are produced. A blush called "Cameo" is a blend of 92% Seyval and 8% Cabernet Sauvignon. Finished with 3%

residual sugar, the "Cameo" is a pleasant if unexciting blush. The red, called "Renaissance," offers something unique. A slightly sweet red wine, "Renaissance" was produced with picnics and barbecues in mind. A blend of 90% Rougeon (purchased from Archie Smith at Meredyth Vineyards) and 10% Seyval, the wine is finished with 1% residual sugar. "People really thought I was crazy when I made this wine," says Dellinger with a smile. "But I've always thought there was a place for a red that you could chill down and serve with ribs. I guess I was right — "Renaissance" is selling as well as any of the wines we make!" As Tarara's vineyard matures, "Renaissance" will be made with Chambourcin instead of Rougeon. If a bit different, the wine does offer pleasing, bright berry fruitiness bolstered by crisp acidity.

To round out the lineup, Tarara will bottle a wine called "Cabernets." A proprietary blend of Cabernet Sauvignon and Cabernet Franc, the wine will strive to achieve the style and complexity of the Bordeaux wines that are made from the same grapes. A barrel taste of the components from the estate's three-year-old vines was remarkably deep and concentrated. Look for a potential winner in years to come.

Any tour of the Virginia wine country must now include a trip to Tarara. Visitors will not only see a state-of-the-art facility and sample fine, well-made wines, they can also take advantage of an absolutely delightful setting. Several picnic pavilions dotting the landscape and a large tasting deck looking toward the Potomac complete an all-round fantastic visit.

INCIDENTALLY . . .

In keeping with the family nature of the operation, Tarara's labels boast artwork created by one of the Hubers' daughters, Martha. Visitors can also see the creative talents of Martha's sister, Karen, when they visit the winery; all of the basketry on display in the tasting room, produced from grape vine cuttings gathered on the property, was created by this Virginia artist.

The name Tarara is actually Ararat spelled backwards. Mount Ararat, the resting place of Noah's Ark in Turkey, was chosen as an appropriate moniker for the Huberts' retirement spot.

DIRECTIONS

From Leesburg, follow Route 15 north for approximately 8 miles. In the town of Lucketts, turn right onto Route 662 and proceed 2.3 miles to Tarara on the left.

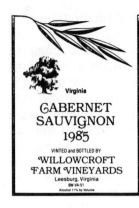

Virginia

GABERNET
SAUVIGNON
1985

VINTED and BOTTLED BY
WILLOWCROFT
FARM VINEYARDS
Leesburg, Virginia
BW-VA-51
Alcohol 11% by Volume

Willowcroft Farm Vineyards

ADDRESS: Route 2, Box 174A
Leesburg, VA 22075
PHONE: (703) 777-8161
OWNERS: Lew and Cindy Parker
WINEMAKER: Lew Parker
TOTAL ACRES: 5
CASES/YR: 1,000
HOURS: Saturday and Sunday 12-5, weekdays by
    appointment

If you are looking for the Virginia winery that is the shortest drive from Washington, DC, visit Willowcroft Farm Vineyards. Located just under an hour west of Washington in Leesburg, Willowcroft is a small, charming operation owned and run by the Parkers, Lew and Cindy.

The couple, with their two daughters, bought the property and moved into its colonial farm house in October of 1979. Lew, a financial director for a biological research firm in Fairfax, had no previous experience as a farmer. He spent many hours driving his new, longer commute to work, each day trying to decide how to develop his new farm. In the Spring of 1980, he planted forty vines just as a fun experiment. The following winter, when all but two or three died, he did not give up. "I made the mistake the next year of trying again!" Choosing as a new site to plant on the gently sloping grade above their barn, Lew began planting the vines that now make up his 5-acre vineyard. By 1984, the Parkers had obtained their Farm Winery License and undertook their first crush.

"It's actually pretty funny," says Lew, an amiable, low-key man. "I wish I could say that I had a grand scheme for all this, or that I've always had this burning desire to work the land and make wine. But actually, the winery just sort of happened. Cindy and I have always enjoyed wine, our property seemed well-suited for grape growing, and winemaking just seemed like a fun thing to do!"

Cindy is in charge of marketing the wines which, according to this dynamic and outgoing individual, "pretty much sell themselves. We've been so fortunate that our first vintage was well received. Our reputation has spread mostly by word of mouth."

At this time, Willowcroft's wines can be found either at the winery or at selected fine restaurants and wine shops in the Leesburg area.

THE VINEYARD

Willowcroft Farm is actually located on the top of Mt. Gilead, a few miles south of Leesburg. More a hill than a mountain, Mt. Gilead slopes gently upwards to a height of 750 feet above sea level. This elevation places the vineyard such that it enjoys a beneficial temperature inversion. Warm summer days are slightly cooler and winter days are slightly warmer than surrounding lower areas. The site also enjoys excellent southern exposure and good airflow from the prevailing westerly winds. From the top of the vineyard (which is the top of the mountain), visitors can enjoy a wonderful view of the Loudoun Valley to the south and the Blue Ridge Mountains beyond.

Dave Collins, the only person employed by Willowcroft to help Lew and Cindy out, manages the winery's 5-acre vineyard. His training as a horticulturist at Virginia Tech prepared him well for the job of caring for vinifera grape vines. As seen below, 3.5 acres of the Parkers' land are devoted to Chardonnay, 1 to Riesling, and .5 to Cabernet Sauvignon. The only departure from the winery's focus on vinifera vines is the three rows planted to the white French-American hybrid Seyval. The winery purchases small amounts of each of the four varieties each year to supplement its own crop.

GRAPE VARIETIES AND ACREAGE

Variety	Vinifera	French/Amer. Hybrids
Chardonnay	3.5	—.—
Riesling	1.0	—.—
Cabernet Sauvignon	0.5	—.—
TOTALS	5.0	0.0

THE WINES

The winery facility at Willowcroft, which currently produces 1,000 cases annually, is a model of efficiency and high technology on a small scale. Located on the "basement" level of the farm's barn, it is situated below ground level and is well insulated on two sides by earth. Two neat rows of jacketed stainless steel tanks allow Lew, who makes the wine, to carefully control fermentation temperatures. A small area at the back for aging wines in American oak barrels and a narrow workbench along one side for all the necessary lab work complete this cozy but eminently workable winery.

All of the white wines at Willowcroft are fermented cool, at about 55° F. None are put through *malolactic fermentation* (a secondary fermentation that softens a wine's acids but can rob it of fresh fruitiness). The regular Chardonnay and Seyval receive brief aging in American oak (about six weeks), while a Reserve bottling of Chardonnay spends roughly twice as long in the barrel. Riesling is fermented slowly and "stopped" with about 2% residual sugar. ("At least that's what I shoot for," says Lew. "Halting a wine's fermentation by dropping the temperature to a point where the yeast can no longer function is sort of like trying to stop a speeding Mack truck—sometimes it just wants to keep going!")

Spicy, smoky oak is quite evident in the nose of Willowcroft's Reserve Chardonnay. For the 1988 version, the strong theme of oak flavors is balanced by fairly round, almost buttery apple fruit. The wine finishes with bright, refreshing acidity. The regular bottling for the same year offers similar characteristics but with less intensity. The winery's Rieslings have tasted drier than the 2% residual sugar would lead you to expect. This is due to the ample balancing acidity, which makes this a refreshing, crisp wine.

Willowcroft's Cabernet is vinified in a traditional manner, with skin content lasting for seven to ten days at "as high a temperature as I can get" to maximize color and fruit extraction. Lew has, in past vintages, experimented by blending Chambourcin (a red French-American hybrid) into the *cuvée* in a proportion of about 15%. "I liked the blend quite a lot. The Chambourcin softened the wine in much the same way Merlot softens the classic Bordeaux." In the last several years, however, Willowcroft has not been able to find a source from which to purchase the Chambourcin, and has ended up bottling 100% varietal Cabs.

Willowcroft has experienced a bit of a roller coaster ride with its Cabernet Sauvignons. Starting in 1984, a fairly simple, straightforward wine in a style more reminiscent of Beaujolais than Bordeaux was produced from immature three-year-old vines. Just a vintage later, however, the '85 Cabernet showed what a difference a year can make. It possessed an intense, purple/black color and tight, young, juicy flavors with raspberry, blueberry, and cassis fruit dominating. In successive years, the Cabernets showed continued improvement until, in 1988, foul weather at harvest contributed to a less-ripe crop. Maintaining their integrity and commitment to quality, the Parkers chose to bottle this pleasant, light, cherryish wine under the label "Claret," rather than honoring it with the designation of Cabernet Sauvignon.

The winery produces a pleasant blush wine as well. When grape supplies permit, this wine is made from Cabernet Sauvignon. A true *blanc de noir*, the wine is made by fermenting the *free run juice* of the Cabernet grapes, resulting in a pretty pink/copper-colored wine that is fresh and crisp, possessing attractive berryish fruitiness.

INCIDENTALLY . . .

The Parkers have recently completed a new tasting room on the upper level of the barn. Retaining the rustic nature of the structure, it offers visitors impressive views of the Loudoun Valley and the distant Blue Ridge range.

DIRECTIONS

From Leesburg, go south on Route 15. Turn right on Route 704, then immediately left on Route 797. Follow this dirt road 3.1 miles to the winery on the right.

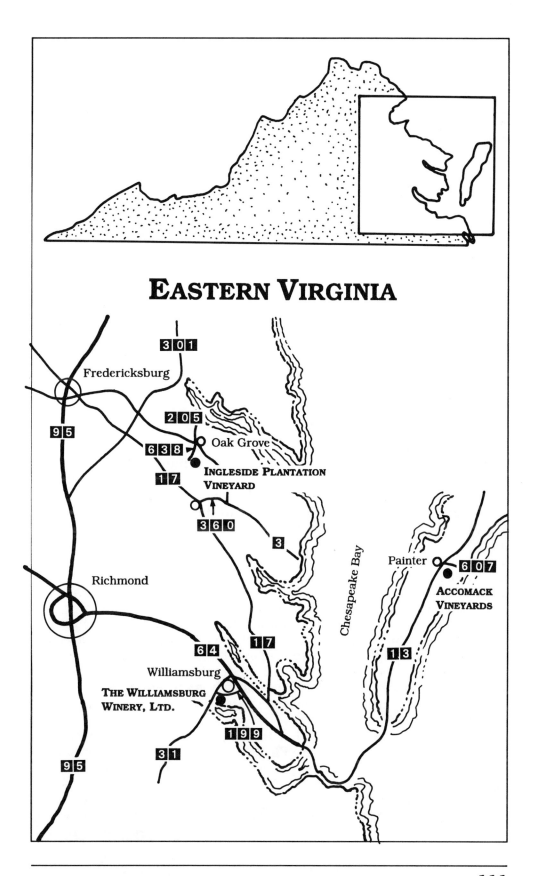

EASTERN VIRGINIA

301

Fredericksburg

95

205

638

Oak Grove

INGLESIDE PLANTATION
VINEYARD

17

360

3

Chesapeake Bay

Painter 607

ACCOMACK
VINEYARDS

Richmond

17

64

13

Williamsburg

THE WILLIAMSBURG
WINERY, LTD.

199

95

31

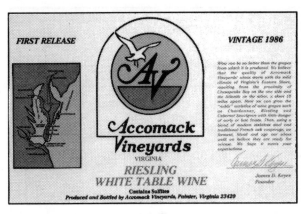

Accomack Vineyards

ADDRESS: P.O. Box 38
Painter, VA 23420
PHONE: (804) 442-2110
OWNERS: Jim and Gerry
    Keyes
WINEMAKER: Jim Keyes
TOTAL ACRES: 2
CASES/YR: 2,100
HOURS: Tuesday through
    Sunday 10-4

On the Presidents' Birthday holiday in February 1975, Jim and Gerry Keyes left their Washington, DC area home to spend a long weekend on the Eastern Shore. Besides taking a break from their busy careers, the journey had another specific objective: to begin looking for a piece of land upon which they could retire and, perhaps, grow grapes. Exactly twelve years later, to the weekend, the Keyes opened Accomack Vineyards and realized their dream. With the opening of the winery, Accomack became the first and only bonded winery on the Eastern Shore. According to Jim Keyes, this fact represents the real story behind Accomack.

Locating vineyards in close proximity to large bodies of water has been a strategy employed by winegrowers for centuries. In Europe, the great vineyards of Bordeaux enjoy the moderating effects of the nearby Atlantic Ocean, while some of the best vineyards in Germany depend on the broad waters of the Rhine River to diminish the harshness of winter. In this country, the Napa and Sonoma regions experience the daily cooling effects of fog and moisture off the San Francisco Bay, and in New York, both the Finger Lakes growing region and vineyards on the eastern tip of Long Island place great emphasis on the importance of nearby water.

The reasons behind all this are quite simple. In the summer, the sun warms the land and rising hot air draws fresh, cooler air off the water. In the winter, the water retains warmth longer than the land and radiates this warmth to nearby land, causing it to stay several degrees warmer. The effect is one of moderating extremes. Summers stay cooler, allowing grapes to ripen slowly and gently. Winters stay warmer, so vineyards experience relatively less damaging winter-kill and frost.

Accomack Vineyards, located in the southernmost region of the Delmarva Peninsula in Painter, Virginia, enjoys each of these beneficial effects. That section of the peninsula is just 10 miles wide and is thus extremely close to both the Atlantic Ocean and the Chesapeake Bay. Summer evening temperatures drop by 15 to 20 degrees from daytime highs, allowing grapes to cool and retain their natural acids. This is a luxury not enjoyed by most Virginia growers, says Keyes, where hot and humid summer evenings increase the likelihood of grape rot and disease. Because of these advantages, Jim predicts that the Eastern Shore may likely develop into the premier winegrowing region in the state.

Jim's interest in wine began as a consumer in the late 1960s. Over a seventeen-year career as an official in the Foreign Service of the State Department, he received broad exposure to the wines of the world. Gradually, Jim's specific interests turned toward viticulture and he joined a number of wine clubs. Appreciating the special needs of vinifera grapes and understanding what conditions are necessary for the production of premium quality fruit played a big part in his and Gerry's decision to retire on the Eastern Shore and establish their vineyard.

Accomack has had two winemakers in its short history as a winery. For 1986, young Tom Payette managed the production. Tom had studied winemaking at Virginia Tech and had apprenticed with Jacques Recht at Ingleside Plantation Vineyard before landing his first winemaking post at Accomack. In the spring of 1987, when Tom decided to start his own operation (Riverside Winery in Rapidan), Jim Keyes had to search for another winemaker. After consideration, Jim decided he would take the helm, again under the guidance of Jacques Recht. Using a high-tech approach, the two communicate regularly via computer terminals.

THE VINEYARD

The Keyes have an estate vineyard of 2 acres planted exclusively to Merlot. A somewhat delicate, thin-skinned grape, Merlot is extremely difficult to grow in hotter, more humid parts of the state. On the Eastern Shore, however, Accomack's vineyard is thriving.

GRAPE VARIETIES AND ACREAGE

Variety	Vinifera	French/Amer. Hybrids
Merlot	2.0	—.—
TOTALS	2.0	0.0

Two other growers on the Eastern Shore supply Accomack with the vast majority of the grapes it needs for wine. While the eventual goal of Accomack is to produce wines exclusively from grapes grown on the Eastern Shore, the winery now supplements its harvest with a small amount of Seyval and Chardonnay purchased from other parts of Virginia.

THE WINES

Accomack spreads its 2,000+ case production over five bottlings. Their Chardonnay is fermented in temperature-controlled stainless steel dairy tanks and is aged for one month in French oak. To soften the natural acids, the wine is encouraged to complete a secondary *malolactic fermentation.* The Riesling is finished medium sweet with 2% residual sugar. For everyday drinking, the "Old Dominion White" offers a Chablis-style dry table wine created by blending 67% Seyval and 33% Chardonnay.

Of the three whites, the Riesling has offered the most consistent quality. It has a very pale straw color, is light bodied, and possesses crisp acids to balance the sugar. Its flavors are reminiscent of peaches and honey, with a bit of background earthiness. The "Old Dominion White" offers pleasantly crisp, slightly herbaceous fruit.

Two vinifera reds are produced at Accomack—a Cabernet Sauvignon and, Jim's pride and joy, his estate bottled Merlot. Both wines receive similar treatment. After spending seven days fermenting in contact with the skins, the wines are pressed and then spend up to a year aging in French oak. Of the two, the Merlot has shown superior quality and consistency. The 1988 bottling offered light but pure sour cherry fruit, framed by firm acids and some astringency. Toasty oak warms and softens the overall impression. It will be interesting to see how these wines develop with bottle aging.

If not showing spectacular results in its first vintages, Accomack has certainly verified Jim Keyes' claim that fine vinifera fruit can be successfully grown on the Eastern Shore, especially the tricky Merlot.

DIRECTIONS

Accomack Vineyards is a bit out of the way, sure. But on your next trip to the shore, keep in mind that it is just a pleasant drive north from Virginia Beach or south from Ocean City, Maryland. From either direction, follow Highway 13. In Painter, take Route 607 east (towards the ocean) for 1/2 mile to the winery on the right.

Ingleside Plantation Vineyard

ADDRESS: P.O. Box 1038
Oak Grove, VA 22443
PHONE: (804) 224-8687
OWNERS: The Flemer Family
WINEMAKER: Jacques Recht
TOTAL ACRES: 53
CASES/YR: 18,000
HOURS: Monday through Saturday
10-5, Sunday 12-5

It was the summer of 1980. Carl Flemer's experiment of planting a vineyard in 1976 was about to bear fruit—literally. Owner of a successful nursery business on his 2,500-acre Ingleside Plantation near Oak Grove, Carl had sent his son Doug to France to pick up a few hints on how to make wine and, if he was lucky, persuade a winemaker to leave his native land and make wine in Virginia.

Meanwhile, retired Belgian enologist Jacques Recht and his wife Liliane were busy sailing up the Potomac River. A year and a half earlier, the two had sailed away from Jacques' twenty-five year career as a European winemaker, consultant, and professor in their self-built catamaran to circumnavigate the globe. Their adventure took them around Spain, Africa, the Canary Islands, the Caribbean and, through a quirk of fate, the Chesapeake Bay. A friend had given Jacques a copy of James Michener's novel *Chesapeake*, and Jacques had whiled away many of his hours at sea reading about what he calls "this fascinating region."

It was a hot, hazy, muggy summer afternoon when the Rechts dropped anchor at the small town of Kinsale. Upon meeting some of the locals, Jacques was told about a nearby neighbor who had been growing grapes there along the Potomac. Carl Flemer was introduced to Jacques at a dinner party and the two began to get to know one another.

Flemer began to discuss Recht's past. Most recently, he had been a professor of enology at the Fermentation Institute at Brussels University, possessing an advanced degree in enology himself. Prior to that, he had been a winemaker and consultant at numerous well-known chateaux in Bordeaux. During the late 1960s, Recht had even been a Vice President at the American consulting firm of Booz-Allen when he was hired to revamp the wine and grape industries in Algeria. Could it be that Carl Flemer might convince this eminent professional to help him out at Ingleside?

"We were a bit tired of sailing," says Jacques, a benevolent, wise-looking man. "I agreed to stay for three weeks to help with the crush. Well," he chuckles softly, "three weeks turned to three months, which turned to three years. Eight years later, I'm still here!"

Yet there is no disappointment in his voice. On the contrary, Jacques' bright blue eyes light up when he speaks of helping Virginia become a respected wine-producing region. "It has been fun being a pioneer in a new land. Unlike California, Virginia has seasons! We have a climate here which is much like the Loire Valley or Bordeaux," adds Recht, "and we are already proving that we can produce very good wines here, more in the style of Europe than California."

Over his years at Ingleside, Jacques and the two Flemers have overseen the expansion of the winery facility, the purchase and installation of new equipment, and an almost doubling of vineyard acreage—nearly all expansion being plantings of vinifera varieties.

Carl and Doug Flemer can be praised for not trying to rein in their winemaker. On the contrary, they both urged Jacques to accept his first offer to consult with another Virginia winery. Understanding that the reputation of an industry cannot be built around just one good operation but around many, they have willingly shared Jacques on many occasions in hopes that the entire state could benefit from his considerable talents. Over the years, Recht has played a significant role in helping to establish numerous wineries up and down the east coast, and specifically tutored three of Virginia's bright young prospects: winemakers Deborah Welsh of Oakencroft Vineyard, Tom Payette of Riverside Winery (and previously Accomack Vineyards), and Debbi Dellinger of Tarara Vineyard. He also contributes numerous articles to leading wine magazines, has hosted a number of research programs in Virginia for the Bordeaux University in France, and is in the process of writing a book on "Chateaux Winemaking."

Jacques and Liliane Recht are now permanent fixtures on the Virginia wine scene, and the whole eastern industry is the better for it. They've built a new house near the Potomac and have established an experimental 5-acre vineyard of their own using the low 18-inch cordon trellis of Burgundy. And all because a couple of wandering sailors read a Michener novel and decided to change their course towards the Chesapeake.

Doug Flemer will never forget the moment. "Here I was in France, searching in vain for a winemaker. I get a telegram from my father which says: 'Come home. While you've been away, I plucked a winemaker right out of the Potomac!'"

THE VINEYARD

Ingleside Plantation's vineyards now stand at slightly more than 50 acres. Based primarily around Carl Flemer's original planting of 1976, the vineyard is still roughly 70% French-American hybrids. As displayed below, the largest plot is devoted to the white hybrid Seyval (12 acres) followed by the white hybrid Vidal (10 acres). Fifteen acres of vinifera vines were planted since Jacques' arrival; 10 to Cabernet Sauvignon and 5 to Chardonnay. Significant acreage of red hybrids include Chambourcin and Chancellor. Rounding out the vineyard is 6 more acres planted to numerous hybrid varieties including whites Villard Blanc and Rayon D'or and reds Chelois, Foch, and DeChaunac.

GRAPE VARIETIES AND ACREAGE

Variety	Vinifera	French/Amer. Hybrids
Seyval	—.—	12.0
Vidal	—.—	10.0
Cabernet Sauvignon	10.0	—.—
Chardonnay	5.0	—.—
Chambourcin	—.—	4.0
Chancellor	—.—	3.0
Miscellaneous	—.—	9.0
TOTALS	15.0	38.0

In speaking of the growing region, Jacques states, "One of the reasons I decided to stay here was that it reminded me of Bordeaux, where I had spent so much of my life." Indeed, the sandy-loam soil and its location on a slight ridge between the Potomac to the north and the Rappahannock River to the south specifically recalled the Entre-deux-mers appellation of the Bordelais.

In fact, enjoying the moderating effects of such large nearby bodies of water, the region earned special viticultural status from the U.S. Bureau of Alcohol, Tobacco and Firearms in 1987. Now called the Northern Neck-George Washington Birthplace Viticultural Area, this region runs along a 100-mile northwest-southeast peninsula bordered on two sides by the aforementioned rivers and on the east by the Chesapeake Bay. With its snowfall less severe, its frost-free days greater, and its temperature more even and moderate than the Piedmont region to the west, this appellation now supports sixteen commercial grape growers and the one bonded winery.

"This is why we can support vinifera so well here. The climate is mild. I feel like I can produce a Cabernet much more elegant, lean and refined, like the Medoc, than those hot-weather wines of California," adds Jacques.

THE WINES

Jacques Recht has brought to and uses at Ingleside Plantation a wide and diverse mastery of winemaking techniques. Assembling red wines in the Bordeaux method, fermenting cool, crisp whites that emulate the style of the Loire, barrel-fermenting and aging Chardonnay in the Burgundian fashion, and using the *carbonic maceration* (whole berry fermentation) technique to produce a Beaujolais Nouveau-styled wine, Jacques works to the limits of his abilities. To top it off, he even produces two *méthode champenoise* sparkling wines, a blanc de blanc Brut and a Rosé, which have earned high praise up and down the east coast.

To be sure, he is equipped at Ingleside with state-of-the-art tools: jacketed stainless steel fermentation tanks, a heat exchanger, and both French and American small oak cooperage for aging. "But wine-making is also a subtle art," says Jacques in his soft French accent. "You make wine by chemical testing, true, but also by your senses and careful tasting."

Perhaps the most important art Jacques continually strives to perfect is that of blending. "Especially with hybrids, which can be somewhat one-dimensional, I try to assemble complementary elements in hopes of creating subtle, complex wines."

For example, after several years of bottling a 100% varietal Seyval, Ingleside has produced a new wine called "Chesapeake Blanc"—a 90% Seyval, 10% Chardonnay blend. "I've tried to hit on a wine like the Muscadet of the Loire. The Chardonnay helps to lighten the overall effect." Cool-fermented and touching no oak, the wine is crisp, slightly grassy, with delicate fruit flavors of pears and apples—a perfect match with regional seafood.

Another exciting new blend is the "Chesapeake Claret," a *cuvée* of 90% Chancellor and 10% Cabernet Sauvignon, which receives eight months of aging in American oak. It is a clean, fruity, medium-bodied table wine with a crisp structure and vivid cherry fruit, all enhanced by the spiciness contributed by the oak.

But the true star, and the pride of Jacques Recht, is Ingleside's Cabernet Sauvignon. A classic Médoc blend of Cabernet Sauvignon, Merlot, and Cabernet Franc (proportions vary depending on the vintage), the wine spends fourteen to eighteen months in French Nevers oak, and is only fined with egg whites prior to bottling. While lighter bodied than many of its brethren, the wine more than makes up for its lack of sheer weight with lots of subtle berry and cassis fruit. Elegant, refined, with soft-round tannins and creamy vanillan oak notes, the 1983 and 1984 versions helped put Virginia on the Cabernet map. Look for more recent releases to offer more of the same.

Jacques, while aging his Chardonnays for six weeks in new French Nevers oak, also puts the wine through a secondary *malolactic fermentation*. This Burgundian practice creates softer, rounder wines with notable buttery qualities. Ingleside's Chardonnay is medium-bodied with apple and cinnamon flavors and a delicate oaky veneer.

The only other vinifera table wine is Ingleside's semi-sweet Riesling, made from purchased fruit. A variety Jacques feels is not well-suited to Virginia ("It's a bit too hot in most parts of the state"), Ingleside's is pleasant, a bit awkward and heavy, but still an interesting version of the variety.

Four generic hybrid blends offer pleasant everyday drinking at very affordable prices: the "Virginia Chablis" (a crisp, bright blend of Villard Blanc and Vidal), "Virginia Blush" (a pleasant, slightly grassy blend of Seyval, Vidal, and Chambourcin), "Virginia Rosé" (Chambourcin and Vidal), and "Virginia Burgundy." The latter is the most interesting of the lot—a blend of Chambourcin, Chancellor, and a touch of DeChaunac, Foch, and Chelois. It is light, exuberantly grapey, and completely enjoyable. Ten percent of the wine is produced by using whole berry/carbonic maceration with the Chancellor in order to produce extra fruity aromas and flavors. For the rest of the wine, skin contact is kept to a minimum during fermentation to avoid the heavy, herbaceous qualities sometimes contributed by red hybrids.

Finally, Ingleside's Champagnes are delightful examples of the European-style sparklers that can be produced in the mid-Atlantic. Explains Jacques, "You need high acid, low pH grapes grown in a cool climate to make great Champagne. By picking Chardonnay and Pinot Noir early here in Virginia, we can make wonderful méthode champenoise wines." Ingleside's Brut is lean and austere, with tart green apple fruitiness and pronounced yeasty, toasty notes. A Rosé version is also made by adding either small amounts of Cabernet to the cuvée or by adding some Pinot Noir that was fermented in contact with the skins.

INCIDENTALLY . . .

Quite a controversy ensued between the U.S. BATF and Carl Flemer after the latter submitted his petition to request special viticultural status for the region where Ingleside is located. Carl felt that the most recognizable geographic characteristic of the region was that it was the birthplace of George Washington, America's first President. The BATF, however, felt that the term "Northern Neck" was a more commonly used title. Even though seventy-four of the eighty-one commenters to the government's Notice of Proposed Rulemaking took sides with Mr. Flemer, the Feds took the path of compromise—thus creating perhaps the longest titled appellation in the country: The Northern Neck-George Washington Birthplace Viticultural Area!

DIRECTIONS

Take Interstate 95 to Route 3. Travel east to Oak Grove, then proceed south on Route 638 for 2.5 miles to entrance on left.

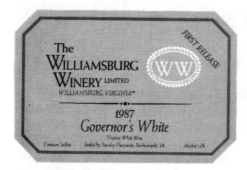

The Williamsburg Winery, Ltd.

ADDRESS: 2638 Lake Powell Road
Williamsburg, VA 23185
PHONE: (804) 229-0999
OWNERS: Patrick and Peggy Duffeler
& Associates
WINEMAKER: Steve Warner
TOTAL ACRES: 78
CASES/YR: 28,000
HOURS: Tuesday through Sunday 10-5

It seems fitting that, in a spot where some of America's earliest settlers struggled against the elements in an attempt to grow wine, a modern winery has finally sent down its own roots. Nestled in the heart of some of this country's richest historical lands, the Williamsburg Winery lies just a stone's throw from both Colonial Williamsburg and Jamestown.

While the colonists failed miserably in their attempts, today's Williamsburg endeavor shows promise to succeed wonderfully under the dynamic leadership of Patrick and Peggy Duffeler. The couple have assembled a team of eminently qualified professionals in enologist Steve Warner and viticulturist Eric Capps, and have invested heavily in what is already becoming one of the showcase wineries in the state.

The Duffelers bring a certain international flair to the Virginia wine community. Born in Brussels in 1942, Patrick was exposed to the fine wines of the world at an early age. His family lived, at various times, in France and Germany as well as Belgium. As a young adult, Patrick moved to Rochester, New York so that he could study at the University of Rochester and work at Eastman Kodak. But after working in the graphics department for several years, he developed an affinity for economics, finance, and marketing and, in the end, he received his formal degree in business. It was at the University that Patrick met Peggy, and shortly after graduation the couple were married.

For the next twenty years, the Duffeler family enjoyed an exciting and cosmopolitan lifestyle. Beginning in 1969, Patrick worked for Philip Morris where he was given responsibility for marketing, including sports development. The company sponsored, among other things, Formula I racing teams, and Patrick took charge of organizing operations through the international racing circuit. In 1976, Patrick began consulting with Revlon where he marketed that company's fragrance products around the world. For three years, the Duffelers lived on the Mediterranean coast of Spain.

By the fall of 1981, Patrick and Peggy had had enough of the gypsy lifestyle and longed to settle down and live a more normal life with their two sons. They looked to the United States, and Virginia specifically, as a likely place to purchase some land and perhaps explore the possibility of farming. After looking at more than fifty possible properties, the Duffelers chose their present 300-acre estate along the James River in Williamsburg.

It was not until 1984 that Patrick and Peggy began "entertaining the thought" of growing grapes and producing wine. "Wine had always been in the background of my life, growing up and living for so long in Europe as I did," he explains. "When we began observing the surge in the Virginia industry, we naturally wanted to become a part of it."

After having soil samples analyzed, they planted their first 3 acres to Chardonnay in 1985. By the next year, it was full steam ahead. Patrick began organizing a corporate partnership with a few Williamsburg neighbors, started looking into leasing arrangements with various Virginia vineyards, and began recruiting his team.

"I viewed the challenge much like those before my Formula I racing teams in Europe," says Patrick. "In order to compete, I had to assemble the best team in the state." As winemaker, Patrick wanted Steve Warner. "I had tasted the 1984 and 1985 Merlots and Cabernets from Montdomaine Cellars," he continues. "Those are world-class wines, and I knew that the man who made them must be something special." Patrick tracked down Steve Warner at Chateau Morrisette and made him an offer that he "was pretty sure Steve couldn't refuse."

Next, he located a young viticulturist named Jeanette Smith. A horticulture graduate from Virginia Polytechnic Institute, Jeanette had experience working in several Virginia vineyards, and had most recently worked for the state of New York providing extension assistance to growers on Long Island.

By the fall of 1987, their winery license was in hand, 10 more acres of grapes were in the ground, and the first crush of the Williamsburg Winery was underway.

Plans today look to extensive and ambitious growth. Over the course of 1988, the Duffelers finished renovating their Georgian farmhouse and a winery was completed with state-of-the-art equipment valued at over $500,000. More acres have been planted to grapes each year, bringing the estate vineyard total to over 75 acres. Additionally, the corporation purchased the Somerset Vineyard near Charlottesville, a well established property producing premium Chardonnay and Riesling and has planted another 8.5 acres at Montpelier, home of James Madison. If that weren't enough, the Duffelers are also drawing up plans for a European-style, sixty-room hotel.

"The trick is to blend realism with your dreams," explains Duffeler. Through careful planning, judicious investment in excellent staff and equipment, and calculated, cautious growth, the Williamsburg Winery seems destined for great things.

THE VINEYARD

The Duffelers and Jeanette Smith are extremely optimistic about the future of their vineyard in Williamsburg. The primary advantage of the site is its proximity to water. The Duffelers' property is less than 30 miles from the Atlantic Ocean, less than 15 miles from the Chesapeake Bay, and borders directly on the James River, which is more than 2 miles wide at that point. These large bodies of water serve to moderate temperatures, especially in winter, so that tender vinifera vines have a much better chance for long, healthy lives. Enjoying benefits similar to Ingleside Plantation on the Northern Neck and Accomack on the Eastern Shore, Williamsburg finds itself in climatic Zone 8, one step warmer on the scale than Charlottesville, for example, which is in Zone 7.

The soil in this part of the state tends to be lighter and better drained, and Williamsburg's vineyard is also perched on a slight ridge, about 30 feet higher than surrounding land, so air flow is improved.

The Duffelers have focused the vast majority of their plantings on vinifera varieties, led by Chardonnay and Cabernet Sauvignon. When Somerset Vineyard was purchased, an additional 12 producing acres of Chardonnay was obtained, as well as a source for Riesling (9 acres).

GRAPE VARIETIES AND ACREAGE

Variety	Vinifera	French/Amer. Hybrids
Chardonnay	40.5	—.—
Riesling	9.0	—.—
Cabernet Sauvignon	11.7	—.—
Merlot	12.5	—.—
Seyval	—.—	2.0
Cabernet Franc	2.0	—.—
TOTALS	75.7	2.0

The ample rainfall coupled with the area's rich soils tends to make grapevines grow vigorously. Thus, vines will produce excessive shoots and foliage, causing the fruit and interior leaves of the canopy to be shaded. To counteract this problem, viticulturist Eric Capps practices extensive shoot thining and leaf pulling to open up the canopy. The inital vineyards were planted at the rate of 623 vines per acre (10-foot row spacing with 8 feet between vines); however, Eric has taken advantage of the excess vigor and increased the spacing to 14 feet between rows with a divided canopy. This "V"-type trellis system accommodates the excess vigor and allows better exposure of fruit and interior sunlight. This system also increases aeration and decreases the amount of hand labor.

To ensure a reliable source of water for the young vineyard, a drip irrigation system was installed. The ability to irrigate the older, bearing vines through dry periods also prevents "berry bursting" when the rain does return.

THE WINES

Thirty-three-year-old Steve Warner was born in San Mateo and raised in Madera, California, in the heart of the San Joaquin Valley. As an undergraduate studying crop science at Cal Poly-San Luis Obispo,

Steve happened to take one course on winemaking and immediately fell in love with the subject. The following spring, he enrolled in the graduate enology program at Fresno State University, a mere 20 miles from his hometown. He received his Masters degree in 1984.

While the University of California at Davis receives worldwide respect for its enology and viticulture programs, many insiders admit that Fresno State may even surpass Davis in its ability to provide practical applied training. Upon graduation, Steve looked for the best avenue to apply what he had learned. Rather than picking up a job in California as an assistant to someone else, Steve preferred the idea of heading east where he could be given sole responsibility for a winery's production. Learning by doing, Warner landed the winemaker job at Montdomaine Cellars in Charlottesville for the '84 and '85 vintages, and then moved on to Chateau Morrisette for 1986. He joined Patrick and Peggy Duffeler in time to oversee the 1987 production.

Steve Warner's skills teamed with the Duffelers' vision and resources are already proving to be a dynamite combination. Warner assisted the Duffelers with both the design of the winery facility and the selection of equipment. Today, along with the usual impressive array of temperature-controlled stainless steel fermenters and rows of French oak barrels, Warner also has such high-tech tools at his disposal as a must chiller (which quickly lowers the temperature of newly crushed grapes, thus preserving freshness) and dejuicing tanks (which allow winemakers to hold certain wines, such as Chardonnay, in contact with their skins prior to fermentation, and permit wineries to extract greater proportions of clean *free-run juice* from their musts).

The Williamsburg Winery offers visitors a lineup of seven wines: four varietals and three lower-priced blends. Three Chardonnays are produced—a regular bottling, an "Acte 12" Chardonnay, and a special "Vintage Reserve." For the regular Chardonnay, two-thirds of the wine is fermented in stainless steel while one-third is fermented in French Allier oak. After spending a short period of time resting *sur lie*, the barrel fermented wine is blended back with the main batch. Both the initial releases of this wine, in '88 and '89, were fresh, crisp, and possessed slightly buttery apple fruit touched lightly by vanillan oak.

The "Acte 12" Chardonnay, which is named for the act of Virginia's House of Burgesses in 1619 directing Virginians to plant vines, is 100% oak aged and 30% barrel fermented.

The "Vintage Reserve" Chardonnay, on the other hand, is entirely barrel fermented using French oak. Unlike its counterpart, this wine is permitted to complete a secondary *malolactic fermentation*, which reduces the wine's overall acidity and adds complex buttery notes. The wine is aged on its fermentation *lees* for a full four months to add further complexity. The goal is to create a bigger, toastier, more assertive and complex wine.

Both a Cabernet Sauvignon and a Merlot are produced by Williamsburg. Steve ferments both of these wines in contact with their skins for seven to ten days. To add extra varietal fruitiness, Warner allows approximately 10% of the fruit to be fermented uncrushed, as whole berries. The reds spend ten to fourteen months in both American and

French Nevers oak. At the time of this writing, only the 1988 Merlot had hit the market. Produced from young vines, the wine possesses bright, clean cherry fruit in a light/medium-bodied frame. Pert acidity and toasty oak complement the fruit flavors.

Nearly as exciting as the varietal wines are Williamsburg's blended table wines. Joining the current movement of combining vinifera wines with wines made from French-American hybrids, Warner has created surprisingly delicate and complex quaffers that can be offered at very affordable prices. The debut release of the winery, called "Governor's White," is a mix of 55% Riesling and 45% Vidal. It is fermented slowly at a very cool 45° and is finished with 1.5% residual sugar by arresting the fermentation by chilling. The "James River White" is made by taking the *press juice* from the winery's Chardonnay and combining it with Seyval. With final proportions of about 40% Chardonnay and 60% Seyval, the wine is fermented entirely in stainless steel and is bottled crisp and bone dry. Finally, the "Plantation Blush" is a combination of 70% Riesling and 30% Foch (a red French-American hybrid). It, too, is fermented cool in stainless steel and finished with approximately 2% residual sugar. Of the three, the "Governor's White" has shown the most pleasing consistency, with delicate citrus blossom aromas and clean grapefruit and peach flavors. Like Linden Vineyards, Williamsburg has demonstrated how well Riesling and Vidal complement each other.

It seems clear that the Williamsburg Winery will become a showcase for the Virginia industry. Given the emphasis on top-notch quality and the readily-accessible market in Colonial Williamsburg, it is hard to imagine that it can miss.

DIRECTIONS

From Colonial Williamsburg, take Route 31 toward Jamestown. Turn left on Route 199, then right on Brookwood Lane. At Lake Powell Road, turn left and proceed to winery.

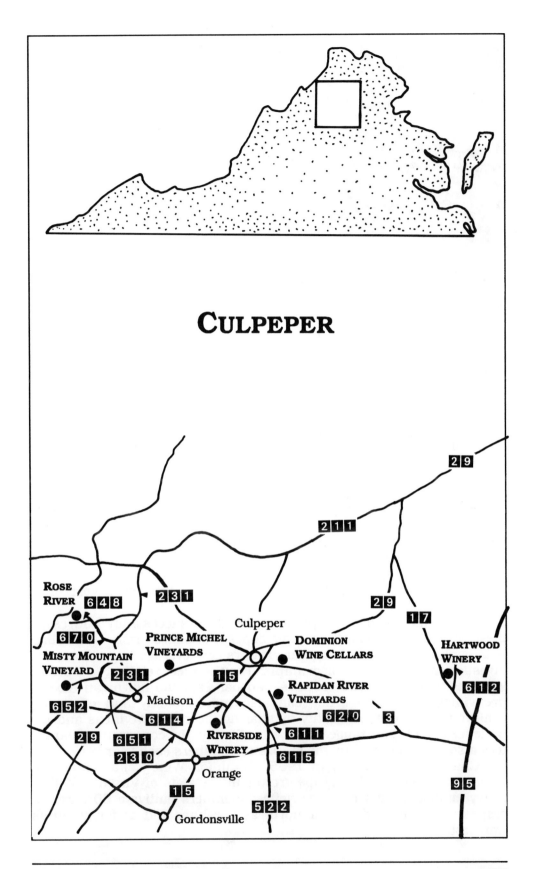

CULPEPER

ROSE RIVER 6 4 8
2 3 1

6 7 0
PRINCE MICHEL VINEYARDS

MISTY MOUNTAIN VINEYARD
2 3 1

6 5 2

2 9
6 5 1
2 3 0

Madison

6 1 4

1 5

RIVERSIDE WINERY

Orange

1 5

Gordonsville

5 2 2

Culpeper

2 1 1

2 9

DOMINION WINE CELLARS

RAPIDAN RIVER VINEYARDS

6 2 0

6 1 1

6 1 5

3

2 9

1 7

HARTWOOD WINERY

6 1 2

9 5

Dominion Wine Cellars

ADDRESS: P.O. Box 1057
Culpeper, VA 22701
PHONE: (703) 825-8772
OWNERS: Cooperative owned by twenty
      winegrowers/stockholders
WINEMAKER: Alan Kinne, consultant
TOTAL ACRES: 60
CASES/YR: 10,000
HOURS: Tuesday-Sunday 12-5

If you're driving on U.S. Route 29 just north of Culpeper and look west towards the foothills of the Blue Ridge, you'll very likely notice a strikingly beautiful, contemporary chateau-style structure surrounded by lush vineyards. Please don't scratch your head and drive on. Stop. You'll be letting yourself in on one of the most innovative and promising wine ventures in the state of Virginia.

Dominion Wine Cellars is a winery cooperative—one of only three in the entire country. The idea for a cooperative was conceived in response to a number of constraining "givens" facing vineyard owners and aspiring winery owners:

• Beginning a new winery is extremely risky, especially in the east, due to a tough, chauvinistic wine-drinking public and an often harsh, variable climate;

• Beginning a winery also involves a huge capital investment for land, equipment, and construction; and

• Beginning a winery immediately presents cash flow problems, since new vines won't even produce a crop for three years after planting, and wines from that crop aren't marketable for nearly an additional year after that.

• For the grape grower, let alone the aspiring winery owner, another problem is finding someone to purchase your crop year after year.

The formation of a cooperative structure successfully addresses these problems through the simple concept of shared risk. By pooling both capital and energy, member-growers can leverage larger loans for investing in equipment, for example. They can feel relatively secure in knowing that one or two growers' bad harvests will not mean the entire vintage is a loss. They can also more quickly and efficiently achieve improved wine quality by sharing the collective ideas and experiences of a broad range of growers. Finally, the cooperative guarantees a source that will buy the grapes of members each year.

Chartered in January of 1985, Dominion Wine Cellars now has twenty members, each a grape grower in the state of Virginia. With a heavy emphasis on vinifera varieties, members cultivate 60 acres of grapes from vineyards as far north as Leesburg and as far south as Amherst.

At harvest time, through a very carefully scheduled and choreographed process, these growers deliver their harvests to the winery facility in Culpeper. Not only is the slate-blue multi-level winery beautiful to look at, it is also stocked with state-of-the-art equipment. Twelve uniquely designed tall and cylindrical Italian stainless steel fermentation tanks, each temperature-controlled, tower above the winery floor. A completely sterile bottling line is located nearby. A comfortable tasting room on the second floor affords a bird's eye view of the fermentation room, and outside a spacious deck for sipping and picnicking permits nice views of the surrounding countryside.

All this energy and effort would be for naught unless Dominion could find a winemaker with the skills to pull it all together. Since its inception, the winery has benefited from the talents of three leading enologists.

In Steve Reeder, an energetic young man who is never at a loss for words, Dominion found a successful resolution to that problem for its first vintage. Steve, who received his training at the University of California at Davis, brought to Dominion seven years of professional experience. His résumé reflected work in both California (at Alexander Valley Vineyards and Kirigan Cellars) and in the eastern United States (at such places as Glenora Wine Cellars and McGregor Vineyards in New York's Finger Lakes and Penn Shore Vineyards near Lake Erie in Pennsylvania). Reeder designed much of the winery's layout and made all of the wines from the 1986 crush.

A bit of a wanderer, Reeder left Dominion in the winter of '87 to follow new opportunities in Pennsylvania. The members of Dominion conducted a nationwide search for an able replacement and found one in Russell Hearn. A native of Australia, Hearn brought an international flair to Dominion, as well as a diverse background in winemaking. He was educated down under at Roseworthy Agricultural College and then worked at Houghton's Wines Ltd. as cellarmaster. Not a stranger to eastern U.S. winegrowing, however, Hearn had previously served as winemaker and operations manager at Commonwealth Winery in Plymouth, Massachusetts.

After overseeing operations for the '87 through '89 vintages, Hearn departed. To fill his shoes, Dominion has hired veteran winemaker Alan Kinne as consulting enologist.

The early growth of Dominion, with its cooperative structure, has been fascinating to witness. If future years are as successful as the first few have been, the potential certainly exists for Dominion to become a showcase winery for the state of Virginia.

THE VINEYARDS

In all, the twenty member/growers of the cooperative cultivate 60 acres of vinifera vines located in sites literally all over the state. The bulk of the planting is dedicated to Chardonnay (30 acres) and Riesling (20 acres). An acre of Gewurztraminer rounds out the whites. For the reds, Dominion members grow Cabernet Sauvignon, Merlot, Cabernet Franc, and Pinot Noir.

Selected French-American hybrid varieties are purchased for blending with vinifera grapes in Dominion's "generic" line of white, blush, and red table wines.

GRAPE VARIETIES AND ACREAGE

Variety	Vinifera	French/Amer. Hybrids
Chardonnay	30.0	—.—
Riesling	20.0	—.—
Cabernet Sauvignon	7.0	—.—
Gewurztraminer	1.0	—.—
Merlot	1.0	—.—
Cabernet Franc	0.5	—.—
Pinot Noir	0.5	—.—
TOTALS	60.0	0.0

Just after completing his first crush at Dominion, Reeder and I discussed the contractual arrangement with member/growers. "As with all situations where wineries purchase grapes under contract with growers," he explains, "there is a built-in incentive for growers to boost production in order to elevate profits . . . sometimes at the expense of grape quality. The key difference here, though, is that the grower has a direct stake in the wines made from his grapes. If the quality of the final product is not there, we all lose."

Continuing, Reeder explained, "One of the greatest advantages Dominion has is the opportunity to evaluate which grapes grow best in different parts of the state. We are positioned to direct future plantings based on our growers' experiences. If one region of the state or one type of micro-climate works best for Cabernet, for example, I could see growers planting just that variety or even grafting existing vines over to that variety." Such a system presents Dominion with the opportunity to follow the European system of grape growing, where whole regions are devoted to one variety that performs best there.

THE WINES

Dominion offers visitors a very well thought-out array of wines to choose from. Namely, they offer a broad line of "premium" wines, ranging from white to red, dry to semi-sweet, and a line of lower priced "everyday" table wines. The former are all made from 100% vinifera varieties, while the latter are very promising blends of vinifera and French-American hybrid grapes.

Dominion's Chardonnays are partially barrel-fermented. Early vintages have been lean and crisp, with subtle lemon and citrus fruit and toasty oak notes highlighting the aromas and flavors.

The more noticeable, striking wines have been the Rieslings. Two styles are offered—a dry (.8% residual sugar) Alsatian-type wine appearing under the label "White Riesling," and a semi-sweet (2.8% residual sugar), Germanic wine called "Johannisberg Riesling." While

the former is nice but a bit narrow, it is the Johannisberg that receives the most praise. Fermenting extremely slowly (8 weeks) at very
cold temperatures (45° F) has produced wines of significant delicacy.
Early vintages have possessed a nose that is floral and rich with
scents of honeysuckle and apricots. In the mouth, ripe fruit flavors are
well balanced and linger in the finish. The '86 Johannisberg was a
Riesling of truly unusual proportions for Virginia, a state that is often
too hot and humid to produce fine examples of this varietal. While
later vintages have not always lived up to the promise of the initial release, Dominion's Rieslings still offer some of the better renderings of
this grape available in Virginia.

Referring to Dominion's lower-priced everyday wines as generic
does not really do them justice. In its "White," Dominion has produced
a remarkably attractive, effusively fruity, slightly grassy wine reminiscent of a mid-range California Sauvignon Blanc. Made from a blend of
Seyval and Chardonnay, the wine fills both nose and mouth with utterly clean and refreshing scents and flavors. Given its low price, it
must rate as one of the best values in the state.

The "Red," too, is an extremely enjoyable wine. A blend of Chambourcin and Cabernet Sauvignon, it represents another fine example
of just how good vinifera/hybrid blends can be. Deep ruby with youthful purple edges, the nose is dominated by spicy, smoky oak. Smoky,
medium-bodied fruit of black cherries and berries is tight and narrow
in its youth, but promises to soften into a supple, easily drinkable
wine in a year of so. Again, strong, almost tarry oak frames the wine
on the palate.

Only the "Blush" falls short of its exciting generic partners. An unusual blend of Pinot Noir, Seyval, and Cabernet Sauvignon, this wine
exhibits too much of the red varieties' herbal, vegetal qualities and not
enough fruity, berry character.

While the blends making up these wines will probably change
slightly with each vintage, look for Dominion's "everyday" wines to offer consistently fine quality at a very fair price.

INCIDENTALLY . . .

During the summer of 1990, the owners of Dominion Wine Cellars entered into a management agreement with the Williamsburg Winery.
That winery's dynamic founder, Patrick Duffeler, now oversees all aspects of Dominion's planning, winemaking, management, and distri-
bution. The most immediate change made by Duffeler was to redesign
Dominion's label. Future plans call for changing the makeup of the
winery's blended wines (which will be renamed "Blanc de Blanc,"
"Blanc de Noir," and "Claret").

DIRECTIONS

Driving south on Route 29, just north of Culpeper, take exit at Routes
522 and 3. Turn right one-quarter mile to McDevitt Dr. Turn right
again to Winery Avenue and Dominion on right.

HARTWOOD WINERY
RAPPAHANNOCK BLUSH
Virginia Table Wine

BOTTLED BY HARTWOOD WINERY
FREDERICKSBURG, VA   BW–VA75

Hartwood Winery

ADDRESS: 345 Hartwood Road
Fredericksburg, VA 22405
PHONE: (703) 752-4893
OWNERS: Jim and Sharon Livingston
WINEMAKER: Jim Livingston (with
    consultation from Lee Reeder)
TOTAL ACRES: 7
CASES/YR: 1,200
HOURS: April through December, Wednesday
    to Sunday 11-5

Jim and Sharon Livingston, both school librarians in Prince William County, took a slow and methodical course to becoming winegrowers in Virginia. Born and reared in east Tennessee, their Bible Belt upbringing did not expose them to much wine. But after moving to northern Virginia in 1969, they were exposed to and began actively learning about it. The Livingstons joined the Fredericksburg chapter of the American Wine Society. They also, just for fun, began growing some vines in their back yard.

But like so many other vintners in the mid-Atlantic, what began as an innocent foray with a few vines transformed into a passionate obsession. A neighbor of the Livingstons learned of the couple's interest and offered a 4-acre field next to his home as a vineyard site. In 1981, one of the acres was planted to seven varieties of French-American hybrids. The following year, two more were planted to the same cultivars. After consulting with a fellow Wine Society member, well-known Virginia viticulturist Lucie Morton Garrett, two varieties were identified that seemed to be performing especially well. In 1983, the total acreage was converted to these—Seyval and Vidal.

Over subsequent years, Sharon and Jim learned their craft. They took viticulture courses from Linden Vineyards' Jim Law at Fairfax Community College. They joined the Virginia Vineyards Association. Sharon was elected president of the group and served in that capacity for two years. The couple successfully produced large, healthy crops of grapes that were sold to Burnley Vineyards for several vintages.

It was only natural that the Livingstons began thinking of the logical next step. Could they, like so many others, operate their own winery? One presumes the answer "yes" was arrived at quickly. Vacation property at Lake Anna was sold in order to purchase a 12-acre lot a few miles northeast of Fredericksburg in the community of Hartwood. Planting was begun in 1985 and continued over the next two years. By April 1989, with license in hand and winery construction completed, Hartwood Winery opened its doors and its owners officially became members of the continually expanding Virginia wine industry.

THE VINEYARD

At this writing, 7 acres are producing at Hartwood with 3 remaining acres available for planting. The Livingstons also lease and manage another 5-acre vineyard at a nearby location.

The couple suffered an early setback with their estate vineyard— an initial 3-acre planting of Cabernet Sauvignon succumbed to the pernicious virus Crown Gall. The land was replanted to sturdy, reliable French-American hybrids — the white Vidal and red Chambourcin.

GRAPE VARIETIES AND ACREAGE

Variety	Vinifera	French/Amer. Hybrids
Chambourcin	—.—	3.5
Vidal	—.—	3.5
TOTALS	0.0	7.0

The growing site chosen by the Livingstons is located well east of the rolling piedmont slope of the Blue Ridge Mountains. This location possesses both advantages and disadvantages when compared to the more numerous vineyards surrounding Culpeper. On the plus side, Hartwood escapes the damaging frosts that often afflict other vineyards when frigid mountain air slides to lower elevations along the eastern slope of the Blue Ridge. On the minus side, the relatively flat Fredericksburg area is quite a bit hotter than neighboring regions to the west and east. For this reason, some of the more delicate cold-climate varieties like Riesling cannot be grown as successfully. To take advantage of the heat, the Livingstons plan to try again with Cabernet Sauvignon in the coming years.

THE WINES

For their first vintage, 1988, the Hartwood winery facility was still under construction. The Livingstons' grapes were processed at the winery of their friends, the Reeders of Burnley Vineyards. Making wine here also allowed the couple to benefit from the tutelage of proven Burnley vintner Lee Reeder. Production is being gradually transferred to the Hartwood winery.

Six wines in all are produced by Hartwood: two dry whites, two semi-dry whites, a blush, and a red. For dinner wines, a Chardonnay and a Seyval are offered. Both are fermented at cool temperatures in stainless steel, and both spend a short time aging in small American oak cooperage. In order to retain crisp, fresh fruitiness, neither wine is put through a secondary *malolactic fermentation*.

A Riesling is made from purchased grapes. It is finished with 2.5% residual sugar. Slightly less sweet is the Hartwood "Rappahannock White," a blend of 90% Vidal and 10% Seyval finished with just under 2% residual sugar. Both wines are sweetened by adding a *sweet reserve* of unfermented juice just prior to filtration and bottling. This approach is becoming widely used throughout the mid-Atlantic and is praised as one that adds not only sweetness but a vibrant dose of fresh fruitiness. The "Rappahannock Blush" is an interesting blend of 60% Riesling and 40% Foch. From the Foch, a grape notorious for its inky purple color, only the *free run juice* was used, thereby creating the pleasant deep rose color.

Finally, Hartwood offers a 1988 wine called "Claret." A 100% Cabernet Sauvignon wine, the "Claret" is actually made from the Livingstons' three-year-old vines that were subsequently ripped out due to the Crown Gall virus. The fruit from these immature vines produced a simple, light-bodied, pleasantly fruity wine. In future years, the Livingstons hope to produce a more robust red dinner wine from Cabernet grapes.

INCIDENTALLY . . .

A tour that includes Hartwood Winery should also set aside ample time to visit the many historic Civil War battlefields in the area. The Livingstons will gladly discuss such an itinerary with their guests over a pleasant glass of Hartwood wine.

DIRECTIONS

From Interstate 95, near Fredericksburg, take Route 17 north. Drive for 5 miles until Route 612 is reached (Hartwood Road). Turn right and proceed 1.5 miles to winery on left.

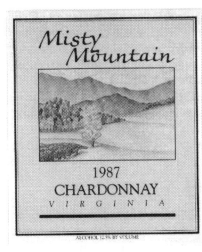

1987
CHARDONNAY
V I R G I N I A

ALCOHOL 12.5% BY VOLUME

Misty Mountain Vineyard

ADDRESS: Star Route 2, Box 458
Madison, VA 22727
PHONE: (703) 923-4738
OWNERS: Michael J. Cerceo
WINEMAKER: Jeff Grady
TOTAL ACRES: 9
CASES/YR: 1,000
HOURS: Monday-Saturday 11-4, Sunday by
    appointment

Misty Mountain Vineyard had its origin in one man's dream to find his family a summer home. Michael J. Cerceo, a physicist living and working in northern Virginia, was searching for a place to escape the rigors of his busy profession—a quiet place, out in the country, where he, his wife, and their five children could relax and do, say, a bit of farming. This was in 1982. Eight years later, the Cerceos have their summer home and farm, located in the rolling hills above Madison. But things certainly aren't any less busy!

"As I was looking for a location," explains Michael, an intense, energetic man, "the only crop that made any sense, economically, was grapes. Now, I come from an Italian family, and I grew up loving wine, so that seems like a good idea. Well, one thing leads to the next, and now, not only do I have my career as a physicist, but I also have the winery!"

The Cerceos bought their property in January 1983 and four months later began planting 2.5 acres of Johannisberg Riesling. Over the next two years, as the vines were maturing, Michael turned his attention to remodeling the farm's house and to turning an old barn into a modern, well-equipped winery.

By 1985, Michael was ready to start gearing up the winery. To help get started on the right foot, he contracted with Belgian winemaker Jacques Recht of eastern Virginia's Ingleside Plantation Vineyard. "I have the utmost respect for the man. He is, in my opinion, the most knowledgeable enologist in the state, for that matter, the country," he adds. Jacques helped to design the winery and advised them regarding necessary equipment.

By July 1986, when the winery was bonded, one part was still missing. "We had no winemaker for the '86 crush!" explains Cerceo. But Jacques knew of a young man from his native Europe who was apprenticing at nearby Prince Michel Vineyards. Eric Brevart was recruited and managed the winery's first commercial vintage. A former English teacher in France, Eric did not come to this country equipped with any specific wine background, just a good palate and an intense interest in Virginia's growing industry. "Under Jacques' tutelage, Eric did a terrific job our first year," says Cerceo. Still a bit of a wanderer, however, Eric left Misty Mountain in the summer of 1987 to pursue wine interests in California. Back in the region again, you can now find Eric making wine at Piedmont Vineyards in Middleburg.

After Eric's departure, Cerceo hired another newcomer to wine—Jeff Grady. A former policy analyst with the U.S. General Accounting Office, Jeff has a degree in organic chemistry from the University of Virginia and has been tutored, like his predecessor, by Jacques Recht.

THE VINEYARD

Located at 1,250 feet above sea level, Misty Mountain's vineyard site is a promising one. Protected by surrounding mountain ranges, its rows line an eastern-facing slope that receives gentle warmth from morning sun. However, after the first 2.5 acres of Riesling suffered higher than acceptable damage during the winter of 1983, Cerceo decided some advice would help ensure success of future planting. Both Joachim Hollerith of Prince Michel and Rapidan River wineries and Archie Smith III of Meredyth Vineyards in Middleburg were consulted on laying out the rest of the vineyard.

By the spring of 1987, with the winery remodeled and their first vintage settling and aging safely inside, Misty Mountain began its second major phase of vineyard development. A rich array of varieties was added, including 1.5 acres of Chardonnay, 2 acres of Cabernet Sauvignon, 1 of Merlot, and a small amount of Cabernet Franc for blending. As seen in the table below, 2 additional acres of the white French-American hybrid Seyval were also planted, bringing total acreage to 9. Until these new acres begin producing, Misty Mountain will continue to supplement its harvest with purchased fruit.

GRAPE VARIETIES AND ACREAGE

Variety	Vinifera	French/Amer. Hybrids
Riesling	2.5	—.—
Cabernet Sauvignon	2.0	—.—
Seyval	—.—	2.0
Chardonnay	1.5	—.—
Merlot	1.0	—.—
TOTALS	7.0	2.0

THE WINES

Misty Mountain divides its production across an ever-changing array of wines. All whites are fermented in stainless steel tanks with temperatures controlled by pumping fermenting *musts* through a glycol *heat exchanger*. All reds and Misty Mountain's Chardonnay receive judicious oak aging in French Limousin oak.

To date, the winery's Chardonnays and Merlots have offered the most interest. Two Chardonnays are produced: a "Reserve," which is entirely barrel fermented, and a regular, which is fermented in stainless steel and then aged in oak. The "Reserve" Chardonnays have shown fairly big, ripe apple fruitiness and abundant toasty oak. The regular Chardonnay, while less intense, offers slightly cleaner fruitiness. The Merlots, especially the winery's inaugural '86 bottling, have displayed deep purple color, a dense nose of cherry, cassis, and a bit of mint, and clean, focused, medium-bodied flavors that mirror the aromas.

Other wines produced include "Virginia Chablis," a 90% Vidal/10% Riesling blend that offers crisp, neutral, slightly citrusy flavors, a 100% varietal Riesling, a Cabernet Sauvignon (with 15% Merlot blended in), and a blush wine.

INCIDENTALLY . . .

For the future, Michael is contemplating the development of a larger winery facility and visitor center on Route 29 near Madison. The current location, while scenic, is not readily accessible to visitors and is thus only open by appointment.

DIRECTIONS

Follow Route 29 to Madison (15 miles south of Culpeper), then take Route 231 north. At Route 651 turn left, then go right on Route 652. At Route 698, turn left. Winery is at the end of the road.

VIRGINIA

Chardonnay

1986 VINTAGE VIN BLANC
Grown, vinted and bottled by VaVin, Inc., Leon, Virginia
Contains sulfites   Alc. 12% by vol.

Prince Michel Vineyards

ADDRESS: Route 4, Box 77
Leon, VA 22725
PHONE: (703) 547-3707
OWNERS: Omni Corporation
WINEMAKERS: Joachim Hollerith and Chris
        Johnson
TOTAL ACRES: 110
CASES/YR: 25,000
HOURS: Daily 10-5, except major holidays

Prince Michel Vineyards, located conveniently off Route 29 in Leon, Virginia (just 10 miles south of Culpeper), offers visitors an opportunity to see one of the most high-tech, state-of-the-art winery facilities operating in the east. This is no small, one-man operation. This is a corporate-backed, big-bucks endeavor that has spared no expense in its pursuit of quality winegrowing in Virginia.

Since its beginnings in 1984, Prince Michel has built a beautiful brick visitor center, winery museum, gift shop, and tasting room, an efficiently designed winery capable of handling production of 50,000 cases per year, and has planted the largest vineyard in the state.

Now owned by the Omni Corporation, Prince Michel Vineyards was the brainchild of two men—Norman B. Martin of Culpeper and Jean LeDucq of Paris, France. In 1983, with plans developed and land purchased, they still were in need of an experienced winegrower who could make all of their plans work. Together, they approached and recruited Joachim Hollerith of nearby Rapidan River Vineyards.

Joachim was, in 1978, just finishing up his coursework in enology and viticulture at the Geisenheim University in Germany (the preeminent school for this type of study in that country), when he was approached by Dr. Gerhard Guth, a surgeon from Hamburg. It seemed that Guth was just setting out to start a vineyard and winery in America. Joachim, coming from a family who had been involved with winemaking for some 300-plus years, thought this sounded like a good opportunity. For the next five years he worked to establish a 25-acre vinifera vineyard at Rapidan River Vineyards and made wine for that winery's first three vintages.

Joachim was appointed winemaker and general manager of Prince Michel in 1983 and immediately set out to begin the winery's vineyard planting. Joachim also oversaw and directed the purchase of the winery's sophisticated equipment, which today includes not only impressive rows of temperature-controlled stainless steel fermentation tanks and stack upon stack of French oak barrels, but also a Braud automatic harvesting/spraying/leaf trimming machine, a 10-ton pneumatic bladder press, and a sterile bottling line capable of processing 3,000 bottles per hour.

Coincidentally, in 1985, Rapidan River Vineyards was put up for sale. Already seeking opportunities to expand, Martin and LeDucq purchased the operation. Joachim was appointed to manage and make wine at Rapidan in addition to his responsibilities at Prince Michel. With the doubling of his duties, it was clear that Joachim would need some help. Prince Michel brought on a second winemaker. Alan Kinne, himself a veteran of ten years of winemaking in Virginia and on Long Island, served in that capacity until 1990. Today, Chris Johnson assists with winemaking responsibilities.

THE VINEYARD

Prince Michel Vineyards grows only varieties from the noble family of grape—vitis vinifera. Under the direction of Joachim, the present vineyard was planted in three phases: 40 acres in 1983, 50 acres in 1984, and 20 acres in 1985, totalling 110 acres—the largest in Virginia.

Nearly two-thirds of Prince Michel's acreage is devoted to two white varieties, Chardonnay and Riesling. Additionally, a very large plot of Cabernet Sauvignon is grown. Other varieties cultivated include Merlot, Cabernet Franc, Pinot Noir, and Gewurztraminer.

GRAPE VARIETIES AND ACREAGE

Variety	Vinifera	French/Amer. Hybrids
Chardonnay	41.0	—.—
Cabernet Sauvignon	28.0	—.—
Riesling	27.0	—.—
Merlot	7.0	—.—
Pinot Noir	4.0	—.—
Gewurztraminer	2.0	—.—
Cabernet Franc	1.0	—.—
TOTALS	110.0	0.0

Joachim's viticultural practices follow a different approach than conventional wisdom. Instead of following typical norms of planting 600 to 800 vines per acre, he plants more than 1,400 vines per acre at Prince Michel. This sort of "crowding" is not aimed at increasing total production per acre. Conversely, "high density" planting leads to a smaller yield per vine, producing grapes of greater intensity and higher quality. Because of the number of vines, the vineyard can consistently yield 4 to 6 tons per acre.

Prince Michel's location in the piedmont plain east of the Blue Ridge Mountains places it at a relatively low elevation above sea level — about 650 feet. This fact has not been without consequence. Here the vineyard is exposed to lower winter temperatures and occasional spring frosts, as heavier, colder air flows east down the slopes of the mountains. In 1986, for example, Prince Michel experienced a damaging early frost that led to a 6% bud loss. Joachim has attempted to compensate for this effect by planting as many acres as possible on slopes with southeast exposure. Such positioning exposes vines to the warming rays of early morning sun to mitigate the effects of frost.

THE WINES

While the winemaking style at Prince Michel is evolving each year through careful experimentation, it can be categorized generally as "French" with a touch of German influence. To assist Hollerith, the winery recently retained French enologist Jacques Boissenot to develop Prince Michel's wine program. Boissenot operates a wine lab in Bordeaux and consults for Chateau Lafite and Chateau Margaux. His first vintage assisting at Prince Michel was 1987.

White wines at Prince Michel are either fermented at 60° F in stainless steel or, with certain varietals, barrel fermented. Aging of certain varietals takes place in French Nevers and Allier oak, and several of the finished wines are blends of different grapes. While early vintages saw experimentation with various winemaking techniques, Prince Michel has seemingly hit upon a winning approach employing the advice and consultation of Frenchman Boissenot.

In 1987, Boissenot began a Chardonnay program that dictated that two wines be produced. Today a regular bottling is offered, as well as a "Barrel Select" reserve version, made from the property's oldest vines. The "Barrel Select" is, as its name suggests, entirely fermented in French oak. Upon completion of fermentation, the new wine is left to age on its fermentation *lees* in order to pick up yeasty complexity. The resulting wine is "bigger" than any Prince Michel Chardonnay produced before 1987. The regular Chardonnay is fermented cool in stainless steel and then briefly aged in French oak to produce a crisper, lighter rendition.

This approach has paid dividends. In each year since '87, Prince Michel has released very impressive "Barrel Select" Chardonnays. The wines display nice ripeness, powerful apple and pear flavors, buttery/toasty oak highlights, all bolstered by bright lemony acids. The regular bottlings are significantly improved as well. The '89 version possesses very ripe, forward fruit rounded out with vanillan oak and pert acidity.

Clearly, the winemaking techniques employed with Prince Michel's Chardonnays are French in character. Where Prince Michel's German touch enters is in Joachim Hollerith's traditional use of fining materials. *Finings* are various elements (a clay called bentonite, gelatin, and egg whites are most common), which are added to wine or unfermented *must* in order to aid in the "clearing" process. Since finings are heavier than wine, they sink to the bottom of the tank and while doing so, bond with and carry down many of the solid particles that cloud wine. Different finings remove different particles from wine. For example, bentonite is negatively charged and thus chemically attracts positively charged proteins. Gelatin is positively charged and thus attracts negatively charged tannins.

The judicious use of finings is practically universal in winemaking for it is one method of producing the crystal clear wine we all purchase. Joachim follows the classic German winemaking practice of adding bentonite to the freshly crushed and pressed juice of white wines, enabling him to ferment a clearer, cleaner juice. (Most wineries do not use finings until after wine has finished fermentation.) Joachim then follows up at a later time with two additional finings of the finished wines (one with gelatin and kieselsol, and once more with bentonite), again in the classic German method.

In addition to the two Chardonnays, the winery produces a proprietary blend of 80% Chardonnay and 20% Pinot Noir called "White Burgundy," and a rosé wine called "Blush de Michel." The "White Burgundy" consistently offers pleasant, well-developed, and forward fruit. The presence of Pinot Noir is quite evident, adding a light strawberry note to both aromas and flavors. For this wine, only the clear *free run juice* of lightly pressed Pinot Noir was used in the blend with Chardonnay. Light oak complements this nice wine.

The "Blush de Michel" is consistently one of the best blush wines being made in the mid-Atlantic. It is 85% Riesling/15% Cabernet Sauvignon (for color) and has 1.75% residual sugar. A delightful floral-Riesling nose is followed by clean, crisp fruity flavors touched by a bit of green herbaceousness from the Cabernet.

The winery has not yet released what most would consider a full-fledged Virginia Cabernet Sauvignon. Instead, the last several years have seen the release of a 100% Cab called "VaVin Nouveau." Not a nouveau wine at all, the wine is simply a fruity, light-bodied red produced from the Cabernet of not-yet-mature vines.

In 1990, Prince Michel did release a surprisingly pricey Cabernet clearly crafted to appeal to the upper end of the market. Called "Le Ducq," it is a blend of Cabernets from vineyards owned by Jean LeDucq in Virginia and California. It carries with it a hefty $50 per bottle price tag and seems to beg that Prince Michel be compared, head-to-head, with ultra-premium California wines such as Opus One, Insignia, and Dominus. Time, and critical appraisal of the wine, will tell if this was a wise strategy for Prince Michel to engage in.

INCIDENTALLY . . .

Following a dispute with a California winery using a similar name, Prince Michel's wines will appear under the label, Prince Michel de Virginia.

The gift shop adjacent to the tasting room at Prince Michel is quite special. It features, in addition to the normal T-shirts and souvenirs, beautiful French linens, china and pottery, handmade picnic baskets and other picnic "necessities," gourmet jams and relishes produced locally, and a wide array of crystal wine glasses and other wine accessories.

DIRECTIONS

The winery is located on the west side of Route 29 approximately 10 miles south of Culpeper and 8 miles north of Madison.

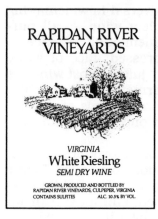

Rapidan River Vineyards

ADDRESS: Route 4, Box 77
Leon, VA 22725
PHONE: (703) 547-3707
OWNERS: Omni Corporation
WINEMAKERS: Joachim Hollerith and Chris Johnson
TOTAL ACRES: 50
CASES/YR: 7,500
HOURS: No tours or tastings; wines available at Prince Michel Vineyards

In 1976, a surgeon from Hamburg, Germany named Dr. Gerhard Guth came to Virginia with a strange idea. After researching the fact that German settlers had tried (and basically failed) to grow grapes and make wine along the banks of the Rapidan River as early as the year 1710, Dr. Guth decided he might want to try the same thing. He already owned a large tract of land in rural Orange County south of Culpeper. Guth gathered soil samples, climate charts, and topographical maps and brought them back to a German friend, Professor Helmut Becker, in the viticulture program at Geisenheim University. Careful study and positive thinking convinced them both that with today's available sprays and technological advances, vinifera grapes could be grown successfully here. By 1978, Rapidan River Vineyards was founded.

To help with his enterprise, Dr. Guth approached a young viticulture/enology student just finishing up his degrees at the Geisenheim University. Joachim Hollerith jumped at the opportunity to help pioneer grape growing in Virginia. He began in 1978 by planting the first vines of what would become Rapidan's 25-acre vineyard.

For five years, Hollerith and Guth built Rapidan into one of the better known vinifera-based wineries in the state. Then, in 1983, Joachim was lured away by the folks at Prince Michel Vineyards to help start their operation in the nearby town of Leon. Business, however, proceeded at Rapidan. In 1984, the vineyard was doubled in size with additional planting bringing total acreage up to 50.

In 1985, with the satisfaction of having successfully established the winery, Dr. Guth decided to move on to other things and put Rapidan River up for sale. As chance would have it, the owners of Prince Michel purchased the winery, and their first move was to reinstate Joachim as general manager and winemaker of Rapidan. After a couple of years of extremely busy transition, while overseeing the operations of the largest and fourth-largest wineries in the state, the continued presence of Joachim Hollerith has lent a stylistic consistency to the winegrowing philosophies at Rapidan River.

THE VINEYARD

With the combined German heritage of Guth and Hollerith, it is not at all surprising that Rapidan's initial focus was on growing white grape varieties, with a heavy emphasis on those of their native land. Of the 25 original acres planted in 1978, 22 were devoted to Riesling, 2 to Gewurztraminer, and 1 to Chardonnay.

In 1984, when the vineyard was expanded, a sizeable number of red varieties were added to broaden the winery's offerings, including 2 acres of Cabernet Sauvignon, 2 acres of Merlot, and 2 acres of Pinot Noir. Nineteen more acres of Chardonnay were also planted. Total acreage now stands at 50, making Rapidan River the fourth largest vineyard in the state.

GRAPE VARIETIES AND ACREAGE

Variety	Vinifera	French/Amer. Hybrids
Riesling	22.0	—.—
Chardonnay	20.0	—.—
Gewurztraminer	2.0	—.—
Cabernet Sauvignon	2.0	—.—
Merlot	2.0	—.—
Pinot Noir	2.0	—.—
TOTALS	50.0	0.0

The Rapidan River, which runs adjacent to the property, is not a large river and therefore does not act to moderate temperatures in regions through which it passes. At the relatively low elevation where the vineyard now stands (150 feet above sea level), frost has created problems from time to time. In April 1985, for example, an unusually late frost killed the early blooming buds of all the Gewurztraminer vines and most of the Chardonnay. The Riesling vines clearly illustrated their growing advantage—since they bud nearly two weeks after the Chardonnay and Gewurz, they were spared any damage from the frost. Thus, for 1985, a good supply of Riesling was produced, but only fifty cases of Chardonnay and no Gewurztraminer.

Frost damage, luckily, only hurts the harvest of the year in which it occurs. "Winter kill," which occurs when temperatures drop to extremes below -10° F, can finish off entire vines for good.

Rapidan River Vineyards follows similar, albeit not as extreme, cultural practices as the newer Prince Michel Vineyards. Joachim has "crowded" an average of 1,200 vines per acre (Prince Michel plants 1,460 per acre) at Rapidan compared to traditional standards of 600 to 800 per acre. Such an approach decreases each vine's individual output and aims to produce individual berries of greater intensity. Overall increases in harvest tons per acre are not the goal; increased quality is.

THE WINES

Today, Joachim and Chris Johnson share winemaking duties at both Rapidan River and Prince Michel. The overt stylistic approach to winemaking at Rapidan is Germanic. Riesling production constitutes

90% of the total annual case production of 7,500 cases. Fermentation takes place at cool 55° temperatures in jacketed stainless steel tanks to preserve delicacy and natural fruitiness, and no Rapidan wines receive any oak aging.

One approach to winemaking which sets Rapidan River apart and is particularly Germanic is how it employs the practices of filtration and *fining*. German winemaking historically stresses the importance of immaculately clean *must* in producing fine wines. The natural juice of freshly crushed and pressed grapes is, if one has ever seen a harvest in progress, very different from the crystal clear wine we eventually see on shop shelves. It is quite cloudy due to a high natural solids content (from pulp and other matter in the grape) and can contain other solids from the picking process including bits of leaves, stems, and even the occasional bug.

Virtually all wineries chill and settle fresh juice in order to let such undesirable solids sink to the bottom of the tank, and then pump the clearer juice into clean tanks for fermentation. Some wineries will actually run the fresh juice through a centrifuge to separate out solids.

The classic German approach is to either run the juice through a coarse filter prior to fermentation or add a *fining* material to the fresh juice. Hollerith fines the fresh juice before fermentation and then filters the finished wines before bottling. While such processes accomplish their goal, there is considerable debate that excessive fining or filtration can literally strip out certain elements that contribute complexity and depth to wines.

Early vintages at Rapidan River caused one to wonder whether such mistakes were ever made. Wines from the early '80s seemed light in body and very delicate (almost thin) in nuance. But by 1986, whether or not that was ever the case, Rapidan succeeded in reaching new heights by producing wines that better balance fullness of fruit and elegance of style.

Today, the winery bottles three styles of Riesling, a dry "Alsatian," a semi-dry "Germanic," and an ultra-dry (unreleased at the time of this writing). While the dry is nice, it is the semi-dry that puts Rapidan ahead of its competitors. The '86, '88, and '89 versions offered some of the best Rieslings ever produced in Virginia. By adding a *sweet reserve* of unfermented Riesling juice to the finished wine, Hollerith has made wines with 1.7% residual sugar. Intense aromas of blossoms and honeysuckle are matched with similar flavors of apricots, peaches, and flowers. Crisp acidity is nicely balanced by lingering sweetness.

The last production of a Rapidan River Chardonnay was in 1986, and it was truly a standout. Light green/pale straw in color, it has a delicate nose of citrus touched by accents of vanillan oak. Delicate, elegant fruit leans to the grapefruit and lemon end of the spectrum, again touched by a deft measure of oak. (From 1987 on, Rapidan has focused exclusively on Riesling and Gewurztraminer, shipping all other Chardonnay fruit to Prince Michel.)

Rapidan's Gewurztraminer is one of the few available in the mid-Atlantic and, in recent years, has established itself as consistently the best. This unusual grape, which ripens to a striking pinkish/gold color, can produce exceptional wines which combine both delicacy and power. The German word "Gewurz" translates into "spicy," describing the variety's unique spicy overtones. The '86, '88, and '89 are each finished semi-dry, and possess terrific rose petal and lichi nut fragrances. In the mouth, intense flavors of apricots, pears, and herbs persist in a long finish.

While the winery suffered through a few rough years of transition in the mid-'80s, recent vintages clearly indicate that things are strongly back on the right track.

DIRECTIONS

At this time, the winery is not open for tours. However, the wines are available in supermarkets, restaurants, and wine shops throughout Virginia and Washington, DC, and in parts of Maryland.

For reference purposes, Rapidan River Vineyards is located southeast of Culpeper. From Route 29, take Route 3 east, then Route 522 south over the Rapidan River Bridge. Turn left on Route 611 and go 4 miles to Route 620. Turn left and proceed 1.3 miles to vineyard on right.

VIRGINIA

Riesling

ORANGE COUNTY

1987
MONTICELLO APPELLATION

PRODUCED AND BOTTLED BY PAYETTE WINERY RIVERSIDE
RAPIDAN, VIRGINIA   BW-VA 69
ALCOHOL 10% BY VOLUME   CONTAINS SULFITES
NET CONTENTS 750 ML

Riverside Winery

ADDRESS: "Riverside" - Route 615
Rapidan, VA 22733
PHONE: (703) 672-4673
OWNER: Elizabeth T. Payette
WINEMAKER: Tom Payette
TOTAL ACRES: 1
CASES/YR: 1,000
HOURS: March through December, Tuesday
through Sunday 11-5

Another of the new wineries that crushed their first grapes in the fall of 1987 is the tiny but charming Riverside Winery, in the heart of the town of Rapidan. Just a quick ten-minute drive southeast of Culpeper, the winery's name describes its situation quite accurately; the home of Elizabeth Payette and her son Tom is perched on a knoll overlooking the bubbling Rapidan River.

The Payettes moved to this house twenty-four years ago and raised a family while working at medical careers in Culpeper. When Tom went to college at Virginia Polytechnic Institute in Blacksburg, he took a course entitled "Wines and Vines" and quickly became hooked. In the few short years that followed, Tom followed an amazingly fast track. He received his Bachelor of Science degree in Food Science Technology, then apprenticed under some of the most important wine-makers in the state, moved on to his first winemaking job at another winery and, remarkably, at the age of twenty-six, found himself running his own!

While at Virginia Tech, Tom studied under Bill Cooler. Learning a great deal about the chemistry and technical lab work required by the discipline, he acted as a teaching assistant when there were no more wine-related courses to take and performed independent studies to further enhance his knowledge. One fall, Tom experimented by making a Riesling through the whole-berry fermentation technique called *carbonic maceration*. Usually reserved for lighter, fruity red grapes, the wine turned out to be, as Tom puts it "fairly bizarre! But I wanted to learn the process, and used the only grapes I could get my hands on—some Riesling from Prince Michel Vineyards." One summer during school, Tom picked up his first practical experience while working at Prince Michel under the direction of German-trained enologist Joachim Hollerith.

Upon his graduation from Virginia Tech in 1985, Tom quickly landed a job as an assistant to winemaker Jacques Recht at Ingleside Plantation Vineyard. Recht, Bordeaux-trained and today one of the more influential winemakers and consultants in the eastern U.S., taught Tom a great deal. "I was able to follow a complete cycle during my eight months at Ingleside," explains the quietly friendly Payette. "I worked the '85 crush, monitored the fermentations, pruned dormant vines in the winter, then helped filter and bottle the '85 whites. I even got to disgorge some of Jacques' champagne!"

In the spring of '86, Tom's work at Ingleside was complete and he was, temporarily, back at VPI assisting Bruce Zoecklin in the school's enology lab. Meanwhile, out on the Eastern Shore of Virginia, Jim Keyes was looking for a winemaker to oversee his first crush at then brand-new Accomack Vineyards. Jim had contacted Jacques Recht for recommendations and Jacques didn't hesitate to give Keyes Tom's number. By May of that year, Payette found himself on the Eastern Shore, tending Accomack's Merlot vineyard and setting up a new winery in preparation for his second harvest.

But while the Eastern Shore is a lovely place to raise a family, or vacation, or retire, it was a bit too isolated and quiet for Tom. Feeling separated from his family and friends, he began planning his next move — a winery in his own back yard. Tom left Accomack in the spring of '87 and quickly began pulling the plans together with his mother. He stripped and converted the family's small barn, picked out, purchased, and installed equipment, and entered into agreements with growers to lease several acres of grapes. By late summer, a license was received and, a few months later, grapes were delivered to begin the process of becoming the first Riverside wines.

THE VINEYARD

While the Payettes' farm totals 8.5 acres, none of the property is especially suitable for growing grapes, especially vinifera varieties. Located in the lower elevation Piedmont, well east of the Blue Ridge foothills, the area experiences bitter cold winter lows and some spring frosts. One slope does have good eastern exposure and, in the spring of 1988, was planted to the red French-American hybrid Chambourcin. The Payettes also have their eye on nearby Moormont Mountain where higher elevations could provide excellent vineyard sites. In the meantime, Riverside will purchase the lion's share of the fruit needed to produce its wines.

GRAPE VARIETIES AND ACREAGE

Variety	Vinifera	French/Amer. Hybrids
Chambourcin	—.—	1.0
TOTALS	0.0	1.0

THE WINES

Riverside Winery bottles just over 1,000 cases, split evenly between a Chardonnay, a Riesling, and a 100% vinifera blush.

The Chardonnay is fermented entirely in jacketed, temperature-controlled stainless steel tanks and then receives brief aging in French oak. The Riesling is also fermented cool in stainless steel. For the Riesling, Payette chooses to use Epernay yeast. This yeast strain, which ferments quite slowly, helps bring out the delicate, aromatic nature of wines and is often the yeast of choice for Riesling. It is also a yeast sensitive to cold temperatures, which allows Tom to chill the Riesling when it reaches 2% residual sugar, thereby halting the fermentation with natural medium sweetness.

Of the two wines, the Riesling displays more interest. It shows faint, fresh, blossomy aromas of pineapple and citrus. In the mouth, it has clean, crisp flavors of peaches, apricots, and pineapple.

The blush is also predominantly Riesling (92%). However, it is fermented at slightly higher temperatures with a different yeast, Prise de Mousse. This yeast emphasizes rounder, more complex flavors in a wine and is often used for Chardonnay. With the Riesling is blended 8% juice from a hodgepodge of red vinifera grapes that vary each vintage depending on availability. In the inaugural 1987 blush, Payette used small portions of Gamay Beaujolais and Zinfandel. This wine, too, has a subdued but clean floral nose, fresh fruity flavors, and a very light copper/pink hue. It is finished relatively dry, with slightly less than 1% residual sugar.

In future vintages, look for a 100% varietal, oak-aged Chambourcin to round out the lineup.

INCIDENTALLY . . .

The label appearing on Riverside's wines is a reproduction of an original mural that was painted on the wall of the dining room in the Payettes' house, which dates back to 1790.

DIRECTIONS

From Route 29 in Culpeper, take Route 15 south. Turn left on Route 614 (Locust Dale) for 4.2 miles, then turn right on Route 615. Proceed for 3 miles to winery on the right.

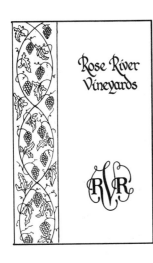

Rose River Vineyards

ADDRESS: S.R. 2, Box 186
Syria, VA 22743
PHONE: (703) 923-4591
OWNERS: Kenneth L. McCoy, Sr. and Kenneth L.
    McCoy, Jr.
WINEMAKER: Kenneth L. McCoy, Jr.
TOTAL ACRES: 6
CASES/YR: 400
HOURS: April through November, Friday-Sunday
    10-5; others by appointment

Dr. Kenneth McCoy, his son Kenneth Jr., and Kirsten Kohl are your hosts at Rose River Vineyards, another of Virginia's newer wineries. With their first commercial crush in 1986, the group successfully achieved a goal that had its roots dating back to 1976.

That year, Kenneth McCoy, a pathologist directing the laboratory facility at Providence Hospital in Washington, DC, was looking to future retirement and wished to set aside some land in a more peaceful, rural setting. McCoy and his son found their present farm nestled in a remote hollow west of Syria, Virginia.

Today, visitors will find at Rose River a charming, very small operation with 6 acres bearing grapes, a tiny barn retooled to perform as a winery, and a recently completed tasting room restored from the original farmhouse. This striking, rustic structure features an original chimney dating back to 1750. An added bonus is the farm's extensive network of trails — one can be followed along the river to an abandoned cabin that graces a forested picnic area, while another follows a 1¾ mile mountain loop.

THE VINEYARD

Once the fields at Rose River were cleared, a vineyard was planted. Started in 1976, the 6-acre vineyard now boasts a diverse group of vinifera and French-American hybrid varieties. Vinifera plantings focus predominantly on Cabernet Sauvignon and Chardonnay, with additional plots devoted to Merlot, Riesling, and an experimental few rows of Zinfandel. Small amounts of Seyval, Vidal, and Cayuga finish up the acreage.

Thus far, the vineyard has experienced considerable success. The site is located at an elevation of 1,000 feet above sea level, thereby enjoying a beneficial temperature inversion. At such elevations, daytime highs are several degrees cooler during the summer than in surrounding valleys, allowing for a slower, more gentle maturation of grapes. Similarly, in the winter, rising warm air leaves the vineyard site several degrees warmer than surrounding lowlands, protecting vines from damaging winter kill.

THE WINES

At this time, a varied array of wines greets the visitor. All grape wines are *estate bottled*: a Chardonnay, a Cabernet Sauvignon, and a "Mountain Blush" are produced. From fruit and honey produced in the surrounding countryside, "Mountain Apple," "Mountain Peach," and "Mountain Mead" are also made.

Kenneth Jr. currently serves as winemaker at Rose River. A self-taught vintner, Ken's most directly related previous agricultural work was managing a nursery producing grafted vinifera vines and as a crop duster on the Eastern Shore of Maryland. For several years prior to turning pro, Ken nurtured his vineyard and honed his winemaking skills with estate-grown fruit.

The tiny winery facility, housed in the renovated barn, rivals Blenheim's converted smokehouses as one of the smallest in the state. Neat, miniature stainless steel tanks are arranged in orderly rows for the fermentation and aging of Rose River wines. Ken chills the entire fermentation room with a powerful cooling system for both fermentation and cold stabilization. At this time, no oak aging is given to any Rose River wines.

Tastings begin with the 100% varietal Chardonnay. Bone dry, crisp, and appley, the wine is clean and light, reflecting its methods of production. The "Mountain Blush" is a blend of a wide variety of grapes and is finished with a couple of percentage points of residual sugar. It has a pleasing rosy/salmon color, and a faint nose of candied berries. Clean, fruity, and crisp, the wine possesses good balance and has a long, palate-cleansing finish. The Cabernet wraps up the table wine selection. The '86 bottling was a big, deeply extracted wine, but also extremely tight and unforgiving. Slightly stemmy berry, plum, and cassis flavors dominate, yet the wine reflects the fact that it was not aged in oak, as it is quite hard and astringent. At this point, the wine seems to want for some oak-aged softening.

More sweetly finished fruit wines offer an unusually pleasant variation to the more typical mid-Atlantic wine tour visit. The "Mountain Apple" is clean and fresh and quite true to the natural fruit. The "Mountain Peach" is also engaging and attractive. Made in extremely small amounts, the winery also offers a honey-based "Mountain Mead."

INCIDENTALLY . . .

For wine tourists who also happen to be rock hounds, the Rose River offers a special attraction. The fairly rare semi-precious stone Unikite can be readily found along the banks of the babbling brook that runs through the estate.

DIRECTIONS

From Route 29 at Madison, take Route 231 north. At Banco, turn left onto Route 670. Proceed 1.7 miles past Syria, past the Graves Mountain Lodge, to Route 648. Turn left and proceed to vineyard.

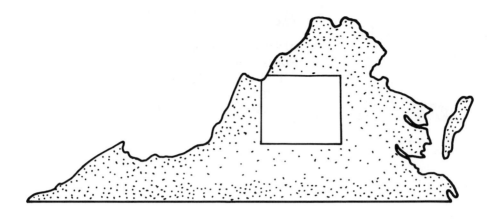

MONTICELLO

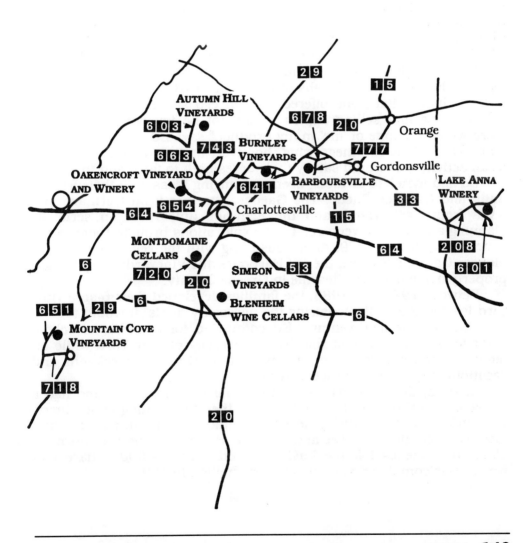

Autumn Hill

Virginia Chardonnay
Monticello Appellation

Dry White Wine
PRODUCED AND BOTTLED BY
AUTUMN HILL VINEYARDS, STANARDSVILLE, VA
BW VA59 *CONTAINS SULFITES*
ALCOHOL 12.5% BY VOLUME

Autumn Hill Vineyards

ADDRESS: Rural Route 1, Box 199C
Stanardsville, VA 22973
PHONE: (804) 985-1600
OWNERS: Avra and Ed Schwab
WINEMAKERS: Ed Schwab
TOTAL ACRES: 8.5
CASES/YR: 1500
HOURS: Daily by appointment only

In the late 1970s, the Schwabs, Ed and Avra, were deeply involved with their careers and the demands of raising their family on Long Island. As their children grew older, however, they began to contemplate certain lifestyle changes. Ed, owner of an interior design business and Avra, a teacher, explored alternatives that might allow them to, as Ed explains, "get more out of life."

While on vacation on the west coast, they looked into apple farming in Washington state and both avocado and macadamia nut farming in California. The Schwabs were intrigued with these possibilities, but concluded that none offered enough ego satisfaction. "I just felt that growing and selling apples would not be involving enough . . . there would be none of 'me' in my product," says Ed, a wiry, energetic man. The option of winegrowing, however, appealed to the Schwabs as an activity that would satisfy their urges both to farm and to create.

Ed and Avra had all along been exchanging ideas with their friends Anita and Gunther Gaede. The Gaedes, Gunther from Germany and Anita from Switzerland, and the Schwabs quickly began seriously planning a joint wine venture. Their explorations brought them to the state of Virginia in 1979. After consulting with the renowned vinifera pioneer Gabriele Rausse, then of Barboursville Vineyards, they bought property north of Charlottesville in Greene County.

Between 1979 and 1983, the families developed their 6-acre vineyard in absentia while acquiring the necessary "tools" it would take to succeed in their new venture. Ed completed forty credits of school work in plant sciences at the State University of New York while attending numerous seminars in winemaking. On spare weekends and vacations they tended to their new vines in Virginia.

In 1983, the Schwabs moved to the farm permanently and had a house built as well as the small facility then functioning as a winery. By 1986, their farm winery license in hand, the families picked and crushed their first harvest and Autumn Hill Vineyards was born. In 1989, the Gaedes left the business, and a new 4,000 square foot winery was completed and open for production in 1990.

THE VINEYARD

The Schwabs and the Gaedes chose the site for their vineyard only after extensive consultation with Gabriele Rausse. He advised them on the micro-climates required for the cultivation of vinifera grapes. "Not everyone agrees with me, but I feel very strongly that if Virginia ever hopes to be considered a great wine region, it must grow only the noblest grape varieties," says Ed.

The site selected is at 600 feet above sea level on a southern-facing slope of the Blue Ridge Mountains. Situated on this hilltop, surrounded by no other adjacent higher ground, the vineyard enjoys good air and water drainage, unobstructed sun exposure, and almost constant breezes. Such air flow has helped Autumn Hill avoid the vine damage other Virginia wineries have experienced from spring frosts which, in still air, tend to gather in pockets at the lowest points of a vineyard. Besides the practical advantages this site offers, the vineyard also affords the visitor wonderful views of the surrounding mountains to the north and west, and of the Virginia piedmont plateau to the east.

At this time, Autumn Hill grows the standard three varieties of vinifera so often seen in Virginia vineyards: Chardonnay, Riesling, and Cabernet Sauvignon. The 8.5-acre parcel is divided such that the largest plot is devoted to Chardonnay (4 acres) with 1.3 acre plantings in Riesling and the balance in Cabernet Sauvignon.

GRAPE VARIETIES AND ACREAGE

Variety	Vinifera	French/Amer. Hybrids
Chardonnay	4.0	—.—
Riesling	1.3	—.—
Cabernet Sauvignon	3.2	—.—
TOTALS	8.5	0.0

In June of 1987, the Federal Bureau of Alcohol, Tobacco and Firearms officially approved a modification to the boundaries of the Monticello Viticultural Area to include Autumn Hill with its neighboring wineries.

THE WINES

The inaugural '86 crush at Autumn Hill yielded 250 cases of wine; a minuscule amount by commercial standards, but an amount the owners were proud of nonetheless. "We take great satisfaction in using our own estate grapes and our plan is to start off slowly and produce premium wines in limited quantities," explains Ed. An eventual goal is to produce 2,000 cases annually.

Autumn Hill will regularly offer four wines: a Chardonnay, a Riesling, a Cabernet Sauvignon, and a Blush wine. The Chardonnay, which is finished bone-dry, differs from many in that it receives no oak aging. This is a stylistic preference of the Schwabs who wish to emphasize the grape's fresh fruitiness. The wines have consistently displayed a clean, light-intensity nose of varietal fruit and, in the mouth, similarly clean, crisp flavors of citrus and green apples.

The Rieslings is a semi-dry (finished with 1.75% residual sugar). This wine is light and pleasant. The semi-dry has a good balance between sugar and acid.

The Blush is a pleasing wine, pale salmon in color and possessing an attractive nose of sweet berries and subtle herbaceousness (a typical and attractive trait of the Cabernet grape). In the mouth, the wine is crisp with candyish berry and cherry flavors and has a supple texture due to the slightly sweet (2% residual sugar) composition. This wine, which was produced from the *free run juice* of the just-pressed Cabernet grapes, is a true *blanc de noir*. The first Cabernet Sauvignon red table wine will be released in 1991. Until that time, the winery's blush wine is a nice picnic alternative that offers more interest than the usual, run-of-the-mill rosé crowd.

INCIDENTALLY . . .

The photograph adorning the label of Autumn Hill Vineyards was taken by Ed and Avra Schwab's daughter, Hilary, a professional photographer. It is a view of the nearby Blue Ridge foothills taken from the families' property.

DIRECTIONS

On Route 29, 6 miles north of Charlottesville, turn left (west) on Airport Road (Route 649). Turn left onto Route 606, then right (north) on Route 743 to Earlysville. Turn left on Route 663, go 1.4 miles, then right on Route 663 for .5 mile, left on 663 for 3.7 miles. Turn right at 603 for 2.2 miles; vineyard entrance on right.

Barboursville Vineyards

ADDRESS: P.O. Box 136, Route 777
Barboursville, VA 22923
PHONE: (703) 832-3824
OWNER: The Zonin Corporation
WINEMAKER: Luca Paschina
TOTAL ACRES: 48
CASES/YR: 12,000
HOURS: Monday-Saturday 10-4

Just a few miles north of Charlottesville, you'll find a winery that is 1) the oldest in the Monticello Viticultural Area; 2) the first winery in the state to produce truly commercial levels of vinifera wine; 3) a winery with a rich European tradition; and 4) a winery which brought to Virginia, in 1976, a level of businesslike professionalism the likes of which the state had never seen before. The winery is Barboursville Vineyards.

The story behind Barboursville begins in Italy where the Zonin family had been involved with viticulture since 1821. Today, the largest privately-owned wine company in Italy, the Zonins are centered in Gambellara and control hundreds of acres of vineyards and eight separate wineries located in all of the famous regions of the country—Veneto, Friuli, Tuscany, and Piedmonte.

In 1976, given the relative strength of the lire on foreign markets at that time, Giani Zonin, thirty-seven years old and president of the family's holdings, decided that investment in the United States would make sense. But the decision to venture into Virginia had its roots much further back than 1976.

In fact, more than two hundred years previously, another Italian began one of the first experiments in growing grapes in Virginia. In 1773, a physician and merchant from Tuscany named Filippo Mazzei set out for the colony of Virginia armed with 10,000 vinifera cuttings and an ambitious plan. Working with Virginia businessman Thomas Adams, Mazzei hoped to establish a successful wine venture in this new world which, in a later letter to George Washington, he praised as "better calculated than any other I am acquainted with for the produce of wine." Upon his arrival, Mazzei was soon introduced to the political leaders of the day, among them a noted wine enthusiast, Thomas Jefferson. Never a man to question his own dreams and goals, Jefferson was so intrigued by Mazzei's idea that he took him out to Monticello, persuaded him to purchase 50 acres adjacent to Jefferson's property, and convinced him to start his vineyard there.

Well, winegrowing success was not to be Mazzei's or Jefferson's. Vinifera vines of Europe had grave trouble growing in the too-hot summers and too-cold winters. Unresistant to disease, rot, and fungus,

Mazzei's vines finally succumbed to the deadly root louse phylloxera. As both Jefferson's and Mazzei's interests refocused on the growing American revolution, the early vineyards were abandoned.

After researching the climate, soils, and topography of present-day Virginia, Giani Zonin was convinced that successful vinifera growing could take place and that modern sprays and viticultural techniques could handle the problems Mazzei and Jefferson were unable to overcome. To direct the task, Zonin chose thirty-one-year-old Gabriele Rausse, an agronomist who had recently graduated from the University of Milan with a degree in plant pathology. The Zonins purchased a 700-acre farm in Orange County that was the former estate of James Barbour, at one time a Governor of the state and a good friend of Thomas Jefferson.

Progress at Barboursville did not proceed smoothly at first, however. Both the U.S. Department of Agriculture and Virginia Polytechnic Institute shunned the project, saying that commercial growing of vinifera was not only unprofitable but probably impossible. Neither liked the idea that the Barboursville venture might excite other farmers into risky investment in vineyard development. State officials also feared a negative potential long-range impact on other traditional crops such as tobacco. Rausse met with resistance as he tried to import European rootstock and cuttings. Even locals appeared confused by the mysterious activity and, in 1979, a fire of unknown origin occurred in the Barboursville winery causing $100,000 worth of damage.

Yet Rausse's hard work and Zonin's investment have paid off. In 1979, despite a burned-out winery, the first Barboursville vintage produced 20,000 bottles of wine — earning Barboursville the shared honor (with Piedmont Vineyards) of producing the first vinifera wines in the state.

In 1981, Gabriele Rausse left Barboursville to begin nearby Simeon Vineyard. To take his place, the Zonins brought in another experienced Italian winegrower, Adriano Rossi. Between 1982 and 1990, Rossi strove to build Barboursville's reputation, especially outside the state of Virginia, by entering wines in numerous national and international competitions.

Starting with the 1990 crush, Barboursville has benefited from the skills of yet another well-trained Italian winemaker. Luca Paschina attended the Institute Umberto Primo in Alba. Prior to joining Barboursville, he held winemaking positions at two wineries in the Piedmonte region of Italy, as well as at Widmer's Cellars in the Finger Lakes region of New York.

THE VINEYARD

While originally the Zonin company had planned for large expansion of Barboursville Vineyards (250 acres had been targeted as early as 1983), actual plantings have plateaued at considerably smaller levels. Yet, at 48 acres, Barboursville still represents one of the largest vineyards in the state.

Nearly half of the acreage is devoted to two of the best-known varieties—Chardonnay and Cabernet Sauvignon. As seen below, Barboursville has focused exclusively on vinifera varieties including Riesling, Merlot, Pinot Noir, and Cabernet Franc. At 4 acres, Barboursville's Gewurztraminer parcel ranks as one of the largest in the mid-Atlantic devoted to this often-difficult variety. Another acre is planted to various experimental varieties such as the white Italian grape Malvasia. Most recently, 5 acres of Sauvignon Blanc, another difficult variety to grow in the east, have been planted.

GRAPE VARIETIES AND ACREAGE

Variety	Vinifera	French/Amer. Hybrids
Cabernet Sauvignon	10.0	—.—
Chardonnay	10.0	—.—
Riesling	5.0	—.—
Sauvignon Blanc	5.0	—.—
Gewurztraminer	4.0	—.—
Merlot	4.0	—.—
Pinot Noir	4.0	—.—
Cabernet Franc	4.0	—.—
Miscellaneous	2.0	—.—
TOTALS	48.0	0.0

One reason for the slower than planned growth has been the constant battle with extreme winter temperatures and late spring frosts. Production levels have varied greatly from more than 8,000 cases to fewer than 5,000 due to weather conditions that have damaged the vineyard.

THE WINES

Despite the support of a multi-million dollar corporation, Barboursville Vineyards has never devoted its capital into creating a glitzy tourist attraction. The workmanlike winery building is constructed simply and functionally with corrugated steel, and the nearby cinderblock tasting room doubles as the winery's office.

"We are a business, and our business is wine production. The real beauty of this place is the vineyards, not the place we make wine. It is as it should be," said Adriano Rossi during an interview prior to his departure.

Certain winemaking techniques follow a decidedly Italian style at Barboursville. Whites are produced very crisp, dry, and fruity without any contact with oak. Reds, as well, tend to be lighter-bodied and emphasize vibrant fruitiness rather than depth and extract. All fermentation is in stainless steel, with a heat exchanger employed to control the temperature of tanks. The only oak used for aging is that used traditionally in Italy, Slavonian red oak from Yugoslavia.

Barboursville currently bottles eight wines—four whites, two reds, and two rosés.

The Chardonnay and Pinot Noir Blanc are wonderful examples of the quality white table wines capable of being produced in the mid-Atlantic. Both are bone-dry, crisp, light, thirst-quenching, and squeaky clean. The Chardonnays produced in recent vintages have blossomy aromas of citrus highlighted by baked-bread yeasty notes. On the palate the wine combines the richness of apples with attractive tartness of yellow grapefruit. The Pinot Noir Blanc is, in part, a true *blanc de noir*. It is made from 80% Pinot Noir and 20% Chardonnay. While showing many of the nice qualities of the Chardonnay, it also has more complex "soil" elements contributed by the Pinot.

Both the Riesling and Gewurztraminer are attractive, well-made wines. The Riesling typically has 10% Malvasia blended in, possesses a floral nose, light-intensity fruit, 1.5% residual sugar, and sometimes an awkward heaviness not uncommon to many Rieslings from Virginia. The Gewurz is produced dry, in the Alsatian manner, and has a medium intense spicy, herbal nose characteristic of the grape.

The Cabernet Sauvignon (which has 20% Cabernet Franc blended in) and the Merlot (which is 15% Cabernet Sauvignon) are quite nice, if lighter than many produced in the state. The winery often releases its Cabernet after lengthy barrel and bottle aging. Therefore, the wines are typically ready to drink upon release. For example, the '82 Cab was well developed with a rich nose of coffee and cassis. In the mouth, soft, round fruit had lost almost all of its tannin. The '83 version had deeper, livelier fruit of berries and plums with a hint of chocolate.

The Merlot spends just four months in oak (in contrast to the Cab, which spends twelve months). It is a lighter-bodied wine that displays bright strawberry, raspberry, and cherry fruit flavors touched by evident herbaceousness.

Both rosé wines are pleasant. The Cabernet Sauvignon Blanc is a blanc de noir made from the *free run juice* of Cabernet Sauvignon (80%) and Cabernet Franc (20%). An interesting companion is the more robust "Rosé Barboursville," which is a darker, heavier true rosé made from a blend of Semillon, Malvasia, Alicante, and Barbera.

INCIDENTALLY . . .

Gracing the Barboursville property and appearing on the winery's label are the ruins of James Barbour's house originally built in 1814. Designed by Thomas Jefferson, the house burned down on Christmas day in 1844 when a candle on the Christmas tree set the house on fire.

DIRECTIONS

From Route 29, travel east on Route 33 to the town of Barboursville. Turn right at Route 20, drive 200 yards and turn left on Route 678. Proceed one-half mile to Route 777 and turn right again. Drive 500 yards to winery entrance on right.

Blenheim Wine Cellars

ADDRESS: Route 6, Box 53A
Charlottesville, VA 22901
PHONE: (804) 293-2761
OWNER: John Marquis
WINEMAKER: John Marquis, Jr.
TOTAL ACRES: 10.25
CASES/YR: 1,000
HOURS: By appointment only

Blenheim Wine Cellars is an extremely small operation and, therefore, is only open to visitors occasionally, by appointment. It is also, however, an extremely interesting place to know about from a number of viewpoints. First, the property possesses a rich and varied history. The house and separate library are both on the National Register of Historic Places and date back to 1745. Located within a short few miles of Thomas Jefferson's Monticello and James Madison's Ashlawn, Blenheim was originally part of a 9,000-acre land grant purchased by John "King" Carter from King George III in 1730 for just 46 pounds, 15 shillings. Over the next 250 years, the property passed through various owners including Carter's grandson, who represented the country in the House of Burgesses, and Andrew Stevenson, who served both as Ambassador to England and on the Board of Governors of the University of Virginia in the early 1800s.

Second, Blenheim has a nifty winery facility, a high-tech operation in miniature. All fermentation, stabilization, filtration, and bottling take place in two buildings no bigger than large closets. The buildings, in their former two century-long lives, served as smokehouses for the various previous owners. Heavily insulated and stuffed to the gills, the smokehouses are equipped with small (5-foot tall) stainless steel tanks, pumps, filters and, for cold stabilization, a cleverly employed deep freezer, used under more conventional circumstances for storing steaks and chops.

Third, visitors can wander through a model 10-acre vineyard. Only about half of the fruit grown at Blenheim is used for its wine; the other half is sold to Monticello Viticultural Area wineries Barboursville and Simeon. In the words of the distinguished Simeon winegrower Gabriele Rausse, "I never visit Blenheim during the growing season. At harvest time, I know that the grapes I purchase will be perfect."

This high praise is directed at and has grown from the labors of John Marquis, Jr., the quiet son of John Marquis, Sr. The two moved to the Charlottesville area in the late 1970s from Ohio, where John Sr. operated a large grain farm. John Jr., who studied chemistry at small Ashland College in Ohio, planted a few grapes in their new home as a hobby. With help and advice from neighboring wineries like Chermont and Montdomaine, John Jr.'s experimental vineyards flourished and his home winemaking skills improved. As so many hobbyists-turned-professional state, "the bug had bitten," and Marquis decided to go commercial. He received his license in August of 1983 and today devotes his full energies to the vineyard and winery.

THE VINEYARD

Blenheim's vineyard was planted in two phases; in 1983 and 1984. Today, a total of 10.25 acres are producing: 7 planted to Chardonnay and 3 to Riesling. In 1985, John Jr. added a .25-acre plot of Cabernet Sauvignon on an experimental basis and, depending on its success, may expand it in the future. All of the Riesling and a little less than half the Chardonnay are sold to other wineries.

GRAPE VARIETIES AND ACREAGE

Variety	Vinifera	French/Amer. Hybrids
Chardonnay	7.0	—.—
Riesling	3.0	—.—
Cabernet Sauvignon	0.25	—.—
TOTALS	10.25	0.0

THE WINES

At this time, Blenheim produces about 1,000 cases (or less), concentrating on just one variety, Chardonnay. John Jr. has been experimenting a great deal in his early vintages at Blenheim. Within each vintage, before blending and bottling, different "lots" of wine will be treated differently (some with no oak, others with varying degrees of oak aging; some filtered and fined, others not, etc.). In these efforts, John is developing his style which, he hopes, will end up "quite Burgundian." For example, his Chardonnay is put through a secondary *malolactic fermentation* to reduce acidity and develop toasty, buttery complexity. While fermented entirely in stainless steel, the wine is aged in French Nevers oak for a relatively brief, one to two month period.

The style of Blenheim Chardonnay is evolving. Early vintages have produced uneven results, but given the dedication and innovation shown by this young man, I would look for continued improvement in years to come.

INCIDENTALLY . . .

The name "Blenheim" also dates back to the mid-1700s when the property was named for Blenheim Palace in England.

While the winery is not generally open to the public, Blenheim wines are available at the gift shop at nearby Ashlawn, the historic home of James and Dolly Madison.

Burnley Vineyards

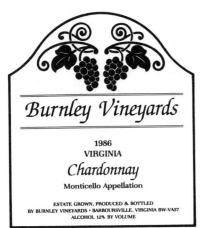

ADDRESS: Route 1, Box 122
Barboursville, VA 22923
PHONE: (703) 832-2828
OWNERS: The Reeder Family
WINEMAKER: Lee Reeder
TOTAL ACRES: 12
CASES/YR: 1,500
HOURS: Wednesday-Sunday 11-5

Burnley Vineyards, located about 15 miles north of Charlottesville, is a true family operation: C.J. Reeder is the General Manager, his wife Patt is in charge of sales, son Lee is the winemaker, and Lee's wife, Dawn, is responsible for tastings and tours.

Between 1976 and 1981, C.J. Reeder was serving as Colonel and Commanding Officer of the U.S. Army Foreign Science and Technology Center in Charlottesville. During this tour of duty, he and his family fell in love with the region and decided to settle there permanently. They purchased the property where the winery and vineyard now stand in 1976 and immediately began planting grapes. The Reeders had planned from the start to grow grapes and sell them to Virginia wineries. In 1981, when C.J. retired, the vineyard was producing grapes commercially for this purpose. That same year, however, Lee was in his second year at Virginia Tech when he decided he wanted to learn the art/science of winemaking. This decision started the ball rolling towards the family's goal of operating a premium farm winery. A short two years later, in April 1985, Burnley (named for one of the early landowners of the area) opened its doors.

Lee performed undergraduate research in wine technology for two years at Virginia Tech and graduated in 1983. While there, he completed special studies on how freezing affects grape quality, and whether added oak chips and oak dust can be successfully substituted for barrel aging of wine. Following graduation, as he was helping his father construct the winery, Lee also took seminar courses from Jacques Recht, winemaster at Ingleside Plantation Vineyard and from Lisa Van de Water, a noted chemist and consultant from The Wine Lab in Napa, California. The experiences, he feels, prepared him well for the rigors of commercial winemaking.

THE VINEYARD

The 12 acres of estate vineyards at Burnley represent some of the oldest vines in the Monticello Viticultural Area. Focusing predominantly on vinifera varieties, the table below shows that 6 acres are planted to Chardonnay, 3 acres to Cabernet Sauvignon, 2 acres to Riesling, and 1 acre to the white French-American hybrid Vidal. Burnley also leases vineyards in the Fredericksburg area as well as on the Eastern Shore of Virginia. Purchased grapes to supplement the estate's crop include Riesling, Vidal, and red French-American hybrids Chambourcin, De-Chaunac, Foch, and Baco Noir.

GRAPE VARIETIES AND ACREAGE

Variety	Vinifera	French/Amer. Hybrids
Chardonnay	6.0	—.—
Cabernet Sauvignon	3.0	—.—
Riesling	2.0	—.—
Vidal	—.—	1.0
TOTALS	11.0	1.0

The Reeders feel they have an excellent site for growing vinifera grapes. Coping with late frosts, which can destroy tender spring buds thus destroying that year's crop, represents the major hurdle for the family. One strategy they employ is lighting bonfires at various spots around the vineyard when especially cold weather is expected. During the winter of 1986 even this effort did not succeed entirely as the vineyard suffered limited damage to some Chardonnay vines. Despite these infrequent setbacks, however, the Reeders feel confident that their vineyard will continue to produce fine fruit.

THE WINES

Production at Burnley is a relatively small 1,500 cases per year. Slow and steady growth has seen the winery double its output each vintage, and the ultimate goal of the winery is to bottle between 4,000 and 5,000 cases annually.

Burnley Vineyards produces six wines. The current stars of the lineup are their Chardonnay, Riesling, and Cabernet Sauvignon. Lee is an extreme advocate of fermenting wines at very cool temperatures in order to preserve their fresh fruitiness. Using temperature-controlled stainless steel tanks, this is a common and preferred practice for white wines in most premium wineries. However, the practice is not usually employed for reds. The common belief is that higher temperatures are required for red wines in order to extract maximum color and fruit character from the skins. Lee's Cabernets (which are 100% varietal) shatter this norm. The wine is fermented at 75° (rather than the normal 80-90°) for four weeks (a rather extended *maceration*). Despite the cool fermentation, a carefully aged '85 bottling possessed a deep ruby color, a nose packed with scents of fresh berries, cherries, and spicy oak, and full flavors completely consistent with aromas. Granted, the cooler fermentation did result in a finished wine of light to moderate tannins, making the wine quite drinkable in its youth. Firm acids, however, will permit this wine to continue to improve with several years of aging. While subsequent vintages have not all lived up to the success of the '85, count on Burnley Vineyards to offer a noteworthy rendition of this grape.

Burnley's Chardonnays are produced in a crisp, fruity style. Again, a long, cool fermentation and a minimal aging of six weeks in American oak produce a wine with bright appley fruit and zippy citrine acidity. In successful vintages, like 1986, this wine exemplifies the high standard of Chardonnay that can be produced in Virginia: wines that are clean and vibrantly fruity like their counterparts of California, yet more lean and elegant, possessing the finer attributes of French white Burgundies.

The Burnley Rieslings consistently offer pleasant drinking. Finished in the German style with 2.5% residual sugar, the Riesling possesses a delicate, floral nose. Medium-bodied flavors of apricot, peach, and grapefruit persist in a long finish. Lee achieves the desired amount of finished sweetness by blending into the wine a *sweet reserve* of fresh, unfermented Riesling juice. Again, Burnley usually succeeds in producing a fine example of Riesling, a variety most winemakers have struggled with in Virginia.

For everyday drinking, Burnley also produces three wines from French-American hybrid grapes. They are called "Rivanna White," "Rivanna Red," and "Rivanna Sunset," named for a river that runs through Charlottesville. The wines are solid, clean, and well made. The white, 100% Vidal, is a crisp, fruity wine that would go well with a wide variety of light foods. The "Sunset," a blush (albeit deeper in color than most) created by pressing the whole berries of Chambourcin grapes and fermenting the juice in the manner of a white wine, has 4% residual sugar, crisp and light berry flavors, and succeeds well as a summer sipper. "Rivanna Red" is a soft, round, fruity wine possessing some herbaceous characteristics. It is a blend of four red varieties: Foch, DeChaunac, Baco Noir, and Chambourcin.

INCIDENTALLY . . .

Burnley Vineyards offers picnic facilities to visitors and a tasting room with a cathedral ceiling and a 30-foot deck overlooking the nearby countryside.

C.J. and Patt Reeder have been deeply involved with the Virginia grape industry since 1976. Patt has served as President of the Virginia Vineyards Association, and at this writing is the Vice President of the Virginia Wineries Association. C.J. has served as Director of the Jeffersonian Wine Grape Growers Society since its inception in 1981.

DIRECTIONS

From Charlottesville, go north 15 miles on Route 20, then go left on Route 641 for .3 miles to winery on left. From Washington, DC or Charlottesville, visitors can also travel on Route 29 and follow the grape cluster signs that appear approximately 15 miles north of Charlottesville, just west of the town of Barboursville.

Lake Anna Winery

ADDRESS: 5621 Courthouse Road
Spotsylvania, VA 22553
PHONE: (703) 895-5085
OWNERS: Bill and Ann Heidig
WINEMAKERS: Bill and Ann Heidig
TOTAL ACRES: 11.5
CASES/YR: 1,000
HOURS: May through September, Saturday
and Sunday 11-5

The inspiration for Bill Heidig's decision to become a winemaker was quite accidental. A wrong communication with his two French-only speaking harvesters resulted in their picking ¾ ton too much Seyval. The buyer for the grapes, Lew Parker at Willowcroft Farm Vineyards, didn't need that much. On that afternoon in 1985, as he was making his long drive back to Spotsylvania County, Heidig wondered what in the heck he was going to do with all these grapes.

When he got home, Bill and his wife, Ann, had two choices: to throw away a truckload of gorgeous fruit, or to stare adversity in the face and make the best of a bad situation. In the end, the couple decided to make a pretty large batch of homemade wine. They scurried around as fast as they could to locate enough containers, and then set about the business of fermenting. A few months later, the Heidigs were quite amazed by the quality of their wine. Could it be that they could be successful winemakers as well as successful grape growers? The answer must have been yes. In June 1990, after a couple of years of careful preparation, Lake Anna Winery opened its doors.

"Whenever we decide to do something, we go whole hog," says Heidig, an impressively large man with bright, white hair. The same was true when, a few years earlier, they decided to grow grapes. Both enjoying active careers in the Washington, DC area, the Heidigs had purchased 75 acres of farmland fronting on Lake Anna in 1972. Several consecutive years of drought had frustrated the couple as they raised traditional crops of soybeans and corn. After consulting with Jim Law of Linden Vineyards, Bill and Ann became convinced that grapes offered a more lucrative future.

"We planted 3.5 acres of Seyval because it was the only vine stock we could lay our hands on," says Bill. "Jim Law also suggested that we plant a small experimental plot of 100 vinifera vines to see how they'd do on the property. We figured that if we were going to go to the trouble of another planting, we might as well make it worth our while." By they time they had finished, 2,000 Chardonnay and Cabernet Sauvignon vines were keeping the Seyval company.

THE VINEYARD

Although Lake Anna's vineyard is situated quite close to the large reservoir of the same name, the Heidigs do not think that the body of water has any influence on this micro-climate. Instead, they attribute their vineyard's success to the gentle rolling hillsides that provide good air drainage. The site has never experienced significant damage from spring frosts.

"I knew I must have a good location because the grapes I sold to other wineries kept getting made into award-winning wines," Bill explains. A regular customer for their Seyval in the late 1980s was Willowcroft Farm Vineyards, a winery that has earned a strong reputation for producing fine examples of this varietal. For 1986, a large portion of the grapes that went into Oakencroft Vineyard's Seyval were from Lake Anna. That wine just happened to be the one President Reagan took to the Soviet Union as a gift to President Mikhail Gorbachev.

Lake Anna currently has 11.5 acres under cultivation. Along with the original 3.5 acres of Seyval are planted 3 acres of Cabernet Sauvignon, 3.5 acres of Chardonnay, and 1.5 acres of Merlot.

GRAPE VARIETIES AND ACREAGE

Variety	Vinifera	French/Amer. Hybrids
Cabernet Sauvignon	3.0	—.—
Chardonnay	3.5	—.—
Merlot	1.5	—.—
Seyval	—.—	3.5
TOTALS	8.0	3.5

The Heidigs have continually experimented with their vineyard techniques. Following the advice of state viticulturist Tony Wolf and Linden vintner Jim Law, they have found that the quality of their Seyval grapes improves significantly when vines are pruned very severely during the dormant season. "I leave so few buds, I'm surprised I don't kill them," says Bill with a chuckle. While the practice decreases overall yields by a third, Heidig believes that the better-balanced sugar, acid, and pH in the remaining grapes is well worth the sacrifice.

The Heidigs have also begun using a fascinating new trellising approach with some of their varieties. The Scott Henry Trellis System, becoming quite popular in parts of Oregon and Washington, uses four bilateral cordons instead of the usual two. Shoots from the top cordons are allowed to grow upwards, where they are tied to catch wires. What is unique, however, is how the shoots from the lower cordons are forced to grow downwards, towards the ground. What results is a larger but thinner canopy of leaves. With more leaves exposed to sunlight and air, disease is inhibited and grape pH is improved. Depending on how this experiment proceeds, the Heidigs may convert more of the vineyard to this system.

THE WINES

Just two wines were produced in the winery's initial vintage (1989): a 100% Seyval and a Seyval-based blend called "Lakeside White." Since their own winery was still under construction during the '89 crush,

Bill and Ann Heidig had their grapes custom-crushed and fermented at Dominion Wine Cellars in Culpeper.

The '89 Seyval, which exhibits clean, crisp, slightly herbal flavors, began its fermentation in temperature-controlled stainless steel tanks. When the still-fermenting *must* reached 5% sugar, it was transferred to small American oak barrels to finish its fermentation. It was allowed to rest *sur lie* for two months to develop yeasty complexity.

The '89 "Lakeside White" was specially crafted with summer vacationers in mind. Lake Anna has become a popular resort area and offers visitors wonderful boating, fishing, and water skiing. For hot summer days, Bill wanted to produce a pleasant, refreshing quaffer. This wine is 90% Seyval blended with a 10% portion that is part Chardonnay and part Riesling. It is finished with 1.5% residual sugar and offers light, pleasant, slightly sweet drinking.

The 1990 growing season saw all of Lake Anna's vines in full production for the first time. Plans call for Chardonnay, Cabernet Sauvignon, Merlot, Seyval, "Lakeside White," and a blush. "The '90 vintage was wonderful for us," Bill explains. "We ended up with very good ripeness in all our varieties." Continuing their commitment to quality, the Heidigs have enlisted the support of well-known mid-Atlantic vintner Alan Kinne as a consultant.

Given the creative energy of its owners, look for Lake Anna Winery to become a mainstay in the Virginia wine community for years to come.

DIRECTIONS

From Interstate 95, take the Thornburg exit. Proceed west on Route 606 for 2.5 miles. Drive straight through the intersection at the town of Snell and continue on Route 208 for 11.5 miles to the winery on the left.

Montdomaine Cellars

ADDRESS: Route 6, Box 188A
Charlottesville, VA 22901
PHONE: (804) 971-8947
OWNER: Bill Greiwe, Chief Operating Officer
WINEMAKER: Shepherd Rouse
TOTAL ACRES: 46
CASES/YR: 7,500
HOURS: Seven days 10-5

Montdomaine Cellars is another winery in the Monticello Viticultural Area that Thomas Jefferson would have been proud of. Located just 15 miles south of Charlottesville, Montdomaine is both conveniently accessible to the weekend wine tourist and provides a wonderful example of the heights of quality Virginia wines can achieve.

Montdomaine's roots reach back to 1977 when airline pilot Mike Bowles planted a small vineyard to vinifera grapes on his Albemarle County property. By 1983, when 40 acres came to maturity, a limited partnership was formed between six major stockholders, and a license was received in time for the 1984 crush.

But while the corporate owners have preferred to remain behind the scenes at Montdomaine, the winemakers have occupied the limelight, and for good reason. For the '84 and '85 vintages, Steve Warner was at the helm. Steve's wines, especially his Cabernet Sauvignon and Merlot, gained critical plaudits for Montdomaine in the first two commercial vintages. Steve has since left Montdomaine to pursue winemaking at two other Virginia operations—Chateau Morrisette and the Williamsburg Winery. Beginning in 1986 and holding to the present, Montdomaine has operated under the direction of another able California-trained enologist—Shepherd "Shep" Rouse.

Shep Rouse brings to Montdomaine a breadth of experience and a flexible expertise that should enable him and Montdomaine to continue successfully in Virginia's variable growing climate. Shep, a native Virginian, first became interested in wine while studying in Germany as a Fulbright Scholar. Leaving his family's Williamsburg home in 1978, he ventured to California where he worked harvests and assisted in the cellar at Veedercrest Vineyards and, the following year, at Mark West Vineyards in Sonoma's Russian River Valley. After picking up this valuable practical experience, Shep knew he needed professional training and enrolled at the University of California at Davis. Shep graduated from Davis in 1982 and landed a job as assistant winemaker at the highly respected Napa producer Carneros Creek Vineyards. After two years of "exceptionally good learning," Shep decided to broaden his background even further. "I figured that I'd never get to the top of my abilities unless I worked with the best people I could find," explains Rouse. For the next two crushes he assisted Richard Arrowood at the prestigious Chateau St. Jean and then at the champagne house of Schramsberg.

By 1986, Shep felt he had the skills to head up his own operation, yet opportunities in California were few and far between. He heard of the vacancy at Montdomaine and quickly landed the job. Now, with several crushes under his belt at the winery, the future continues to look bright for both him and Montdomaine.

THE VINEYARD

A network of six vineyards totalling 46 acres, all in the vicinity of the winery, supplies the grapes to Montdomaine Cellars. The 28 acres surrounding the winery occupy what Shep calls "one of the best sites in Virginia." Sitting on a gentle, southeast-facing slope, the vineyard enjoys good air drainage, early morning sunlight to dry the dew, and shade exposure during the more intense, late afternoon sun. This latter characteristic helps to lengthen the vineyard's growing season, producing grapes of higher quality and character.

"Site selection is clearly the biggest factor in Virginia," says Rouse. "The industry is really in its infancy, and I think a lot of growers have suffered from mis-matching grape varieties with sites."

Only vinifera varieties are grown by Montdomaine partners, with the largest acreage devoted to Chardonnay (23 acres). As seen below, five other varieties share the remaining 23 acres.

GRAPE VARIETIES AND ACREAGE

Variety	Vinifera	French/Amer. Hybrids
Chardonnay	23.0	—.—
Merlot	8.5	—.—
Cabernet Sauvignon	6.0	—.—
Cabernet Franc	4.0	—.—
Riesling	4.0	—.—
Pinot Noir	0.5	—.—
TOTALS	46.0	0.0

"Merlot and Pinot Noir are good examples of grapes which are tough to grow," he explains. "We'll probably phase out the Pinot completely since it is just too susceptible to rot and disease. Merlot, on the other hand, even though it is very sensitive to winter kill and can also be prone to rot due to its thin skin, has been demonstrated to make fine wine in Virginia. Look at Montdomaine's '84 and '85. We have to expect to get only 1 to 1.5 tons per acre from Merlot, which makes it a tough grape to make a profit from."

Expressing sentiments similar to those of Ham Mowbray of Maryland's Montbray Wine Cellars, Shep feels Virginia has just scratched the surface in terms of selecting optimal varieties. "I really would like to see people try to grow Syrah, Nebbiolo, or Sangiovese (the grapes used in the wines of the Rhone, Piedmonte, and Tuscany regions of Europe, respectively). I think the hot summers here would work well with these warm-climate grapes," he explains.

Viticultural practices that Shep directs include two steps aimed at producing more concentrated varietal character. "In the east, we have to pick grapes earlier if we want to maintain varietal delicacy and nuance, say 20° *Brix* for Chardonnay rather than the 23° usually obtained in California. Letting grapes hang longer to get higher sugar levels can contribute intense, heavy, and earthier traits to the wines. We also cluster thin to keep overall production at a low 2 to 2.5 tons per acre. Thus each vine is pumping more nutrients into fewer bunches, leading to more full flavors. Many wineries over-crop and aim for 4, even 5 tons per acre."

THE WINES

The winery at Montdomaine is dug into a hillside so that about half of the facility is below ground level. This design feature allows for cooler ambient temperatures and thus more economical operations inside the winery. To further control temperatures during fermentation, Montdomaine makes use of a portable heat exchanger, rather than having each stainless steel tank temperature-controlled. Working on the same principle as a heat pump or car radiator, wine (either fermenting or being cold-stabilized) is pumped out of the tank through the heat exchanger, where it is chilled, and then back into the tank. The wine is circulated until the desired temperature is achieved. A more economical method than individually jacketed tanks, it is also one that is slightly riskier. "I really have to be on my toes when using the heat exchanger. Every time you move wine, you entertain the possibility of a mistake, say a leak or oxidation," explains Shep. "As long as I'm careful, it's a system that works very well."

Shep also comes from the school of thought that too many winemakers over-process their wines, more specifically, over-filter their wines. There are basically three methods for clarifying wine: filtration, fining, and extended undisturbed aging.

"Just think about it," says Rouse. "Which approach seems less traumatic to the wine? Pumping it through a filter under extreme pressure, or adding finings that slowly drift to the bottom of the tank?" For his Chardonnay, Riesling, and blush wines, Shep will fine the freshly crushed and pressed juice with bentonite and gelatin, thereby clarifying the juice for a cleaner fermentation. This practice allows Shep the luxury of only filtering the wines once, just before bottling. "Most winemakers filter at least twice, and often three or four times," says Rouse.

Typically, Montdomaine bottles two Chardonnays: a regular and a "Barrel Select." The "Barrel Select" is the richer, more attractive of the two. Possessing vibrant, crisp green apple fruitiness framed by ample toasty French oak, this partially barrel-fermented wine is well balanced and impressive.

The regular Chardonnay (sometimes released under the name "White Burgundy") is a lighter styled, lower priced Chardonnay. It possesses yeasty, baked-bread aromas and flavors resulting from extended contact with the fermentation *lees*. Depending on the size and condition of each harvest, Montdomaine will either produce all "Barrel Select" Chardonnay or the two selections.

In the past, Montdomaine has produced three Rieslings: a dry, a semi-dry (1.5% residual sugar), and a semi-sweet (3.5% residual). In the future, Shep would like to produce just one, a semi-sweet 2% residual Kabinet-styled Riesling. Older vintages of Riesling, such as '85, showed impressively, especially the semi-sweet, which displayed a classic "machine oil" nose, silky, viscous texture, and rich fruit flavors of dried apricots and peaches. More recent vintages, like the '87, are also very promising, with nice floral delicacy. Shep sweetens his Riesling by adding a *sweet reserve* of unfermented Riesling juice to the dry-fermented wine just before bottling.

Montdomaine produces both a Cabernet Sauvignon (which is softened with varying proportions of Merlot and Cabernet Franc) and is also the state's largest producer of Merlot (which is bolstered by some Cabernet Sauvignon and Cabernet Franc). The '84 and '85 wines made by Steve Warner were very impressive. The '84 Cab has a deep ruby color, and a rich, full-bodied mouthfeel. Somewhat angular cassis/berry flavors are highlighted by attractive green pepper vegetal notes that are still unfolding and broadening. The '85 Merlot is a fabulously rich, ripe, and fruity wine. Soft and round yet never flabby, it is beautiful now and should age very nicely.

Shep's own Merlots and Cabs illustrate that he, too, knows how to handle these varieties. As a rule, the reds at Montdomaine are produced in the Bordeaux method: *musts* are allowed to remain in contact with the skins for extended maceration (up to four weeks) and then spend twelve to fourteen months in French Allier or Nevers oak. The wines are gently fined with egg whites prior to bottling. In recent years, both regular and "Reserve" bottlings of Merlot and Cabernet have been produced. The Merlots have been very intriguing—the 1987 "Reserve" offers intense cherry/berry fruit, firm acids, and young but supple tannins. The "Reserve" Cab from the same year has an intense, nearly black color, deep closed-in aromas of plum, earth, and oak, and tightly knit, deeply extracted cassis and plum fruit. This wine will need several years for tannins to soften. (Look for the regular bottlings of each to offer lighter intensity, fresh fruit, and earlier drinkability.)

Montdomaine also produces a very attractive blush wine that is one-third Riesling, one-third Chardonnay, and one-third Cabernet Sauvignon. Finished with 1.7% residual sugar, the wine is a light, cheerful sipper—pleasant at every turn.

INCIDENTALLY . . .

On Montdomaine's label appears a reproduction of a detail from the old Monticello Wine Company label, circa 1902.

DIRECTIONS

From Interstate 64, take Exit 24 south and follow Route 20 south for approximately 13 miles. At Route 720, turn right and proceed one-half mile to winery entrance on right.

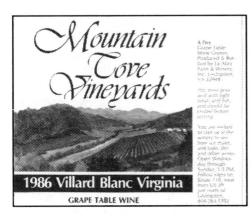

A Dry
Grape Table
Wine Grown,
Produced & Bot-
tled by La Abra
Farm & Winery,
Inc. Lovingston,
VA 22949

This wine goes
well with light
meat and fish
and should be
chilled before
serving.

You are invited
to visit us at the
winery to see
how we make,
and taste, this
and other wines.
Open Weekdays,
day through
Sunday, 1-5 PM.
Follow signs on
Route 718, west
from US 29
just north of
Lovingston.
804/263-5392

1986 Villard Blanc Virginia

GRAPE TABLE WINE

Mountain Cove Vineyards

ADDRESS: Route 1, Box 139
Lovingston, VA 22949
PHONE: (804) 263-5392
OWNERS: Albert and Emily Weed
WINEMAKER: Al Weed
TOTAL ACRES: 12
CASES/YR: 1,500
HOURS: Daily 1-5, closed Monday
and Tuesday January through
March

Like so many of his colleagues in the mid-Atlantic wine industry, Al Weed brought to his current "job" an interesting and diverse professional background, mostly unrelated to wine. A sergeant in the U.S. Army, Al served in the Special Forces in Vietnam between 1962 and 1966. Since then, he has continued to serve in the Army Reserve Special Forces. Schooled as an economist, Al worked at the World Bank and as an investment banker. But it was while he was posted in Amsterdam that he began to envision a different lifestyle for himself, his wife Sui Ling, and his young son and soon-to-be-born daughter.

Tiring of the rigors of a career that forced him to be away from his family frequently, Al began in the early 1970s to look for land in Virginia, the state where he grew up. Wanting to farm, he considered various crops and became interested in the prospect of grape growing when he read about Philip Wagner of Boordy Vineyards in Maryland.

He visited vineyards in Bordeaux and California to study site selection. He also used the findings of George Oberle, an agricultural researcher at Virginia Polytechnic Institute in Blacksburg, who recommended Virginia's central counties of Albemarle, Augusta, and Nelson as the most suitable for viticulture. In 1973, Al purchased his land in Nelson County about 40 miles south of Charlottesville and, joining Archie Smith of Meredyth Vineyards and C.J. Raney of Farfelu Vineyard, became one of the state's first commercial winegrowers.

"Back then things were really tough," describes Weed, a rugged, fit man in his forties. "There was no one to bounce ideas off of, nowhere to buy supplies and chemicals, no one to share equipment with. We were really in the dark."

Planting in both 1974 and 1975, Weed released his first commercial product, 2,000 gallons of a dry apple wine, in 1976. "I don't hesitate to admit that I dumped many a gallon of wine down the drain during those early years," exclaims Weed. "Winemakers today have such an advantage in Virginia with the help the state has provided in supporting the state enologist (Bruce Zoecklein) and viticulturist (Tony Wolf)."

In fact, a significant portion of Al's time since 1973 has been devoted to changing the Virginia scene so that others wouldn't have to face the uncertainty that he and the early pioneers faced. He has been an active lobbyist for the industry in Richmond. He wrote the legislation that established the state's Wine Growers Advisory Board. He was also instrumental in influencing the state's tax code to allow for the favorable tax treatment of wineries' equipment and land.

"The problem for us in Virginia," he explains, "is that we are creating an industry from nothing. Even in New York, there was a long history of grape growing before the premium wine industry evolved. Virginians had to figure out where to plant, what to plant, how to make wine. We've also shot at the high end of the market by planting so much vinifera, so we immediately put ourselves up against the big guys from Europe and out west. I'll tell you, if one of us puts a $10 Chardonnay on the shelf and it's not up to snuff, we hear about it in a heartbeat!"

THE VINEYARD

Not surprisingly, given the timing of his venture into grape growing, Al Weed's vineyard consists only of French-American hybrid varieties. "At that time, there was really no other option," he explains. But he's not at all defensive about what he grows. "Growers and makers of vinifera wine immediately draw themselves into comparison with the best in the world. I am, instead, trying to do the best I can with hybrids and consider them viable as a unique regional product."

As he explains further, "Even vinifera devotees, increasingly, are planting hybrids and using them for blending and creating wines to sell at the lower price end of the spectrum. Realistically, the hybrids offer an economically safer crop, one you can count on each year, and you can produce perfectly fine, everyday table wines."

Planted acreage is split almost exactly between white and red varieties. The biggest plot is to the white Villard Blanc, which joins smaller plots of Vidal and Cayuga to round out the whites. Baco Noir, Chelois, Chancellor, and Villard Noir are the red grapes that fill out Mountain Cove's 12 acres.

GRAPE VARIETIES AND ACREAGE

Variety	Vinifera	French/Amer. Hybrids
Villard Blanc	—.—	4.50
Baco Noir	—.—	2.00
Chelois	—.—	1.50
Chancellor	—.—	1.50
Vidal	—.—	1.00
Cayuga	—.—	0.75
Villard Noir	—.—	0.75
TOTALS	0.0	12.00

Mountain Cove's site is not only beautiful, it is well-suited for grape growing. Most rows are planted on a gentle, eastern facing slope with good air and water drainage and captures the early rays of morning sun. The vineyard is located in a cove, which protects it from severe storms.

THE WINES

Mountain Cove Vineyards produces about 1,500 cases of wine each year, with a projected future capacity of 4,000 cases. The production is spread across six bottlings.

The Villard Blanc is a major focus of the winery. An unusual grape not often seen in the mid-Atlantic, Villard Blanc produces a wine probably closest in style to another white hybrid, Seyval. Al has tried to create a light, delicate wine by adding small amounts of Riesling to his Villard Blanc. The wine typically possesses a rich, full palate and a nice fruity impression of apples and pears. It is almost completely dry with just 0.5% residual sugar.

The "Skyline White" is a sweeter version of the Villard Blanc. A wine made from the same *cuvée* of that grape and Riesling, "Skyline White" is finished with 3.5% residual sugar, and displays similar fruity richness. Neither white produced at Mountain Cove spends any time in oak.

A very pleasant Chianti-style wine is produced under the name "Harvest Red." Made from 100% Chelois, it is simple, straightforward, and direct, with bright cherry and berry fruit and a touch of spicy American oak.

"Skyline Rosé" is a blanc de noir wine made from the *free run juice* of the red varieties Chancellor, Baco, and Villard Noir. Displaying a medium copper/red color and finished with a few percentage points of sugar, the wine is cheerful, clean, and fruity with nice berry notes.

Two fruit wines are also made; "La Abra" Peach and Apple. "La Abra," meaning "The Cove," indicates that locally grown fruit is used to produce these lovely, pleasant quaffers. The Apple, very fresh and luscious, is the better of the two. Both its aromas and flavors are very true to the fresh Pippins and Winesaps from whence it came. The Peach is a bit cloying on the palate, although its nose is fresh and enticing.

Finally, a recent project at Mountain Cove involves making a wine from grapes grown nearby at the Wintergreen vacation resort. There, Peter A. Agelasto has established a 2-acre vinifera vineyard of Riesling, Chardonnay, and Gewurztraminer. Under contract with Agelasto, Al Weed has produced an utterly delightful wine bottled under the Elk Hill Vineyard label and called "Cler Blanc." A blend of the three white varieties, the '87 Cler Blanc has a beautiful nose of delicate spices and spring flowers. On the palate, pert acidity balances the wine's 1% residual sugar. Intense and squeaky clean flavors of apricot and honey fill the mouth. Just 200 cases of the wine are produced for the Elk Hill bottling, and the entire production is quickly sold either at the nearby Wintergreen resort or at Mountain Cove.

DIRECTIONS

Follow Route 29 south from Charlottesville. Just north of the town of Lovingston, go west on Route 718. Follow winery signs for 3.5 miles.

Oakencroft Vineyard and Winery

ADDRESS: Route 5
Charlottesville, VA 22901
PHONE: (804) 296-4188 or (804) 295-
9870
OWNER: Felicia Warburg Rogan
WINEMAKER: Deborah Welsh
TOTAL ACRES: 16.75
CASES/YR: 4,800
HOURS: April-December Monday-
Friday 9-4, Saturday and Sunday
11-5; others by appointment

It only takes a few minutes to drive west from Charlottesville and find oneself out in the country. Off to the left along Highway 601 sits a lovely Polled Hereford farm which also happens to house one of Virginia's promising wineries—Oakencroft Vineyard and Winery.

Like so many wineries in the mid-Atlantic, Oakencroft had its beginnings as the hobby of its owners, in this case Felicia Rogan and her husband, John Rogan, who died in 1990. John, a land developer and owner of the renowned Boar's Head Inn, met and married Felicia in the mid-1970s. When Felicia met Lucie Morton Garrett, a well known Virginia viticulturist, consultant, and author of the book *Winegrowing in Eastern America*, she began to play with the idea of grape growing. She planted her first twenty-five grape vines in 1978. When the plants bore fruit, the couple tried their hands at "garage wine," as Felicia describes it, and liked the results. Subsequent plantings followed each year, and plans for a commercial winery and vineyard were on the drawing board.

It was about this time that current winemaker Deborah Welsh arrived on the scene. A literature major at the University of Virginia, Welsh met Felicia Rogan after answering the Rogans' classified ad for a gardener needed at the farm. She got the job in 1980 and soon found herself tending the Rogans' vines. Subsequently, she also found herself reading everything she could get her hands on about grape growing, having been bitten by the viticulture bug herself.

By 1982, Felicia knew that if her winery were to really take shape, she would need to enlist the help of some of the best talent in the state. Calling once again upon Lucie Morton Garrett, Felicia contracted for an expanded vineyard to be laid out on the knoll rising gently behind what is now the winery facility. Jacques Recht, Belgian enologist, active eastern U.S. consultant, and winemaker at Ingleside Plantation Vineyard on Virginia's Northern Neck, was asked to oversee the conversion of an old smokehouse on the property into a modern winery and to formally train Deborah Welsh in the science/art of winemaking.

By 1983, the setup was complete and the license was in hand. The inaugural crush produced a vintage of just 400 cases of wine, but since then annual production has grown to nearly 5,000 cases.

But, as if getting a winery off the ground wasn't enough work, Felicia Rogan took it upon herself to take a leading role in promotion of not just her own but all of Virginia's wineries. Over the years, she founded the Jeffersonian Wine Grape Growers Society and also chaired the Virginia Wine Growers Advisory Board. In 1984, she was a leader in the successful effort to petition the U.S. Bureau of Alcohol, Tobacco and Firearms for the establishment of the Monticello Viticultural Area, which now contains the state's largest concentration of wineries. More recently, she helped set up the Virginia Wine Museum, which is housed in the historic Michie Tavern just below Monticello, the home of Thomas Jefferson.

All the hard work will be worth it, if Felicia's prediction comes true. Says the outspoken Rogan, "In the next decade, the Virginia wine industry will be the most important in the eastern United States." While that statement might garner some serious discussion among New York winegrowers, no one can deny that the mid-Atlantic future looks very bright indeed.

THE VINEYARD

Today, Oakencroft's vineyard is just under 17 acres. The largest plot is a 5-acre stand of the white French-American hybrid Seyval. Following closely is a 4.75 acre plot of Chardonnay, with further acreage devoted to red vinifera grapes Cabernet Sauvignon and Merlot and, most recently, a new plot of another white French-American hybrid, Vidal. Future plans call for planting of the red French-American hybrid, Chambourcin.

GRAPE VARIETIES AND ACREAGE

Variety	Vinifera	French/Amer. Hybrids
Seyval	—.—	5.00
Chardonnay	4.75	—.—
Cabernet Sauvignon	3.00	—.—
Merlot	2.25	—.—
Vidal	—.—	1.75
TOTALS	10.00	6.75

As Felicia explains it, "We didn't have to agonize over site selection like many others, we just had to pick the best spot on my husband's farm!" While this situation was both convenient and economical, it has had its drawbacks. "We sit in the lower foothills of the Blue Ridge and, frankly, a lot of cold air ends up spilling our way during the winter and spring. All of our vinifera have had some trouble, especially the Cabernet and Merlot," she adds with grim reality. It was for that reason, at least in part, that the stand of Vidal was added to complement the Seyval, which has fared wonderfully.

If it's not the perfect grape-growing site in Virginia, it certainly is one of the prettiest. Sitting atop a gentle knoll, it commands views of the mountains to the west and the impressive red barn/winery below to the east. In front of the winery sits a lovely lake, which serves as home to many a passing Canada goose and blue heron.

To supplement its own harvest, Oakencroft also purchases fruit from other Virginia growers from surrounding Albemarle and Greene Counties, and from a vineyard on Virginia's Eastern Shore.

THE WINES

Under the skilled hands of Deborah Welsh, Oakencroft produces three very elegant wines: a Seyval, a Chardonnay, and a Cabernet Sauvignon.

Especially noteworthy is Oakencroft's Seyval, both in its own right and as an example of one of the extreme styles this wine can display. This wine (actually a blend of 77% Seyval and 23% Vidal), was fermented slowly for five weeks at a cool temperature of 50° F. Fermented and aged entirely in stainless steel, the wine consistently shows crisp, fresh, and lively fruit, with aromas and flavors bursting with bone-dry grapefruit and citrus. A wonderful match with seafood, the wine is a stark contrast to the rich, creamy, oaky Seyvals of producers like Ham Mowbray at Maryland's Montbray Wine Cellars. In their own ways, both wines and styles succeed very well.

The Chardonnay is also a clean, carefully crafted wine. After crushing the fruit, 12% of the *must* is allowed to stay in contact with the skins for eight hours. Explains Deborah, "This contact allows the Chardonnay to extract a bit of extra character and complexity." Seventy-five percent of the wine is then fermented cool in stainless steel tanks, while the remaining 25% is fermented in French Troncais oak and then left to age for three months. A quarter of the Chardonnay from the stainless steel is also transferred to oak for two months. What results is a wine of considerable subtlety. For the last three vintages of the 1980s, Oakencroft's Chardonnays had clean apple blossom aromas, which mingle with faint, buttery oak notes. On the palate, the wine is light bodied yet silky, with lean apple and melon flavors enhanced by creamy, vanillan oak.

Oakencroft's Cabernet Sauvignon typically contains a small, 5% portion of Merlot. It is fermented on the skins for seven days at warm temperatures of 75-80° F in order to fully extract color, tannins, and fruit character. Aged for sixteen months in French oak, the wine is *fined* with egg whites just prior to bottling. The '85, '86, and '87 versions possessed good, deep ruby colors and noses that, with extended aeration, revealed rich cassis and berry scents and sometimes a cleansing impression of mintiness. In the mouth, the wines have shown slightly tart and straightforward flavors. However, a lot of bright, clean cherry and berry flavors, enhanced with a gentle layer of toasty oak, indicate that the wines may develop more complexity with aging.

DIRECTIONS

From Route 29 on the north side of Charlottesville, take Barracks Road (Route 654, which becomes Route 601) west for 3.5 miles to winery on left.

Simeon Vineyards

ADDRESS: Route 9, Box 293
Charlottesville, VA 22901
PHONE: (804) 977-3042 or 977-0800
OWNER: Stanley Woodward
WINEMAKER: Gabriele Rausse
TOTAL ACRES: 7.75
CASES/YR: 800
HOURS: By appointment only

The development of commercial winegrowing in the state of Virginia generally, and in the Charlottesville area specifically, owes a great deal to Gabriele Rausse. While his current role as general manager and winemaker at Simeon Vineyards is relatively low-key, it was in his previous life with Barboursville Vineyards that a great deal of the groundbreaking took place.

A native Italian, Rausse grew up on a grape and dairy farm in Valdagno in the northeast of the country. While attending the University of Milan, he received a degree in agronomy with a special emphasis on plant pathology. At the age of thirty-one, he was approached by Giani Zonin, the president and head enologist of the largest privately owned commercial winery in Italy. The Zonin family of Gambellara had been involved in the Italian wine industry since 1821 and controlled hundred of acres of vineyard land and numerous winery facilities throughout the country, including the famous Veneto, Friuli, Tuscany, and Piedmonte regions. But the services of Mr. Rausse were not needed there. Instead, Mr. Zonin had hand-picked this intense and quietly energetic man to head up the family's latest venture in Virginia.

The selection by the Zonins of Virginia for their new project was by no means coincidental. In fact, the "Italian connection" in Virginia wine history really dates back to the late 1700s and another man famous in the time—Thomas Jefferson.

In 1773, a physician and merchant from Tuscany, Filippo Mazzei, received permission from the Grand Duke of Tuscany to set out for the colony of Virginia to take part in a winegrowing venture. Upon his arrival, and armed with 10,000 vinifera vine cuttings, he was soon introduced to the political leaders of the day, including Thomas Jefferson. Jefferson, a well-known wine enthusiast, became entranced by Mazzei's project and convinced him to buy 50 acres adjacent to Jefferson's home, Monticello. Vineyards were planted and excitement was high but, unfortunately, the experiment failed. Not only did the vines have trouble with disease (resulting from the hot and humid climate) and the root louse phylloxera, but excitement also was rising around another event—the Revolutionary War. Mazzei's (and, as we know Jefferson's) interests turned to politics and soon the vineyards went to ruin. But more about Mazzei in a moment . . .

Due to advances in viticultural technology, the Zonins were, in 1976, convinced that the growing of vinifera grapes was now possible in the mid-Atlantic region. The family purchased a 700-acre farm north of Charlottesville that was formerly owned by another good friend of Jefferson's, James Barbour, at one time the Governor of Virginia. Gabriele Rausse immediately went to work in his new home and began the vineyards for a winery to be named Barboursville.

Rausse'sefforts first met significant resistance from both the U.S. Department of Agriculture and Virginia Polytechnic Institute in Blacksburg. Up to that time, both had shunned vinifera varieties on the grounds that they couldn't be grown profitably in the region and that hybrids were more sensible. Importation of European rootstocks was hindered. There was, in certain circles, the sentiment that Virginia needed to stifle the project in order to protect farmers of more traditional crops like tobacco. Charlottesville citizens were also curious, if not suspicious, of this mysterious Italian project being undertaken. When Rausse imported thousands of concrete posts and began setting up a trellis system that looked more like a cemetery, locals thought he was crazy. But, as Rausse would explain, in Italy they'd never think of using wood posts that would stand only twenty years or so — Barboursville was here to stay.

Contrary to all the naysayers, Barboursville did succeed and, in 1979, produced its first vintage of 20,000 bottles (about 1,700 cases) of wine. This, along with Piedmont Vineyards' small production that year, marked the first Virginia vinifera wines to ever be produced.

By 1981, with two more harvests under his belt and 50 acres producing, Gabriele had tired of the controversy and visibility of the Barboursville project and yearned for a simpler lifestyle. His wishes were granted when Stanley Woodward offered him a job. Woodward, a retired career foreign service officer, happened to own the exact property formerly owned by Filippo Mazzei. Maintaining the same name for the farm that Mazzei used, "Colle" (Italian for "hill"), Woodward had kept the farm productive and had always had his interest piqued by the Mazzei/wine connection. In 1981, he needed a new manager for Colle and, having met Gabriele previously and been impressed with his work, Woodward approached him with an offer to grow grapes on the same soil Mazzei had worked. Gabriele happily accepted.

Over the following years, he quietly set about establishing another vinifera vineyard on Woodward's property and recently had a small but well-equipped winery built. Gabriele also married and now has three young children. While still on the Board of Directors at Barboursville and active as a viticultural consultant to many of the area's new wineries, Gabriele has settled into a peaceful, rewarding, and somewhat reclusive lifestyle. "I am proud of the Mazzei heritage here and love being able to build upon it," he says in his soft, rich accent. "Mr. Woodward gives me the freedom to develop things as I see fit. I have a beautiful family. I am a very happy man." It is a rare pleasure to see such hard work and determination reap such bountiful rewards.

While, for the time being, Simeon Vineyards is open to the public only by appointment, Simeon wines are available at the nearby Simeon Farm Market on Highway 53.

THE VINEYARD

With the freedom and resources afforded by Stanley Woodward, Gabriele has established a vineyard like no other in the state. Perched on a gentle, southeastern slope, Simeon's 7.75 acres are planted to a wonderfully diverse set of varieties. While some of the land is devoted to more traditional varieties like Chardonnay and Cabernet Sauvignon, things get strange after that. As seen in the table below, experimental and difficult to grow red varieties like Zinfandel, Barbera, and Pinot Noir occupy 1.5 acres. An acre of table grape varieties supplies the Simeon Farm Market. By far the largest plot is planted to Pinot Gris—the only such vineyard in the state or in the mid-Atlantic for that matter. In a fascinating experiment, Gabriele has worked with Peter Hatch at nearby Monticello and identified the twenty-five or so original varieties first planted by Thomas Jefferson in the 1700s. A full acre is now being cultivated in these varieties in an effort to bring to life the rich Jeffersonian heritage in the region.

GRAPE VARIETIES AND ACREAGE

Variety	Vinifera	French/Amer. Hybrids
Pinot Gris	3.00	—.—
Cabernet Sauvignon	0.75	—.—
Barbera	0.50	—.—
Chardonnay	0.50	—.—
Pinot Noir	0.50	—.—
Zinfandel	0.50	—.—
Table grapes	1.00	—.—
Jefferson's grapes	1.00	—.—
TOTALS	7.75	0.0

While his vineyard overall is quite experimental, Gabriele has high hopes for many of his vines. Zinfandel and Pinot Noir are, he feels, too susceptible to disease and winter damage ever to produce traditional reds, but could fill a role for blush and blanc de noir wines. Barbera is, however, a relatively thick-skinned, loose cluster variety which could, if it can get through cold winters without too much damage, produce a hearty red wine reminiscent of its Italian relatives.

Planted in 1987, Gabriele is most excited about the Pinot Gris, the famous grape from Italy that produces that country's finest whites, usually called Pinot Grigio. While the variety has very tight clusters, which can fall prey more easily to rot and mold, it does ripen early and thus could be already harvested when fall rains hit the state as they did in 1986, 1987, and 1988.

Gabriele plans to add 6 more acres to the vineyard, all in the Bordeaux varieties of Cabernet Sauvignon, Cabernet Franc, and Merlot.

THE WINES

The first vintage at Simeon, 1986, saw production of only 800 cases of wine in just one varietal — Chardonnay. It was made largely with grapes grown by his neighbor John Marquis at Blenheim Wine Cellars. Gabriele is very pleased with his arrangement at Blenheim, stating that the fruit grown there is "perfect, just beautiful." As his own vineyard matures into production, Rausse will continue to purchase fruit for the bulk of Simeon's production.

To be sure, viticulture has always been Gabriele's first love. But he has also some very strong feelings about how wine should be made and the uses for which it should be produced. "In Italy, we don't drink water with a meal. We drink wine. Wines should always be produced with food in mind—light, crisp, fruity whites; robust, full-bodied but drinkable reds," he explains. Gabriele has never been a fan of the big, oaky style of many California Chardonnays, for example. "Sure they win all the awards, and people sip and analyze every drop in their mouths. But at the end of a meal, there's still half a bottle left! Meanwhile, the same people could drink two bottles of a functional, thirst-quenching, light white like Pinot Grigio! This is better for the meal, and better for sales, too," he adds.

These preferences translate into winemaking techniques including temperature-controlled cool fermentation for whites and use of oak only for reds. Simeon's winery building, a structure modeled after an Italian Palladian villa, is equipped with state-of-the-art Italian equipment.

His decision to grow Pinot Gris is also a calculated one. "From a marketing standpoint, I think it is absurd to offer another Chardonnay when the state already produces over thirty different Chardonnays. Simeon's will be the only Pinot Gris and should attract attention," he says with a smile.

The Chardonnay Gabriele has produced is one he can be proud of. The '86 had a lively, young green-gold color and a clean, precisely varietal nose of Chardonnay fruit—slightly floral with pear and apple notes. On the palate it is broad and ripe yet crisp, with ample green apple and lemon acidity. Subsequent vintages have possessed similar qualities. The wine is, by design, perfectly suited to consumption with light fish or fowl and would match nicely with pasta in cream sauces.

With each passing vintage, Simeon's offerings have expanded. The vintage of 1988 saw the addition of a Cabernet and Pinot Noir to the lineup. Both offered light, crisp texture and bright fruit flavors. Neither would challenge bigger renditions from the West Coast, but both are pleasant sippers.

DIRECTIONS

From Interstate 64, take Exit 24-A (Route 20). Drive south .5 mile to Route 53 and turn left (follow signs to Monticello). Drive past Monticello and turn right at the intersections of Routes 53, 732, and 795. The Simeon Farm Market is located at the intersection; Simeon Vineyards is .25 mile past the market on the right.

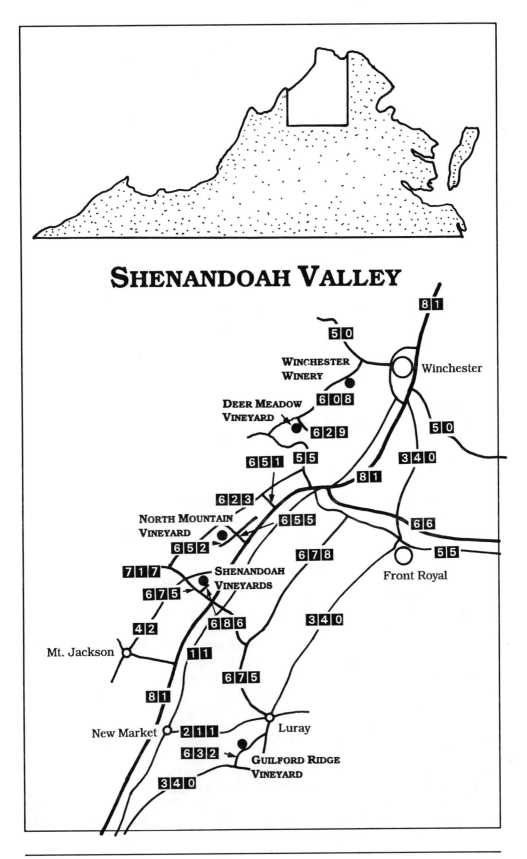

SHENANDOAH VALLEY

DEER MEADOW

Chardonnay

Shenandoah Valley Table Wine

Produced and Bottled by
DEER MEADOW VINEYARD
WINCHESTER, VIRGINIA

750 ml • Contains Sulfites • BW-VA-65

Deer Meadow Vineyard

ADDRESS: Mountain Falls, HC-34, Box 4763
Winchester, VA 22601
PHONE: (703) 877-1919
OWNERS: Charles and Jennifer Sarle
WINEMAKER: Charles Sarle
TOTAL ACRES: 6
CASES/YR: 400
HOURS: March through December, Wednesday-
    Sunday 10-5

The name "Deer Meadow" has taken on an ironic significance to new Virginia vintners Charles and Jennifer Sarle. The winery, which was bonded and crushed its first harvest in 1987, was named for the large herds of deer that roam their property in the northern tip of the Shenandoah Valley near Winchester. While beautiful, these herds have ended up causing the Sarles more than their share of problems.

"It's hard to think of deer as pests," says Charles, a friendly, rugged man with silvery hair and beard. "They're so peaceful and pretty. But, boy, do they like to eat grapes and grapevines!"

As a first strategy to fend off the animals, the Sarles left a long swath of pine trees to separate the family's two vineyard blocks. "We thought that the deer would use this cover as a trail for passing through the property," explains Jennifer. "Instead, they just hid in there and started feeding when we weren't around. We lost, literally, acres of vines." It seems the tender young shoots of growing vines offer a special delicacy to hungry deer.

A second plan involved surrounding both blocks of vines, 6 acres in all, with an electric fence. While this has helped significantly, Charles still estimates that he may have lost as much as 70% of his Seyval crop in 1987 when, one evening, deer were able to enter the vineyard through a gap in the fence.

"We've begun to reconcile ourselves to the situation," he explains. "For most eastern grape growers, rot, humidity, and climate pose the biggest problems. For us, it's deer. We have a lovely, remote spot here in the mountains. Unfortunately, the deer love it as much as we do!"

Charles Sarle came to the Virginia wine industry from a back-ground that was certainly different from any of his colleagues: for more than thirty years, he worked as an engineer in the auto racing business. For many of those years Charles, Jennifer, and their four children lived in Indianapolis where he designed and built numerous turbo-charged engines for Indy 500 racers. When not designing engines for cars, he could often be found racing them himself as a professional driver for the Sports Car Club of America.

Natives of Virginia, Jennifer and Charles bought their present property in 1959 as an investment. The couple were raising their family in Fairfax at the time and grew Christmas trees on the land to help pay the taxes. It was not until the family moved to Indiana that they began to cultivate an interest in grapes.

"As a hobby, I planted about twenty vines in my back yard," explains Charles. "I really enjoyed watching the different varieties grow and learning what it took to make vines thrive."

Upon retirement in 1982, the couple happily moved back to Virginia and began building the winery of their dreams. "We both felt this would be a perfect retirement business," says Jennifer. "We love the outdoors. We love growing things. Charles continues to design and build things for the winery. And, yes, we still love the deer!"

THE VINEYARD

The site the Sarles have chosen to grow the vines has some very promising aspects. Located at 1,100 feet above sea level, the vineyard enjoys a beneficial temperature inversion—winter days are warmer and summer days are cooler than those of their neighbors on the Shenandoah Valley floor. An uninterrupted southeastern exposure also provides the vines with warm morning sun to dry up any unwanted moisture that could lead to rot.

The only problem with the site is its soil. State viticulturist Tony Wolf has taken samples from the vineyard and has determined that Deer Meadow can be classified as predominantly "Burke Drought Prone Soil." In other words, the topsoil layer is quite shallow and tends to dry out very quickly. This condition stunted the growth of Deer Meadow's vines for the first few years, but the Sarles have found ways to compensate for the problem. For two years, the couple mulched the soil around the vines in order to improve its water-holding characteristics. For a more permanent solution, they began installing a drip irrigation system in 1988.

GRAPE VARIETIES AND ACREAGE

Variety	Vinifera	French/Amer. Hybrids
Seyval	—.—	2.0
Chambourcin	—.—	1.5
Cabernet Sauvignon	1.0	—.—
Foch	—.—	1.0
Chardonnay	0.5	—.—
TOTALS	1.5	4.5

Deer Meadow's 6-acre vineyard features a nice blend of vinifera, and both French and American hybrid grape varieties. Chardonnay and Cabernet Sauvignon are the vinifera, while Seyval, Foch, and Chambourcin make up the French hybrids. A favorite from the backyard in Indiana, the native-American hybrid Steuben was also planted in a couple of rows to add a different twist to the selection.

THE WINES

Charles' skills as an engineer were not wasted when it came to constructing the winery at Deer Meadow. The structure was entirely hand-built using the yellow pine from the trees the Sarles cleared when preparing the vineyard site.

Inside, the winery features many of Charles' "inventions." For example, during harvest, all grapes are poured directly into a huge hydraulic press suspended over two large, open-topped, fiberglass-lined concrete fermentation vats. To control fermentation temperatures, Charles also designed a submersible heat exchanger—essentially a large PVC pipe coil through which cooled glycol is circulated. By dunking the coil into the fermenting *musts*, Charles can reduce the temperature of his red wine fermentations.

Charles Sarle strives to create the most complex wines possible at Deer Meadow. For example, to add tannin and subtle herbaceousness to his Seyval, he presses the wine in contact with its stems. The Seyval reflects this, showing a good, viscous body, ripe apple flavors, and deep herbal tones.

The Deer Meadow Foch is an attractive, medium-bodied, and fruity wine. Fermented in contact with the skins a full ten days, with 20% of the full berry clusters included in the must, the wine is surprisingly delicate and nimble. Soft berry and cherry fruitiness dominates both the nose and flavors, which are further enhanced by a bit of background American oak.

Produced as a blanc de noir, the Steuben is an unusual quaffer given the proprietary name "Golden Blush." The grapes' *free-run juice*, which is light red in hue, is transformed during fermentation to a rich orange/gold. Totally dry, the grapey wine gives an impression of sweetness due to its assertive, yet pleasant fruit.

Neither the Chardonnay, Cabernet Sauvignon, nor Chambourcin had been released at the time of this writing.

INCIDENTALLY . . .

Neighbors just a few miles to the north of Deer Meadow on Route 608 are the Smiths at Winchester Winery. For the wine tourist, this proximity offers a special convenience and allows for an interesting comparison of wines from this mountain micro-climate.

DIRECTIONS

From Winchester, drive west on Route 50 for approximately 4 miles to Route 608 on the left. Turn left and proceed for 6.5 miles to Route 629 and veer left. After 1.1 miles, turn right on a small dirt lane and follow signs to winery.

1984

PAGE VALLEY RED

ESTATE BOTTLED
TABLE WINE

FLED BY GUILFORD RIDGE VINEYARD—BW VA-49— VINEYARD ESTAB. I
WEEN THE BLUE RIDGE AND MASSANUTTEN MOUNTAINS—APPELLAI

Guilford Ridge Vineyard

ADDRESS: Route 5, Box 148
Luray, VA 22835
PHONE: (703) 778-3853
(202) 554-0333
OWNERS: John Gerba and Harland Baker
WINEMAKERS: John Gerba and Harland
Baker
TOTAL ACRES: 4
CASES/YR: 200
HOURS: By appointment only

While included within the Shenandoah Valley Viticultural Area, Guilford Ridge Vineyard is actually located in the picturesque Page Valley, nestled between the Blue Ridge to the east and the Massanutten Mountains to the west. A tiny, two-man operation, Guilford Ridge began as Guilford Farm Vineyards in 1971. It is managed by partners John Gerba and Harland Baker and was licensed as a bonded winery in 1983. Both winemakers are still engaged in other careers: John as a planner with the U.S. Environmental Protection Agency in Washington, DC; Harland as a playwright, who recently taught in the Theatre Arts Department at St. Mary's College in Maryland. Harland now combines his playwriting with his "cellarmastering" duties at the winery.

While Harland is at the winery full-time, John must combine his two careers, even though his workplaces are nearly 100 miles apart. Says Gerba, a friendly, soft-spoken man, "I'll work my forty hours, Monday through Friday, and then put in another forty hours of work nearly every weekend of the year as well!" While clearly the escape each Friday evening from the hectic urban life to the quiet rural farm provides respite and peace, he finds just as much pleasure, after a long weekend of pruning vines in the dead of winter, in returning to the warmth and convenience of a modern city like Washington.

THE VINEYARD

In 1971 he took the first step towards this goal by buying into an 85-acre farm near Luray. He named it after a small rural township in Connecticut where he had lived while finishing his graduate work and teaching city planning at Yale University. During his first two years on the Virginia farm, 2,400 vines were planted on 4 acres. Early years were spent experimenting with different grape varieties, trellising systems, production levels, and winemaking styles. The bulk of the crops borne by the young vines were marketed to commercial and home winemakers. In the summer of 1973, John took a "crash course" in viticulture and enology at the University of California at Davis. He has continued to maintain responsibility for vineyard management at Guilford Ridge.

The collective experience gained during this period indicated that the vineyard's soil and climate, influenced by its 1,100 foot elevation and its close proximity to the South Fork of the Shenandoah River as well as major mountain ranges, were all conducive to premium wine-growing.

At this time, Guilford Ridge's 4 acres are planted to a wide variety of grapes, predominantly French-American hybrids, but also some vinifera. Key varieties used in the wines at Guilford Ridge include red *cultivars* Chambourcin, Chelois, Leon Millot, and Cabernet Sauvignon, and white varieties Rayon d'Or, Seyval, and Vignoles. Other varieties grown, which are mainly sold to other sources, include Foch, Baco Noir, and Burdin.

Future planting of 6 to 8 additional acres is planned. While an ardent advocate of hybrid grapes ("They should and will continue to play an important role in the east," claims Gerba), John will focus the expansion on vinifera varieties including reds Cabernet Sauvignon, Cabernet Franc, and Merlot and whites Gewurztraminer and Muscat Canelli (a grape heretofore unplanted in the state but one he feels "in his bones" will succeed gloriously).

Guilford Ridge Vineyard is currently pursuing the establishment of a specific "Page Valley Viticultural Area" under the rules and regulations of the U.S. Bureau of Alcohol, Tobacco and Firearms (BATF). Viticultural Areas, used to designate grape-growing regions with unique geographical, climatological, and soil characteristics, are designed to help consumers identify the origin of wines they purchase. John Gerba feels that the Page Valley, with its higher annual rainfall, its slightly cooler temperatures, and its clay-loam soil, is a growing region significantly different from the nearby Shenandoah Valley. Only time will tell if the BATF agrees.

THE WINES

Guilford Ridge's approach to winemaking is as unconventional in the United States as it is traditional in Europe. Rather than conform to the practice in this country of bottling 100% varietal wines, Gerba and Baker prefer following the centuries-old practice of Bordeaux — the wines at Guilford Ridge are blends of the finest grape varieties grown in the vineyard. Paramount is the winery's long-range goal of producing a distinctive regional product reflecting the Page Valley's optimal grape-growing characteristics.

John and Harland prefer and pursue the art of blending or "assembling" wines for several reasons. "Primarily," explains Gerba, "blends offer a more complex, complete, and well-rounded wine. Using the best fruit from each vintage, grapes are mixed to highlight the best characteristics of each, aiming at a final wine which is balanced."

A second reason for blending, John feels, is that vinifera varieties do not grow true to character in this region of the country. "There are so many wonderful, textbook Chardonnays, Cabernets, and Rieslings grown in other parts of the country. It does not seem an appropriate goal to try to recreate them here. Instead, we're trying to create wines distinct to this region."

Typically, Guilford Ridge produces two wines each year: Page Valley Red and a Page Valley white blend called "Pinnacles." In recent years, a sweetened blend of red and white grapes has also been produced under the name "de Lilah." Only in years where growing conditions are especially favorable will 100% varietal wines be produced. (For example, in 1983, the winery produced a Late Harvest Chelois, which was picked with 35% sugar and bottled with a residual sugar of 9%!)

The Page Valley Red has consistently shown to be quite a remarkable wine, sometimes blending as many as seven varieties. The wine's predominant components are Chambourcin, Chelois, and Cabernet Sauvignon. It is a very deep, ruby colored wine, rich and full-bodied on the palate, possesses light tannins, and offers layers of fully extracted blackberry and currant fruit. A good dose of spicy American oak complements the flavors. In good vintages, such as 1983 and 1987, Page Valley Red ranks among the best red wines produced in the state.

The winery has only recently begun offering its white blend, "Pinnacles." The wine blends varying proportions of up to five varietals, including Rayon D'or, Seyval, Vignoles, and small amounts of Riesling and Chardonnay. Fermented to dryness slowly at cool temperatures, the wine receives only brief exposure to oak. While not offering the same intensity or interest as the Page Valley Red, "Pinnacles" does possess a round, mouth-filling texture, and softly herbaceous apple fruit.

In the future, Guilford Ridge hopes to produce wines that are 100% estate grown. For now, however, the winery purchases about 5 to 10% of its grapes, usually vinifera, to supplement its own crop. Its total production is tiny, just 200 cases per year, making Guilford Ridge the smallest winery in the state of Virginia. Supplies are obviously limited, but wines can be purchased both at the winery and in nearby restaurants.

INCIDENTALLY . . .

A fun spot to visit, guests can picnic at Guilford Ridge farm and enjoy the many unusual animals raised on the property, including African pigmy goats, a Jerusalem Ram and three ewes, wild turkeys, guinea hens, and a llama named Yma-Sue.

On the Labor Day weekend each year, the winery celebrates the new vintage by holding a "Page Valley Fête," which offers musical and theater performances on an open-air stage.

DIRECTIONS

From the traffic-light intersection of Business Route 211 and Route 340 in Luray, turn south on 340 and proceed 4 miles. Turn right (west) on Route 632 and proceed for about 1 mile to vineyard entrance on right.

North Mountain Vineyard

ADDRESS: Route 1, Box 543
Mauertown, VA 22664
PHONE: (703) 436-9463
OWNERS: Dick and Caroline McCormack
WINEMAKER: Dick McCormack
TOTAL ACRES: 10
CASES/YR: 1,000
HOURS: Weekends and holidays 11-5

Back in the mid-1970s, Dick McCormack looked forward to his business trips in California. A public affairs officer for the National Aeronautics and Space Administration (NASA), he would often be called upon to oversee launches of the government's latest rockets and missiles at Vandenberg Air Force Base. While the launches were exciting, they were still work. What Dick really looked forward to were his side trips to the vineyards and wineries in the nearby Santa Ynez Valley in Santa Barbara County. On many an afternoon, while touring and tasting throughout that then-burgeoning wine country, McCormack would fantasize about how nice it would be to farm grapes and make wine when he retired from civil service.

It wasn't until several years later, during a skiing trip in the Shenandoah Valley in 1981, that Dick's fantasy began to take shape. On his way back from a weekend of skiing, McCormack and his wife, Caroline, noticed a sign along the side of the road advertising wine tasting at Shenandoah Vineyards. The two had no idea that wine grapes were being cultivated in Virginia, so they had to stop and check it out. The couple ended up visiting for several hours with Jim and Emma Randel, proprietors of Shenandoah Vineyards. Convinced by the flavorful wines that Shenandoah produced, Dick realized that he needn't leave his home state to become a winegrower. Much to his wife's surprise, he decided that it was time to act.

Later that year, McCormack began looking for suitable property. He discovered that a 30-acre parcel was for sale just a few miles up the road from his newfound friends the Randels. He purchased the lot and by the spring of 1982, 10 acres of grapes were in the ground. Dick McCormack had begun to fulfill his dream.

THE VINEYARD

A novice in the business of grape growing, McCormack soaked in all the advice he received from his new colleagues. The Randels suggested a selection of grape varieties to plant. C.J. and Lee Reeder of Burnley Vineyards helped with advice on an appropriate trellising system. "I never could have done it without the generous help of these people," McCormack states. "Everyone in this state is remarkably supportive."

As detailed in the table below, McCormack settled on three varieties. For reliability, year to year, he decided to plant half his acreage to the French-American hybrids Vidal and Chambourcin. To satisfy his desire to emulate the grape growers he used to visit in Santa Ynez, he planted the other half to the vinifera Chardonnay. Because of some damaged rootstock, Dick suffered an immediate setback—2 of his 5 acres of tender Chardonnay did not make it through the first winter. Those 2 acres were subsequently replanted in Chambourcin.

GRAPE VARIETIES AND ACREAGE

Variety	Vinifera	French/Amer. Hybrids
Chardonnay	3.0	—.—
Chambourcin	—.—	3.0
Vidal	—.—	4.0
TOTALS	3.0	7.0

Located on the lee side of North Mountain, along the western slope of the Shenandoah Valley, McCormack named his new vineyard after its location. The site has worked quite well for him. Vines are planted on gentle slopes facing east and south, thereby enjoying both morning and late afternoon sunlight. While the Chardonnay has suffered some frost damage in certain years, McCormack has usually been successful producing a bountiful crop of high quality grapes. For most of the 1980s, the satisfied customers of Burnley Vineyards, Shenandoah Vineyards, and Winchester Winery purchased his crop.

THE WINES

After several years of grape growing, McCormack began to ponder his options. Selling grapes, while satisfying, was not proving to be remarkably lucrative. Further, he and his wife had each year kept a portion of their crop and made their own wine. Both had been pleasantly surprised by how good their wine turned out. At sixty-two, Dick decided he wasn't getting any younger. If he was going to go all the way, he had better do it now.

After consulting with Richard Vine, well-known eastern viticulturist/enologist from Mississippi State University, McCormack planned his winery. An architect friend developed plans for a facility that recalls a European farmhouse. Construction began in 1989 and by June 1990 North Mountain opened its doors to the public.

For its inaugural season, North Mountain released three wines, called simply "Classic Country White," "Red," and "Blush." The white is 100% Vidal. It was fermented cool and retains 1% residual sugar. Departing from the normal handling of this grape, McCormack encouraged this wine through a secondary *malolactic fermentation* in order to create a more complex, less acidic wine. The 1989 "Classic Country White" is clean and well made. Slightly sweet yet crisp flavors of apricot and peach are quite pleasing.

The "Blush" is 100% Chambourcin and is produced from the *free run juice* of this red grape. Darker than most blushes, it might be more appropriately called "ruby." It, too, is a clean and crisp sipper offering fruity berry flavors.

The "Classic Country Red" was actually purchased in bulk from Archie Smith at Meredyth Vineyards in Middleburg. A 100% Foch wine, Dick custom-blended wines from Meredyth's 1988 and 1989 vintages. The wine is deeply colored (like most Fochs) and possesses fleshy, ripe berry flavors accented well by spicy American oak. What is especially nice about this offering is that it somehow avoids the often herbaceous/vegetal characteristics so common to Foch.

Future vintages will add a Chardonnay to the lineup. (A combination of early frost and late rains did in any hopes for a strong Chardonnay crop in 1989.) Also, McCormack plans to use some of his own Chambourcin to produce the "Classic Country Red" in the future.

At this time, Dick McCormack is overwhelmed, with both excitement and fatigue. "This is a family operation. Maintaining 10 acres and producing and selling wine keeps us all incredibly busy," he says with a smile. "I don't have to tell anyone how we spend our weekends." But McCormack is also filled with the warm glow of satisfaction that comes from achieving one's goals.

DIRECTIONS

From Washington, DC, travel west on Interstate 66 to Interstate 81. Follow I-81 south 10 miles to exit 73 (Tom's Brook). Proceed west for 1 mile on Route 651 to Mt. Olive, then turn south for 2 miles on Route 623. At the junction of Route 655, turn left and shortly turn right on Route 652. Follow signs for .5 mile to the winery.

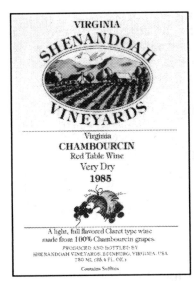

Shenandoah Vineyards

ADDRESS: Route 2, Box 323
Edinburg, VA 22824
PHONE: (703) 984-8699
OWNER: Emma F. Randel
WINEMAKER: Jack Foster
TOTAL ACRES: 45
CASES/YR: 4,000
HOURS: Seven days 10-6

In August of 1977, when Emma and James Randel received their license for Shenandoah Vineyards, what should have been a joyous moment instead became a bit of a nightmare. Coincidentally, in the very same month, the western office of the U.S. Bureau of Alcohol, Tobacco and Firearms (BATF) had awarded a license to another Shenandoah Vineyards in the Sierra Foothills of California. A heated and colorful debate over who should receive exclusive rights to the trademark ensued and was finally resolved by compromise — both wineries were allowed to use the name.

As Emma Randel, a soft-spoken, elegant woman, explains today, "I still think that with the rich history of the Shenandoah Valley, we deserved to win the fight. But we've actually ended up becoming very good friends with the folks in California."

Shenandoah Vineyards is located on the property on which Emma Randel's mother lived as a child. After studying economics at Duke University, Emma met her husband, James, and the two married and raised a family in New Jersey where James was a petroleum engineer for a public utility. In 1974, James suffered a heart attack and the Randels decided that heading for Virginia for rest and recovery made sense. It was at this time that the notion of grape growing occurred to the couple. After two years of tireless reading, research, and study courses, the family planted its first vines on the farm where Emma's mother was born.

At first, the Randels would come down from New Jersey on weekends to tend their vines. As the vineyard matured, however, full-time management was needed and, by 1979, their first grapes were being harvested. The Randels converted the barn on the property into what is now a lovely and efficient winery and tasting room. Shenandoah Vineyards was the sixth winery in Virginia to be bonded, and over the following years the winery enjoyed steady growth and encouraging success.

Sadly, James Randel died in 1985. Emma has since taken over

all aspects of the business and has surrounded herself with talented people. For example, for several years Shenandoah employed Alan Kinne as winemaker. More recently, Shenandoah hired a new winemaker, Jack Foster, who brings to the job six years of experience as winemaker at Cedar Hill Wine Company on the southeastern shore of Lake Erie, near Cleveland.

Emma Randel has become a leading figure in the state industry and has served as Secretary for the Virginia Wineries Association.

THE VINEYARD

Plantings at Shenandoah Vineyards occurred in four phases. The original vineyard, which sits behind the winery on a gentle eastern-facing slope, was planted in 1976. The vineyard in front of the winery was planted in 1981 and then expanded in 1982. Most recently, the 20-acre Stony Creek vineyard just a couple of miles down the road was developed in 1983. Total acreage now stands at 45 acres.

All of the original vines were planted to hardier French-American hybrid varieties. But after several years of learning the ins and outs of grape growing, the Randels focused the majority of remaining expansion on vinifera varieties. At 800 feet above sea level, the site is not high enough to escape the hot, humid summers of Virginia nor the occasional killing frosts of spring. But nearly all varieties have been grown with encouraging success. In fact, the only variety the Randels had to give up on was Pinot Noir, which was too cold-tender.

Today, Shenandoah has 16 acres in vinifera grapes, divided between whites Riesling and Chardonnay and the red Cabernet Sauvignon. The 29 acres of French-American hybrids are divided amongst white varieties Seyval, Vidal, Villard Blanc, and Rayon D'or and reds Villard Noir, DeChaunac, Chambourcin, and Chancellor. Always experimenting, about ten other varieties are also grown in small test plots.

GRAPE VARIETIES AND ACREAGE

Variety	Vinifera	French/Amer. Hybrids
Vidal	—.—	9.0
Riesling	8.0	—.—
Chardonnay	6.0	—.—
Seyval	—.—	4.0
Chambourcin	—.—	3.0
Villard Blanc	—.—	3.0
Cabernet Sauvignon	2.0	—.—
Chancellor	—.—	2.0
DeChaunac	—.—	2.0
Villard Noir	—.—	2.0
Rayon D'or	—.—	1.0
Miscellaneous	—.—	3.0
TOTALS	16.0	29.0

THE WINES

Emma Randel is a firm advocate of wines made from French-American hybrids. "I feel there is a big place in the market for hybrid wines," she explains. "They can, when made well, be delightful, fruity wines, and they're very affordable."

Shenandoah bottles three varietal hybrid wines and four blended wines made primarily from hybrid grapes. The Seyval is fermented dry in stainless steel tanks and then aged briefly in American oak. The Vidal, in contrast, sees no oak and is finished sweet, with 3% residual sugar, by stopping the fermentation. The Vidal is clean, spicy, and fruity, with characteristics somewhere between a nice Riesling and a Gewurztraminer. A real star in the Shenandoah lineup is the Chambourcin. The wine is fermented on the skins for one week and spends eighteen months aging in American oak barrels. Shenandoah's Chambourcin consistently delivers a deeply robust, spicy, hearty wine with smoky black cherry fruitiness surrounded by a strong framework of oak. At $5-7, it is a terrific value for everyday drinking.

Shenandoah places high priority on production of vinifera wines as well. Leading the way is the pleasant, quite Germanic Riesling. Fermented cool in stainless steel tanks, it is finished medium sweet (2.5% residual sugar), possesses an attractive floral nose and lean, racy fruit flavors of grapefruit and melon. While Shenandoah Chardonnays have tended to be a bit over-oaked, the winery is developing a promising reputation for big, flavorful Cabernet Sauvignons. The '83, which is 100% varietal, shows clean berry fruitiness, and reflects rich, toasty flavors picked up during its two-year rest in French Limousin oak. Even better is the Nonvintage Cabernet — a blend of '84 and '85 wine, plus an extra 15% Chambourcin. Contributing a softness and roundness to the overall impression, the Chambourcin's effect is not unlike Merlot added in the traditional Bordeaux cuvées. This wine is big, fruity, and complex.

Four blended wines offer a pleasing contribution to the everyday wine category. The "Shenandoah Blanc," especially, provides delightfully fruity, crisp drinking, and is a deft blend of 25% Riesling and varying proportions of Vidal, Seyval, Villard Blanc, Rayon D'or, and Cayuga. "Shenandoah Rosé" (DeChaunac, Chancellor, Seyval), "Shenandoah Ruby" (DeChaunac, Chancellor, Villard Noir, Chambourcin), and "Blushing Belle," named after Emma's mother (Chambourcin, Chancellor, Vidal, Riesling), complete the lineup.

INCIDENTALLY . . .

While the Randels did not gain exclusive rights to the Shenandoah name for their winery, they did subsequently succeed in petitioning BATF to establish the Shenandoah Valley Viticultural Area in Virginia.

DIRECTIONS

Off Interstate 81, take Exit 71 at Edinburg. Turn west on Route 675 and then right on Route 686. Proceed 1.5 miles to winery on left.

Winchester Winery

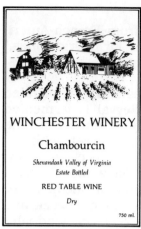

WINCHESTER WINERY

Chambourcin

Shenandoah Valley of Virginia
Estate Bottled

RED TABLE WINE

Dry

750 ml.

Produced and Bottled by
WINCHESTER WINERY, Winchester, VA   BW—VA—52

ADDRESS: Box 188, Mt. Falls Rt.
Winchester, VA 22601
PHONE: (703) 877-1275
OWNERS: The Smith Family
WINEMAKER: Stephen Smith
TOTAL ACRES: 18
CASES/YR: 2,100
HOURS: Wednesday through Sunday 10-5

Winchester, a historic town located at the northern end of the Shenandoah Valley, provides the namesake for this winery, which is also the northernmost winery in the Shenandoah Valley Viticultural Area. Just a short 7-mile drive west/southwest of town lies the 93-acre farm owned by the Smith family. Ray Smith purchased the property in 1972 and began raising cattle as well as several crops such as corn, hay, and apples. In 1974, he decided to diversify his production and planted grapes with the idea of selling the harvest to area wineries.

In the late '70s, the Smiths did just that, but they also reserved some of their crop each year to supply their own home winemaking endeavors. As happens so often, the winemaking bug bit Ray and his two sons Steve and Scott. By 1980, they began planning their own operation and by 1984, they received their commercial license. The winery now produces just over 2,000 cases of wine per year.

Ray, now retired and pursuing his love of painting, has turned over the operation to his sons. Both quiet, intense young men, Steve and Scott have determinedly acquired the knowledge they needed to succeed in this endeavor. By taking courses in horticulture and chemistry, first at a local college and then at Penn State, they now divide responsibilities between winemaking (Steve) and vineyard management (Scott). In 1986, the two completed construction of a new winery building.

THE VINEYARD

Winchester Winery is located 1,060 feet above sea level in a small valley along the eastern slope of the Blue Ridge Mountains. Here, the vineyard enjoys slightly cooler temperatures and slightly less humidity than other growers in the region. Not only do these conditions allow for a longer growing season and slower maturation of fruit, but also less disease and rot. For these reasons, Winchester can get away with spraying their vineyard less often with fungicides and insecticides. Unfortunately, the higher elevation can mean a higher incidence of cold damage in winter. Due to careful experimentation and selection of varieties, Winchester has come through Virginia's coldest winters relatively damage-free.

Winchester grows predominantly French-American hybrids on its 18-acre site and, within this species, a great many varieties. As seen below, the largest plots are devoted to the white hybrid Seyval and the red hybrid Chambourcin (2 acres each). Other whites include the relatively unknown Rayon D'or, the late-ripening Vidal, and Villard Blanc. Red varieties, besides Chambourcin, include hybrids Villard Noir, Chancellor, Baco Noir, and Chelois. The only vinifera varieties grown are Riesling, with 1.5 acres under cultivation, and a .5-acre experimental plot of Chardonnay.

GRAPE VARIETIES AND ACREAGE

Variety	Vinifera	French/Amer. Hybrids
Chambourcin	—.—	2.0
Seyval	—.—	2.0
Riesling	1.5	—.—
Rayon D'or	—.—	1.0
Villard Blanc	—.—	1.0
Vidal	—.—	0.75
Villard Noir	—.—	0.75
Baco Noir	—.—	0.50
Chancellor	—.—	0.50
Chardonnay	0.5	—.—
Chelois	—.—	0.50
Miscellaneous	—.—	7.0
TOTALS	2.0	16.0

A full 7 acres are currently planted to a miscellaneous mix of hybrid varieties, which are either sold to other wineries or are used sparingly at Winchester, including Foch, Verdelet, and Aurora. The Smiths are beginning to graft these acres over to varieties that have enjoyed greater success such as Riesling, Seyval, Vidal, Rayon D'or, and Chambourcin.

Winchester uses their own grapes for the majority of their wines but purchases small amounts of Vidal and Seyval to supplement their crop.

THE WINES

The wines at Winchester demonstrate just how good French-American hybrids can be. The vineyard's higher elevation allows for cooler temperatures and a longer growing season, resulting in grapes that mature slowly and develop more intense varietal character. All grapes are harvested in the early morning hours in order to preserve freshness and natural acidities.

Steve Smith is a devotee of cool fermentations for his whites, but he achieves this goal in a slightly different manner. The winery does not own the expensive cooling systems that circulate glycol in "jackets" wrapped around the stainless steel fermentation tanks. Instead, since the winery is rather small and is well-insulated due to the fact that it is below ground level, Steve simply chills his entire winery to the desired temperature with a powerful air conditioner. This works just fine while fermenting at 45-50° F, but working in the winery can be a bit chilly during cold stabilization when Steve lowers the temperature to 28° for several weeks.

For the dry white table/food wine category, Winchester offers its Seyval. Steve shoots for a Chardonnay-style wine by fermenting the Seyval at slightly higher temperatures and then aging the wine briefly (two months) in American oak. Fifteen percent Vidal is blended into the wine to enhance its fruity nose. Winchester's Seyval can be a rich, attractive version of this varietal. It is quite dry, displays focused, slightly herbal fruit, and is rounded off with a nice impression of oak.

Winchester's other varietal white is Vidal. This wine sees no oak and is finished slightly sweet in a Germanic style (1.5% residual sugar). Fifteen percent Seyval is blended to add body. It has a floral, mineral nose reminiscent of a Riesling and possesses crisp, lively flavors of grapefruits. It is a nice wine for either light meals or sipping.

Perhaps the most charming wine produced is simply called "Winchester White." It is a blend of the obscure Rayon D'or (85%) and Seyval (15%). Like the Vidal, it is finished with 1.5% residual sugar and is bottled young with no oak aging. The wine has a more pronounced floral perfumed nose than the Vidal, and has refreshing citrus and melon flavors. At approximately $5 per bottle, it is a very affordable and pleasant everyday wine.

The "Winchester Rosé" is a *blanc de noir* wine made from the red hybrids Baco Noir and Foch. Blanc de noir, referring literally to the process of making a white wine from red grapes, involves pressing the grapes gently and then separating the *free run juice* from the grape skins and processing it as you would a white wine. In this way, the wine can often (depending on the grape) pick up a tint or blush of color from the skins, while retaining the fresh fruitiness and lighter body of a white. The "Rosé" has a medium salmon/orange color and presents simple, pleasing berry flavors and crisp acidity. It would make a fine picnic wine.

Winchester offers only one red, but what an impressive one it can be! It is made predominantly from the grape Chambourcin (with 12% Chancellor blended for complexity), probably the most promising red hybrid being grown in the mid-Atlantic. Fermented at 75-80° on the skins for one week and then barrel-aged for one year in American oak, the wine is a deep ruby color. Its light berryish nose only begins to hint at the depth the wine offers in the mouth. It is robust and full-bodied, with round, ripe fruit flavors of black cherries and berries. It finishes nicely with complementary layers of smoky, spicy oak.

Winchester releases only a small amount of vinifera wine each year: 100% varietals Riesling and Chardonnay. Neither wine has shown as consistently as the French-American hybrid bottlings.

DIRECTIONS

Follow Route 50 west out of the town of Winchester for approximately 4 miles. Turn left on Route 608 and drive 4.2 miles to winery on the left.

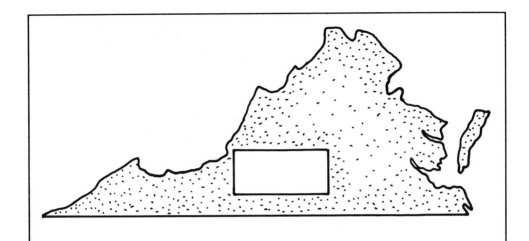

SOUTHERN VIRGINIA

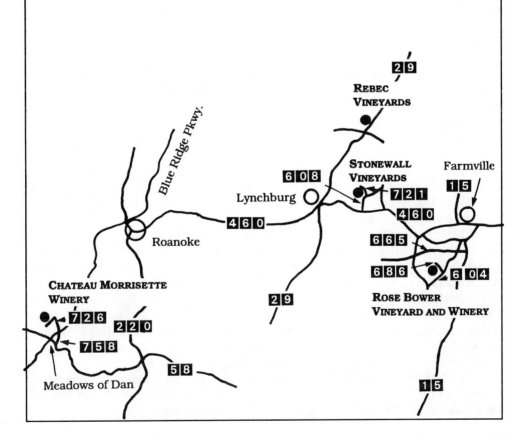

Produced and Bottled by Chateau Morrisette Winery
Meadows of Dan, Virginia USA

19 86

CHÂTEAU MORRISETTE

White Riesling

VIRGINIA

Alcohol 10.5 percent by volume

Chateau Morrisette Winery

ADDRESS: P.O. Box 766, Blue Ridge
    Parkway
Meadows of Dan, VA 24120
PHONE: (703) 593-2865
OWNERS: The Morrisette Family
WINEMAKER: Robert Burgin
TOTAL ACRES: 33
CASES/YR: 8,500
HOURS: Seven days 11-5

Although it is not conveniently close to a major metropolitan area and is located farther south and west than any other Virginia winery, Chateau Morrisette is the perfect winery to visit while touring the state's gorgeous Blue Ridge Parkway. Perched on the sloping top of Buffalo Mountain, the vineyard and winery sit just a mile off the Parkway, near mile post 172, about 5 miles north of the historic Mabry Mill. At 3,500 feet elevation, Chateau Morrisette is also the highest vineyard in the mid-Atlantic and thus possesses its own unique micro-climate—recognized as such by the U.S. Bureau of Alcohol, Tobacco and Firearms when the 8,000-acre region was designated the "Rocky Knob Viticultural Area."

Chateau Morrisette is owned and operated by father and son, William and David Morrisette. Home wine hobbyists, the Morrisettes became caught up in the growing Virginia industry in the mid-'70s and planted their first 2 acres of French-American hybrids vines in 1978. When these vines thrived, the Morrisettes expanded by purchasing extensive acreage adjacent to the Blue Ridge Parkway, by beginning to convert a house on that property into a winery and visitor center, and by planting nearly 45 acres of new vines in 1981. After consulting with leading viticulturists, it was decided that vinifera varieties would not only survive but, most likely, flourish at 3,500 feet given the region's cooler, less humid summer weather.

The Morrisettes have since paid dearly for that decision: after four promising growing seasons and two successful vintages (the winery was bonded and produced wine from the 1983 crush), the devastating winter of 1985 hit. With temperatures dipping to -32° F and, in its exposed site where the wind chill factor was recorded at -100° F, all of the vinifera and many of the French-American hybrids in the vineyard were killed. David estimates losses at about half a million dollars. "A setback like that really makes you want to throw in the towel. But, over time, we adjusted well and things look brighter than ever," he admits.

The family acted quickly to compensate for its losses by arranging lease/purchase contracts with growers in Charlottesville, Long Island, and California. These arrangements kept the winery afloat.

More important, the setback inspired William and David to re-think their long-term grape-growing strategy. Not wanting to expose the winery to similar future risk, the Morrisettes declined to replant vinifera in the original vineyard, but replaced and expanded upon plantings of the hardier French-American hybrids at this high altitude spot. For the vinifera, a new site was located and purchased along the eastern slope of the mountains at a more suitable elevation—1,200 feet above sea level. Chardonnay, Riesling, Cabernet Sauvignon, and Merlot were planted and have recently begun bearing fruit. As David describes, "We literally lost four years and a lot of money because of that winter blast in 1985. But, in retrospect, we may even be better off now. For the hybrids, I think we've got the best site in the state with its cool and low-humidity growing season. For vinifera, we're low enough on the mountain to be protected from heavy winter damage, but high enough to enjoy a temperature inversion and healthy vinifera growing conditions."

David knows whereof he speaks. Between 1981 and 1983, while Morrisettes' vineyard and winery were being developed, he attended Mississippi State University and received degrees in enology and viti-culture. Under the direction of leading eastern viticulturist Richard Vine, the Mississippi State program is fast gaining credit for helping to rejuvenate the southern Muscadine wine industry. In 1983, David was the third student to graduate from the program. During his studies, he apprenticed at Thousand Oaks Winery in Mississippi.

THE VINEYARDS

As it stands today, Chateau Morrisette's mountaintop vineyard has approximately 21 acres of vines. As displayed below, French-American hybrid plantings consist of large plots of white varieties Vidal and Seyval, with smaller plots devoted to red varieties Chambourcin and Foch and the native-American grape Niagara.

Farther down the mountain, an 18-acre vineyard has been developed consisting of 7 acres of Chardonnay, 5 acres of Cabernet Sauvignon, 4 acres of Merlot, and 2 acres of Riesling.

GRAPE VARIETIES AND ACREAGE

Variety	Vinifera	French/Amer. Hybrids
Vidal	—.—	10.0
Chardonnay	7.0	—.—
Cabernet Sauvignon	5.0	—.—
Seyval	—.—	5.0
Chambourcin	—.—	4.0
Merlot	4.0	—.—
Riesling	2.0	—.—
Foch	—.—	1.0
Niagara	—.—	1.0
TOTALS	18.0	21.0

To supplement their own harvest as new plantings mature, the Morrisettes have looked to a new, exciting source of grapes—a grower in the Winston-Salem area of North Carolina named Jack Kroustalis. Kroustalis, who hopes to open a winery himself in the future, is one of the few pioneers in that state who has chosen to grow only vinifera varieties. "I am very pleased by his produce," explains David. "Not only is his fruit beautiful (Chardonnay, Riesling, Cabernet Sauvignon, Merlot, and Gamay Beaujolais), but his growing conditions are actually more similar to ours than previous leased vineyards. He may be in a different state, but if you look at a map, we're a lot closer to him than we are to Charlottesville!" For this reason, David expects no major stylistic changes in these Chateau Morrisette wines produced from this North Carolina source. Due to labeling laws of the U.S. Bureau of Alcohol, Tobacco and Firearms, these Chateau Morrisette wines will have to be designated "American" since the majority of the fruit used was grown outside of Virginia state boundaries.

THE WINES

For the 1986 vintage, Chateau Morrisette enjoyed briefly the services of winemaker Steve Warner. Regarded by many as one of the most skilled winemakers in Virginia, Warner had worked previously at Rapidan River Vineyards in 1983 and in 1984 and 1985 produced very noteworthy wines at Montdomaine Cellars in Charlottesville. After the 1987 harvest, Steve left to join the Williamsburg Winery.

For the wines of 1987 through 1989, Richard Carmichael was brought on board to handle the winemaking responsibilities. A Californian by training, Carmichael received his graduate degree in enology from Fresno State University. Most recently, Robert Burgin has taken over winemaking responsibilities.

Many of the winemaking approaches used by Steve Warner (also a Fresno State graduate) proved so successful that David Morrisette wanted to continue using them at the winery. For example, Rieslings are fermented excruciatingly slowly at the very cold temperature of 42° F. Once dry (which takes several months), a *sweet reserve* of unfermented Riesling juice is added back to finish the wine with 2% residual sugar. What can result from this technique is a Riesling of delicate intensity and good concentration. For the '86 vintage, floral, blossomy aromas literally leap out of the glass. Wonderful, mouthfilling peach and apricot flavors are immaculately clean, delightfully crisp, and linger long after the wine is swallowed.

In his Chardonnays, David wants a big, richly styled wine. So, after starting fermentation in stainless steel tanks, one-half of the *must* is transferred to French Limousin oak to complete fermentation, whereupon it is left to age *sur lie* for six months. The other half of the Chardonnay is also left to age on its fermentation *lees* to allow for added toasty complexity. Surprisingly, the wine was not allowed to complete *malolactic fermentation* (an accomplishment in its own right given all the wine's lees contact) in order to balance complexity with fruitiness. Once again, the '86 vintage produced a beautiful Chardonnay that reflected its care in upbringing. Round, buttery, and fat, the wine fills the nose and mouth with fresh apple and pear flavors, lemony citrine acidity, and a deft, measured toasty oakiness framing all the other flavors.

Between 1983 and 1985, Chateau Morrisette also produced 100% varietal wines from Seyval and Vidal. But a new strategy for hybrid/vinifera blends was begun in 1986 with the addition to the product line of White Burgundy and "Trilogie" table wines. After a comparative tasting, the move seems a good one, given the added complexity of blended wines and the unfair yet generally difficult marketability of wines called Seyval, Vidal, etc. The "White" is a blend of 35% Seyval, 30% Vidal, and 35% Chardonnay. Light, dry, crisp, and nicely fruity, the wine combines interesting clean peach and grapefruit flavors with the slight grassy herbaceousness associated with Seyval. It is a real value. The "Trilogie" is a blend of Merlot, Cabernet Sauvignon, and Chambourcin.

Turning back to the vinifera, Chateau Morrisette hopes to continue offering both a Cabernet Sauvignon and a Merlot. Until estate vineyards begin producing fruit of acceptable maturity, Chateau Morrisette will use purchased fruit. For 1986, Cabernet Sauvignon and Merlot grapes from California were used to produce two big bruisers. Extended skin contact and lengthy aging in French oak resulted in wines of significant power, with lush, deep fruit, hard yet not out-of-control tannins, and pronounced green pepper and olive herbaceousness.

Finishing off the line are two fun, very popular wines. The Chateau Morrisette "Blush" is made from various combinations of grapes depending on the vintage. In 1987, the wine was made from 100% Gamay Beaujolais grown in North Carolina. The only dessert-style wine at the winery is also one of its most popular. "Sweet Mountain Laurel" is a 100% Niagara wine fermented cold and stopped with 5% natural residual sugar. It is clean, crisp, and grapey and is produced in such a limited supply that customers are only allowed to buy three bottles per person!

INCIDENTALLY . . .

Chateau Morrisette boasts one of the lovelier tasting rooms in the mid-Atlantic. Rustic knotty pine floors and walls, a huge rough-hewn stone fireplace, and a spacious deck offering westward views of distant West Virginia are its major charms. Additionally, a French-Continental restaurant on the premises serves lunch and dinner in a romantic French-country atmosphere.

DIRECTIONS

Driving south of Roanoke on the Blue Ridge Parkway, find Chateau Morrisette Winery near mile post 172, 4.5 miles north of the Mabry Mill.

TABLE WINE PRODUCED AND BOTTLED BY REBEC VINEYARDS, AMHERST, VA. CONTAINS SULFITES.

Rebec Vineyards

ADDRESS: Route 3, Box 185
Amherst, VA 24521
PHONE: (804) 946-5168
OWNERS: Richard and Ella Hanson
WINEMAKER: Richard Hanson
TOTAL ACRES: 4
CASES/YR: 420
HOURS: Daily 10 to 5, March-December

The name "Rebec" was chosen to represent another of the newest wineries in the state of Virginia. The word has a very special meaning to owners Richard and Ella Hanson. The rebec is a medieval 13th century stringed musical instrument; sort of a cross between a guitar and a cello. (A sketch of the instrument appears on the winery's label.) As a forerunner of the violin and a descendant of the ancient Arabic rebab, the Hansons feel that "the rebec represents the balance and pleasure that music and wine have given the western world."

Licensed in the summer of 1987, Rebec Vineyards conducted its first commercial crush that fall and opened its doors to the public in the spring of 1988. For Richard, a retired quality control engineer for General Electric, the winery is the product of several years of serious planning and no small amount of sweat and hard work. Among other things (like planting and developing his 4 acres of grapes), he and his family tore down and then rebuilt a circa 1800 tobacco barn now housing the wonderfully rustic winery and tasting room. As he describes it, the barn had been so well built that it "came down like it didn't want to come down!" The original siding from the barn was preserved and now provides the siding for the winery.

The Hansons had been home winemakers for thirty-five years when, in 1969, they were transferred to Ireland for two years. It was there that they suddenly had increased access to the fine wines of Europe and they continued to develop their palates.

Towards the late '70s, back with GE in Amherst, Virginia, the couple began thinking ahead toward their retirement activities. At the time they were living in "Mountain View," an estate listed in the Historic American Building Survey of the Library of Congress, which Ella inherited from her grandparents, together with 70 acres of farmland. Given their interest in wine and the budding Virginia wine industry, the idea of growing grapes seemed more and more appealing.

In 1980, with the helpful consultation of Gabriele Rausse (the pioneering Italian winegrower then of Barboursville Vineyards), the Hansons planted 2 acres of vinifera vines. Five years later, 2 more acres were added to complete the present 4-acre site. And two years after that, with all vines bearing and the winery completed, Rebec was ready to roll, and the Hansons were proudly prepared to share their wine with the public.

THE VINEYARD

Rebec Vineyards produces grapes from a 2-acre plot of Chardonnay, an 1.25 acre plot of Cabernet Sauvignon, a half acre of Riesling and, departing from the norm so prevalent in Virginia, a quarter acre of Gamay Beaujolais. (A few Merlot vines are also present to use for blending with the Cabernet.)

The vinifera have prospered quite well for Rebec. Only in the winter of 1985, when temperatures dipped to -15° F, did the Chardonnay sustain any significant bud damage. Richard is especially fond of his Gamay Beaujolais grapes. The vines grow well in his site. A granite underlayer in the subsoil seems to provide the vines with the proper drainage, nutrients, etc. Unfortunately, the grape's cluster is a very tight one, like its clonal parent the Pinot Noir. Thus, as the grapes ripen and swell, they are very susceptible to bursting and then rotting, especially after late-season rains. For this reason, Hanson has trouble getting the Gamay Beaujolais to ripen past 18-19° *Brix*. In good years, though, he has been very pleased with the wines he's produced from this variety.

GRAPE VARIETIES AND ACREAGE

Variety	Vinifera	French/Amer. Hybrids
Chardonnay	2.0	—.—
Cabernet Sauvignon	1.25	—.—
Riesling	0.5	—.—
Gamay Beaujolais	0.25	—.—
TOTALS	4.0	0.0

Visitors to Rebec may recognize the trellising used by Richard Hanson; it is like that of Barboursville Vineyards, Simeon Vineyards (the present home of Gabriele Rausse), and Autumn Hill Vineyards (another operation that benefited from Rausse's tutelage). Rebec has trained vines to the Cassara system. In this approach, vines are placed back to back, on either side of a sturdy post, and are allowed to grow to the first wire, at which point they form cordons running in opposite directions.

THE WINES

Rather than purchasing expensive temperature-controlled stainless steel tanks, Richard Hanson figured his winery was small enough to try other, more creative approaches. His regular, unjacketed stainless steel tanks (impressively small compared to those of most wineries) are arranged in a room he chills with a powerful air conditioner. While fermenting new wines, he keeps the entire winery chilled to

50-60°. In an especially ingenious move, Richard is able to cold stabilize his whites by moving the 100 to 125 gallon tanks to an old dairy truck parked out back of the winery. The refrigerated compartment of the truck can be chilled to 25° F very efficiently, thus allowing Hanson to precipitate *tartrates* and stabilize the wines before bottling.

Rebec produces three varieties for the commercial market, all from grapes grown in its own vineyard: Chardonnay, Riesling, and Cabernet Sauvignon. (Richard will reserve the Gamay Beaujolais for himself and further experiments.) The Chardonnay is fermented to dryness in stainless steel and then aged briefly in American oak barrels. It presents mild appley fruit and abundant toasty oak character. The Riesling is produced in a Germanic style, with 1.5% residual sugar, by adding a *sweet reserve* of unfermented Riesling juice to the wine prior to bottling. The wine is clean and displays slightly sugary, candy-like fruitiness. Finally, the Cabernet is fermented in contact with the skins for ten days and spends about one year aging in American oak before its release. This wine offers the most interest—the '87 version is a deep purple/black color and shows good extract and concentration.

INCIDENTALLY . . .

If anyone tastes any similarities between Rebec wines and those of nearby Stonewall Vineyards, it may be more than a coincidence. For the few years preceding the licensing of his own winery, Richard Hanson sold his Cabernet Sauvignon and Chardonnay to Howard and Betty Bryan down at Stonewall.

DIRECTIONS

Driving on Route 29, Rebec Vineyards can be found on the west side of the highway approximately 5 miles north of Amherst and 11 miles south of Lovingston.

Rose Bower Vineyard and Winery

ADDRESS: P.O. Box 126
Hampden-Sydney, VA 23943
PHONE: (804) 223-8209
OWNERS: Tom and Bronwyn O'Grady
WINEMAKER: Tom O'Grady
TOTAL ACRES: 10.5
CASES/YR: 2,000
HOURS: March-December, Tuesday-Sunday
1-6; please call ahead for appointment

While scanning a map of Virginia, you would not expect to find a winery or vineyard in tiny Hampden-Sydney, situated in the southern-central portion of the state. On the contrary, not only does Rose Bower Vineyard and Winery call the location home, but one other winery and eight other commercial growers in the surrounding counties occupy the newly proposed Appomattox Plateau Viticultural Area. The false presumption that weekend wine touring does not exist in southern Virginia would also deny enthusiasts the chance to meet one of the more colorful, interesting individuals in the state's industry today.

Tom O'Grady, looking something like a latterday Ernest Hemingway with his full salt-and-pepper beard and piercing blue eyes, is the owner, winemaker, and vineyard manager for the 10.5-acre Rose Bower Vineyard and Winery. But like so many other winegrowers in the mid-Atlantic, Tom, with his career as a winemaker (a full-time job in itself) has another full-time career as well. A respected poet and scholar, Tom O'Grady is currently a poet-in-residence at nearby Hampden-Sydney College and has over the last twenty years taught writing and literature courses at numerous colleges and universities including Johns Hopkins and the University of Delaware. A prolific writer himself, Tom has had his poetry published in literary magazines, anthologies, journals, and books. Tom has also devoted a great proportion of his time in recent years to studying and translating the work of Nobel Prize-winning Czech poet Jaroslav Seifert. Mingling his dual careers, O'Grady also once wrote and published a sonnet sequence entitled "Establishing a Vineyard," and has recently published a book-length essay entitled "Wine Making Itself."

In the mid-1970s, Tom O'Grady "was an avid devotee of the 'back to earth movement'" and moved to the southern Virginia countryside when he received an appointment at Hampden-Sydney College. Also a fan of fine wine, he began in 1974 to plant a vineyard as a sidelight. With each passing year, more land was cleared, more vines were planted, and more success was encountered as an amateur winemaker. By 1979, with several acres mature and producing, O'Grady applied for and received a commercial winery license. Today, along with his wife Bronwyn (an English teacher at Longwood College) and two sons, Ethan and Ryan, Tom welcomes a steady flow of visitors to his lovely, bucolic homestead.

THE VINEYARD

Tom O'Grady works hard at trying to educate people about the suitability of this region of the state for growing grapes. "The Appomattox Plateau," he explains, "experiences about 3,200-3,300 *degree days* each growing season, which is about the same level of warmth as St. Helena in Napa Valley." Tom attributes this surprisingly cool microclimate, which averages 300-400 fewer degree days than the surrounding area, to a gap in the Blue Ridge near Long Mountain and Lynchburg through which cool air spills eastward to lower elevations. Rose Bower now sits about 500 feet above sea level. With slightly cooler evenings and slightly less humidity, Tom feels his vineyard experiences reduced rot and disease.

To help nudge climatic conditions in a more favorable direction, Tom has also installed a wind machine, which he bought used in the Napa Valley. Actually a big motorized airplane propeller that towers above the vineyard on a 50-foot pole, the machine helps move air on humid or rainy days to ward off rot and on frigid nights to inhibit the formation of frost.

Rose Bower's vineyard is located on a very pretty site, surrounded on all sides by thick forests. Now totalling 10.5 acres, it represents a broad range of both French-American hybrids and vinifera varieties. The two largest plots are devoted to Chardonnay and Riesling with 2 acres each. Other white varieties include hybrids Vidal, Seyval, and Rayon D'or. For the reds, vinifera Cabernet Sauvignon, Cabernet Franc, and Merlot are planted to small parcels along with hybrids Chancellor, Chelois, Foch, and Baco Noir. While small amounts of fruit have been purchased to supplement Rose Bower's crushes, Tom hopes that all wines will be *estate bottled* from 1988 on.

GRAPE VARIETIES AND ACREAGE

Variety	Vinifera	French/Amer. Hybrids
Chardonnay	2.0	—.—
Riesling	2.0	—.—
Rayon D'or	—.—	1.0
Seyval	—.—	1.0
Vidal	—.—	1.0
Baco Noir	—.—	0.5
Cabernet Sauvignon	0.5	—.—
Chancellor	—.—	0.5
Chelois	—.—	0.5
Foch	—.—	0.5
Cabernet Franc	0.5	—.—
Merlot	0.5	—.—
TOTALS	5.5	5.0

THE WINES

Given the number of varieties he has to work with, it is not surprising that Tom O'Grady produces a wide range of wines. What is surprising are the numerous and diverse experimental winemaking techniques he uses and that he can do so much in what has to be one of the tightest winery work areas in the mid-Atlantic. With the fermentation pad occupying a small shed-like addition to his house and his barrel room, with barrels stacked three-high to the ceiling in the basement, every inch of space is efficiently used to create eleven separate bottlings.

"I feel that I'm obligated to experiment and manipulate every single variety," says Tom. "In the grand scheme of things, winegrowing in Virginia is really in its infancy, and with hybrids especially there's no complete understanding of what techniques work best with what varieties."

For example, Tom produces two unusual dessert wines: "Le Bon Sauvage," a 100% late harvest Seyval picked at relatively high ripeness of 24° *Brix* and sweetened after fermentation to 6% residual sugar, and "Le Bateau Rouge," a red, port-styled wine made by foot-stomping Cabernet Sauvignon, Chancellor, and sometimes Chelois, which is allowed to ferment for an extended period in contact with the grape skins and, usually, the stems. *Chapitalized* to raise fermentable sugar levels, the wine finishes with 14% alcohol and spends two years in oak.

A 100% Foch "Nouveau" is also produced in a light, fruity style by removing the fermenting *must* from the grape skins after just a few hours of contact. The "Briery Lake" Vidal is also 100% varietal, is fermented cool in stainless steel tanks and sweetened just slightly to .75% residual sugar by adding a *sweet reserve* of unfermented Vidal juice. It is a crisp, clean wine displaying fruit at the pear and apple end of the spectrum rather than citrus like so many other Vidals. A dry-styled Seyval is also produced.

One of the most successful wines produced by Tom O'Grady is called "Hampden Forest Claret." Made from 65% Chancellor and 35% Cabernet Sauvignon, the wine is another example of the exciting red wines that can be assembled by blending red hybrids with vinifera varieties. The Claret has a cherry fruit nose touched by herbal notes, and in the mouth its medium-bodied fruit blends cherries, spicy oak, and green olive herbaceousness for a lively and enjoyable glass of wine.

Varietal vinifera wines include a clean, appley, rich, partially barrel-fermented Chardonnay, a crisp, floral Riesling blended with 15% Gewurztraminer and sweetened to 2% residual sugar by adding a sweet reserve and, harvest permitting, small quantities of Cabernet Sauvignon (which is usually blended with about 10% Merlot). Both of these classic Bordeaux varieties have, unfortunately, not fared well during harsh winters.

Finally, two nice sipping picnic wines complete the lineup: "Blushing Bride," which is 90% Vidal and 10% Foch, and a gutsier "Rosé O'Grady," which is a more deeply colored blend of 50% Chelois and 50% Rayon D'or.

INCIDENTALLY . . .

Tom O'Grady likes to host festivals that are aimed at educating the public about the various phases of winegrowing. He therefore schedules at least two fêtes each year—a spring "Budbreak" and an autumn "Harvest" festival. Sometimes, later in the fall, he will also hold a "Festival Nouveau" to celebrate the release of that vintage's Foch Nouveau. Tom has built a lovely gazebo smack in the middle of the vineyard and encourages guests to use it for picnics and even an occasional wedding. Most recently, the O'Gradys have just completed construction of a six bedroom "Oak Chalet" for guests. The structure boasts a 26-foot high great room with a glass wall overlooking a 10-acre lake.

DIRECTIONS

From Farmville on Route 460 (which runs east to west between Petersburg and Lynchburg), take Route 15 south and turn right onto Route 665 at Worsham. Proceed 3 miles and bear left on Route 664. Go 2 miles and turn right onto Route 686. Rose Bower is on the right, 1.5 miles down 686.

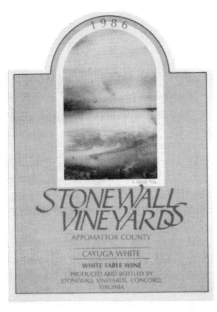

Stonewall Vineyards

ADDRESS: Route 2, Box 107A
Concord, VA 24538
PHONE: (804) 993-2185
OWNERS: Larry and Sterry Davis
WINEMAKER: Bart Davis and Howard
    Bryan
TOTAL ACRES: 7.5
CASES/YR: 2,600
HOURS: Wednesday through Sunday 1-5,
    March-December; others by
    appointment

In the fall of 1990, Stonewall Vineyards was purchased by the Davis family—Larry, Sterry, and son Bart. Currently in charge of telemarketing for duPont in Wilmington, Delaware, Larry Davis has his eyes on retirement in the coming years. An amateur winemaker for more than ten years, he decided that becoming a professional vintner would offer a challenging second career.

But to fully understand Stonewall Vineyards, one must meet its founders, Howard and Betty Bryan. The couple epitomize the phrase "southern hospitality." Soft-spoken, warm, and friendly, the two had welcomed visitors to their absolutely charming vineyard and winery, situated in a dense forest on the Appomattox Plateau 15 miles east of Lynchburg, since 1983.

Up until 1980, the Bryans had devoted their full energies to the rigors of raising a family and to their careers; Howard, a products manager for a nuclear engineering firm in Lynchburg and Betty, a sixth grade teacher. In 1966, while Howard was still in the Marines, they purchased a plot of land out in the country as an investment. "We really didn't know what we'd do with it at first," explains Howard. "Raising tobacco or corn just didn't seem too exciting." Then the idea of growing grapes occurred to them and seemed both more interesting and more promising.

In 1973, a tiny test plot of thirty vines was planted ("While long gone now, this experiment did allow me to learn which six varieties I didn't want to grow—Aurora, Baco Noir, Chelois, Delaware, Foch, Rayon D'or—and let us practice with four different pruning systems!" describes Howard) and everything took off from there. First, the Bryans built a lovely log home on the farm and moved in permanently. Next, a serious planting took place in 1980, and three years later when the vines began producing, they obtained a commercial license and concluded their first crush. They chose the name Stonewall Vineyards because the Stonewall Creek runs through a section of their farm.

THE VINEYARD

The Appomattox Plateau (at the moment being considered for its own viticultural area status by the U.S. Bureau of Alcohol, Tobacco and Firearms) is situated at 760 feet above sea level. The region experiences surprisingly arid summers and, therefore, less humidity than some parts of the state. This, in turn, results in fewer problems with various rots that can plague vineyards.

Before the Bryans planted their vineyard in 1980, they felt it important to consult with an expert. For this task, they called on now-famous Virginia viticulturist Lucie Morton Garrett. She helped with site and grape variety selection, and trellis design, and her advice, according to Howard and Betty, "was sterling. Every variety she suggested has thrived. The only one *I* chose I'm going to have to rip out!" Indeed, the vineyard reflects the careful forethought of an experienced viticulturist.

Ms. Morton Garrett advised the Bryans to focus the bulk of their planting on two white hybrid grapes—one French, the other an American developed in New York at the Geneva Experimental Station in the Finger Lakes. A full 3 acres were planted to both Vidal and Cayuga. The latter is not grown much in the mid-Atlantic but has shown extreme promise for its ability to ripen in a wide range of climates and has proven to be resistant to disease. For red wine, Lucie advised Chambourcin. One acre was planted to this variety, which is fast becoming the red French-American hybrid of choice throughout the east. Because of the risk involved in growing vinifera generally, and the untested nature of the Appomattox Plateau specifically, the Bryans were advised to plant just a .5-acre test plot to Chardonnay, Riesling, and Cabernet Sauvignon.

GRAPE VARIETIES AND ACREAGE

Variety	Vinifera	French/Amer. Hybrids
Vidal	—.—	3.0
Cayuga	—.—	3.0
Chambourcin	—.—	1.0
Cabernet	0.5	—.—
TOTALS	0.5	7.0

Most varieties have grown very well. The Bryans were especially thrilled with the Vidal and Cayuga due at least in part to the use of a high wire, bilateral cordon trellis system. This approach both promotes improved air flow around the vines (critical for drying out fruit and leaves after rain) and exposes the vines' canopy of leaves to optimal sunshine, thereby maintaining healthy pH levels in ripening grapes.

The Chardonnay and Riesling suffered repeated frost damage and were phased out. The variety chosen by Howard, Verdelet, also performed sporadically over the years and was eventually pulled out.

At this time, the Davis family's plans call for doubling the size of Stonewall's vineyard. Future expansion will be devoted to the varieties Chambourcin, Cabernet Sauvignon, Cabernet Franc, and Chardonnay.

THE WINES

Stonewall produces just under 3,000 cases of wine annually in its small, efficiently designed winery facility. But don't let the small size mislead — Stonewall has invested in high-tech equipment to ensure maximum quality. White wines are all fermented in jacketed, temperature-controlled stainless steel tanks. Cool fermentation emphasizes the delicate fruit qualities in both Vidal and Cayuga. Additionally, for those varieties that receive oak aging, the focus has been on using French oak from the forests of Nevers. Only Chambourcin spends its time in American oak.

Vidal, as described within these pages, is proving to be a most versatile grape. Stonewall Vineyards is one spot where visitors can see two versions, each vinified toward opposite ends of the enological spectrum. A semi-dry Vidal is produced in the manner most typically chosen for the grape. It is fermented quite cool to retain its delicate, fruity aromas, is brought up to 1.25% residual sugar by adding a *sweet reserve* of unfermented juice to dry wine, and is then sterile filtered and bottled young. The wine is very Riesling-like with a floral nose and crisp apricot and peach flavors.

The dry Vidal is a truly unusual, engaging wine. It is fermented warmer, around 70° F and, like a Chardonnay, is left for several months on its fermentation *lees*. Frequent stirring of the lees contributes yeasty complexity. The wine is then aged briefly in French Nevers oak. The dry Vidal has a deeper gold color than its semi-dry counterpart, and has a less pronounced nose of fruit accented by a slight toasty oakiness. In the mouth it is still quite lean, more so than a Chardonnay, but displays bright citrus and lemon flavors overlaid by ample vanillan oak. It is an enticingly different sort of wine exemplifying the versatility of the grape.

The Stonewall Cayuga is also a very nice wine. Produced in the same manner as the semi-dry Vidal, it is a very pale straw, nearly clear color, has a light citrus nose, and is clean, crisp, and thirst-quenching. While not as delicate and fruity as some New York Cayugas (due, no doubt, to the warmer climate in Virginia), it still offers very pleasant drinking.

For red wines, Stonewall produces a deep, gutsy "Claret" and an utterly charming Chambourcin. The "Claret," a blend of 78% Cabernet Sauvignon, 12% Merlot, and 10% Cabernet Franc (with just a bit of Chambourcin) is fermented in traditional open-topped vats, and the rising cap of skins is "punched down" and stirred three times a day for seven days. The wine is then *racked* into French oak barrels and spends fifteen months aging. In strong vintages such as 1984 and 1986, the wine has a deep ruby color, young chewy flavors of berries and cassis, and surprisingly soft tannins all wrapped up in a smoky, tarry, black licorice oak veneer. It is brash and bold and not for the faint hearted.

The Chambourcin is vinted in a very non-traditional way for the variety. It is fermented as a white wine—free run juice only is pumped into stainless steel where it is kept at low temperatures to preserve fruitiness. The newly fermented wine is placed in American oak for three months and is then bottled young. Despite the lack of skin contact, the wine has good ruby color (not surprising, since red hybrids tend to be quite inky and freely give up their red pigment). While its nose is quite neutral (again, typical of Chambourcin and perhaps its only shortcoming), the flavors are full, berryish with a nice touch of spicy oak. It is a very nice, light/medium-bodied everyday table wine.

Rounding out the lineup are the "Vin Clochard" (French for "wine of the drunk"), a blush wine made of mainly white hybrids colored by Chambourcin and a touch of Cabernet, and a 100% Verdelet.

Finally, for dessert and holidays, Stonewall also makes a Mead called "Pyment." Following an old English recipe, honey, grape juice (in this case, Vidal), cloves, peppercorns, and skins of bergamot (a citrus fruit like an orange) are all fermented together, very slowly, for nine months. Honey added back sweetens the wine to 6% residual sugar. The wine has a slight honey-haze (normal for Meads) and is mouthwateringly viscous, filled with ripe apple, lemon, and pear fruit overlaid by spicy "potpourri" aromas and flavors. Perfect for fireplace sipping!

INCIDENTALLY . . .

While the Bryans have sold Stonewall Vineyards to their new friends, the Davises, Howard Bryan's imprint will still be apparent in Stonewall's wines. He is currently the winery's consulting winemaker and is teaching young Bart Davis the tools of the trade.

DIRECTIONS

From Lynchburg, drive east on Route 460 approximately 10 miles to Route 608. Turn north (left) and drive 6 miles to Route 721 and turn left. Winery is first driveway on left.

WINE TOURING IN NORTH CAROLINA
AN OVERVIEW

From the standpoint of sheer variety, you would be hard pressed to find any state in this country that can offer the wine tourist as interesting and diverse an experience as North Carolina. That's right, North Carolina. True, there are not too many wineries there and yes, many, many miles separate the few the state has. But where else can you find vitis vinifera, French-American hybrids, native-American hybrids, and vitis rotundifolia, all cultivated and vinified within one state's borders?

North Carolina does not have many wineries, but it does have all types. Far to the west in Asheville, a multi-million dollar operation can be found at the Biltmore Estate. A lovely attraction even without its winery, this grand spectacle owned by the Vanderbilt family offers a gorgeous chateau styled after those famous in the Loire Valley of France. Creating an estate in the true French tradition, the Vanderbilts have built a huge (by any state's standards), state-of-the-art winery, complete with an imported French winemaker, Philippe Jourdain. Committed to wine produced in the classical methods, the Biltmore Estate has made an impressive effort to cultivate only the noblest varieties, vitis vinifera, by planting a 100-acre vineyard.

A hundred and fifty miles to the northeast, a winery on a completely different scale has been pulled together by a small group of professionals who turned a hobby into a second profession. Organized by two individuals, Mallory Chambliss and Jerry Pegram, the Germanton Vineyard and Winery was formed when six amateur growers of French-American and native-American hybrids in the Winston-Salem area pooled their harvests and capital into a joint effort. While extremely small, this winery does offer the wine tourist a charming opportunity to visit a do-it-yourself boutique winery producing high quality wines from hybrid varieties.

But it is another 150 miles or so to the southeast that things get really interesting. Here, the mysterious grapes of the native species vitis rotundifolia (otherwise known as Muscadines) are grown and vinified into wine that will certainly shock the tastebuds while opening the eyes of all but the most experienced wine buffs. And before anyone turns their nose up at a wine called Scuppernong while they sip their noble Chardonnay, please be advised that serious wines are being made under the direction of David Fussell at Duplin Wine Cellars and at the Southland Estate Winery along the eastern third of the state. The unique grapey, musky, spicy flavors of Muscadines are different, but that is because they are made from grapes about as different from vinifera as you can get. They are also, however, made from grapes that have a true native heritage in this country, which both vinifera and French-American hybrids lack.

North Carolina is home to the nation's first cultivated wine grape. From the logbook of Giovanni de Verrazzano, the Florentine navigator who explored the Cape Fear River Valley for France in 1524, comes an account of having seen "Many vines growing naturally there . . ." and that "without a doubt they would yield excellent wines."

In 1584, Sir Walter Raleigh's explorers, Captains Phillip Amadas and Arthur Barlowe, wrote of North Carolina coasts "so full of grapes as the very beating and surge of the sea overflowed them . . . in all the world, the like abundance is not to be found."

And in 1585, Governor Ralph Lane stated in describing North Carolina to Sir Walter Raleigh that "We have discovered the main to be the goodliest soil under the cope of heaven, so abounding with sweet trees that bring rich and most pleasant gummes, grapes of such greatness, yet wild, as France, Spain, nor Italy hath no greater . . ."

By the early 1700s, German-Swiss settlers began the first serious vinification of Muscadines, modifying their European approaches to accentuate the unique flavor and aroma of the native grapes. Sidney Weller's Medoc Vineyards became the nation's first commercial winery in 1835, producing sixty barrels of wine annually from its 12 acres of white and black Muscadines in Halifax County. Believing that Scuppernong was the "finest wine in the world," Paul Garret became the state's most successful vintner. His special blend called "Virginia Dare," produced at his five wineries, was the nation's largest selling wine at the turn of this century. By 1909, however, the growing and successful industry was dealt a death-blow by the adoption of state-wide prohibition.

Well, as we know, prohibition no longer exists and yes, North Carolina is back in the wine business. Clearly, for those truly interested in wine for its variety and diversity, a trip to North Carolina must be experienced.

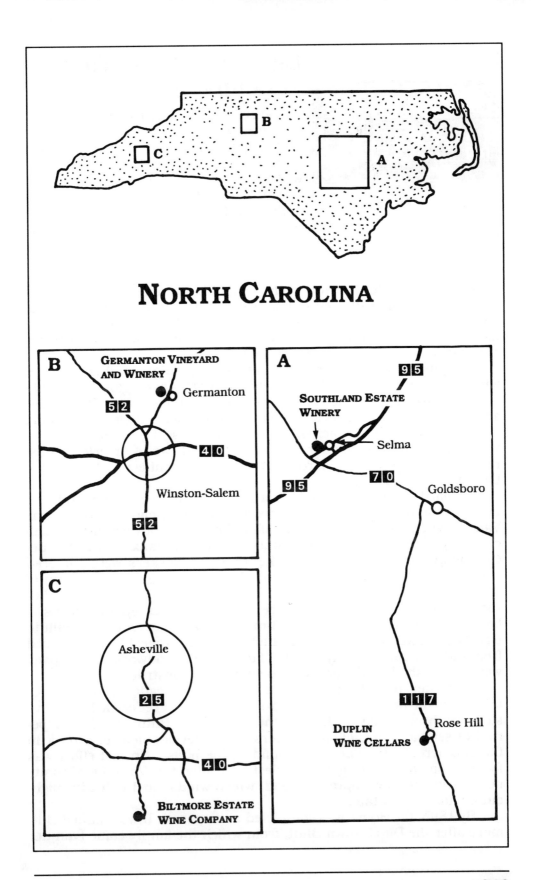

NORTH CAROLINA

B GERMANTON VINEYARD AND WINERY

52

Germanton

40

Winston-Salem

52

A

95

SOUTHLAND ESTATE WINERY

Selma

95

70

Goldsboro

C

Asheville

25

40

BILTMORE ESTATE WINE COMPANY

117

Rose Hill

DUPLIN WINE CELLARS

CHATEAU BILTMORE.

CABERNET SAUVIGNON
NORTH CAROLINA
PRODUCED AND BOTTLED BY BILTMORE ESTATE WINE COMPANY
ASHEVILLE, NC 28803 BW-NC-32 ALCOHOL 11.5% BY VOLUME
VINTAGE 1983
◆I N A U G U R A L◆R E L E A S E◆

Biltmore Estate Wine Company

ADDRESS: The Biltmore Estate
Asheville, NC 28803
PHONE: (704) 274-6280
OWNERS: The Cecil Family
WINEMAKER: Philippe Jourdain
TOTAL ACRES: 108
CASES/YR: 40,000
HOURS: Monday-Saturday 11-7, Sunday 1-7

No trip to Asheville, North Carolina would be complete without a visit to the sumptuous Biltmore Estate. But upon your visit, be sure to allow the better part of an entire day, for you will be seeing not only a handsome, state-of-the-art winery, but the monumental chateau, ornate gardens, and deep forests of the Estate.

The history of the Biltmore Estate and its unique and unexpected winery begins in the mid-1880s, when George Washington Vanderbilt (1862-1914) visited Asheville. Loving the mountains of the Blue Ridge and the temperate climate so much, he purchased a huge tract of land encompassing 125,000 acres, including Mt. Pisgah. To plan and develop the Estate, Mr. Vanderbilt commissioned two of America's most renowned designers—Richard Morris Hunt as architect and Frederick Law Olmsted as landscaper.

Richard Morris Hunt, the first American to receive an architectural degree from l'École des Beaux Arts in Paris, chose to model the Vanderbilt's new country manor after the great 16th century French chateaux of the Loire Valley: Chambord, Chenonceaux, and Blois. Beginning in the summer of 1890, hundreds of workers were gathered from the surrounding area and from Europe to begin construction of the Biltmore House. Over the next five years, construction of the 250-room mansion took place, which required several exceptional steps to be taken. For example, a special 3-mile railway span had to be built to transport materials to the site, including limestone blocks shipped from Indiana. Additionally, a brick factory and woodworking company were established on the grounds to supply the construction.

A master of naturalistic landscape and a leader of the parks movement in America in the mid-19th century, Frederick Law Olmsted was brought on to develop the grounds at Biltmore. Over a period of several years, Olmsted oversaw the development of a park in the 250 acres immediately surrounding the house. Special effort was focused on the house gardens, designed after the Vaux Le Vicomte near Paris, and the Approach Road, which winds for 3 miles throughout the forested Estate.

By 1895, the House was completed and opened. It was named Biltmore after the Dutch town Bildt, from which the family came (van der

Bildt), and the English word "moor," meaning rolling, upland country. As the building was being completed, the Vanderbilts traveled throughout Europe gathering literally thousands of art treasures—tapestries, sculptures, engravings, bronzes, paintings and portraits, wood carvings, porcelains, and furniture—to adorn the modern palace.

After Mr. Vanderbilt's death in 1914, and upon the marriage of his daughter Cornelia to John Francis Amherst Cecil, the Biltmore House became the Cecils' residence. Over the years, much of the original estate had been deeded to the U.S. government for the establishment of the Pisgah National Forest, and sections were sold for development of the Blue Ridge Parkway. In 1930, the Cecils opened the Biltmore House and Gardens to the public. The Estate now comprises approximately 8,000 acres.

A generation later, William A.V. Cecil (the current president and owner of the house) decided that the establishment of a winery would be "in keeping with my grandfather's intention to maintain a working estate in the European tradition." Several viticultural experiments were conducted and the feasibility of a vineyard was verified. In 1971, the planting of a vineyard to French-American hybrids was begun, followed in a few years by experimentation with vinifera varieties.

To find a winemaster to oversee the serious development of this endeavor, Cecil went to France and found Philippe Jourdain of Provence. Jourdain, who had graduated from Algeria's National School of Agriculture in 1955 with a degree in agricultural engineering and in 1957 with a degree in enology, was busy with running his family's vineyard, Société Pourtet Jourdain in Carcassonne, France. In addition, he was teaching enology and viticulture at Carcassonne's Lycée Agricole. Cecil persuaded Jourdain to consult with the Estate beginning in 1977. By 1979, Jourdain was convinced that Biltmore, given its location, offered a unique viticultural challenge. Given the enormous resources upon which to draw, it provided a wonderful winemaking opportunity, so Philippe moved to Asheville to become the Estate's permanent winemaker.

The winery visitors see today opened to the public in May 1985. It is a beautiful, rambling "village" of buildings, expanded and renovated from the Biltmore's original dairy barn, which now encompasses more than 90,000 square feet of work area. It is graced by a striking clock tower. Visitors are led through an impressive and informative tour featuring kiosk displays and murals explaining the winemaking process, a winemaker's calendar, a theatre presentation of the history and culture of wine and of the Biltmore Estate and Winery, a walking tour of the winery's fermentation room, aging/barrel room, bottling line, and champagne facility, all ending in a spacious and pleasant tasting room decorated with stained glass windows by John LaFarge, mentor to Louis Comfort Tiffany.

THE VINEYARD

Not unlike those parts of Virginia along the eastern slope of the Blue Ridge, the Biltmore's Asheville location provides the opportunity for the successful cultivation of vinifera grapes. Its climate is temperate with warm summer days and cool, crisp nights, with humidity levels that remain quite low compared to the piedmont regions to the east. However, at an elevation of 2,200 feet above sea level, Biltmore is also subject to rare extremes of temperature — winter lows can dip well below 0° F.

With the arrival of Philippe Jourdain, Biltmore began an ambitious vinifera program. Throughout the 1980s, each year has seen more varieties introduced and more acres planted. The goals from the beginning were to diversify the vineyard in order to learn which varieties fared best in this untested region, and to increase volume so that a flexible and diverse crop could be harvested each year. That way, a bad year for one variety would not adversely impact the overall harvest.

A 35-acre lake was constructed near the vineyard to provide irrigation for both the summer droughts and, more important, for frost control. Since the region can have frost as late as May 15th (well after most varieties have sent out their young, tender shoots), water spraying of the vines to battle frost is a necessity in the early spring.

By 1985, an impressive 108-acre vineyard had been established with plans for further expansion. Acreage was devoted primarily to Chardonnay (31 acres), Cabernet Sauvignon (28 acres), and Riesling (25 acres). A staggering array of other plantings rounded out a vineyard whose diversity did not exist anywhere in the mid-Atlantic. Pinot Noir, Cabernet Franc, Sauvignon Blanc, Gamay, Merlot, and Gewurztraminer filled out the rest of the vinifera parcel, with French-American hybrids Villard Blanc, Vidal, and Seyval completing the vineyard.

GRAPE VARIETIES AND ACREAGE

Variety	Vinifera	French/Amer. Hybrids
Chardonnay	31.0	—.—
Cabernet Sauvignon	28.0	—.—
Riesling	25.0	—.—
Pinot Noir	6.0	—.—
Cabernet Franc	4.0	—.—
Sauvignon Blanc	4.0	—.—
Villard Blanc	—.—	3.0
Gamay	2.0	—.—
Merlot	2.0	—.—
Vidal	—.—	2.0
Gewurztraminer	0.5	—.—
Seyval	—.—	0.5
TOTALS	102.5	5.5

But in the winter of 1985, disaster struck. An intense freeze, the likes of which had not been recorded for over 100 years, hit the eastern seaboard. In the mountains of Asheville, temperatures dropped to

-20° F for an extended period. This event literally killed most of the Biltmore Estate's vineyard, dealing a serious blow to the otherwise spectacular growth of the enterprise.

Today, the Biltmore and Ted Katsigianis, vineyard manager, are replanting and redeveloping the vineyards. Says Philippe, "The freeze was, clearly, an enormous setback. But also a fluke—the worst in 100 years. So we will go on. We did learn some lessons. For example, Sauvignon Blanc could not stand the cold and died off quickly. Therefore, we are incorporating this knowledge into our new vineyard."

While the old vineyard is being replanted, Biltmore is also establishing new vineyards in alternative locations, which it is hoped will be less vulnerable to colder temperatures. The precise breakdown of new grape acreage was not available at the time of this writing.

THE WINES

Because of the devastating freeze, the next few years will see Biltmore primarily producing wines from purchased grapes. These wines appear under the "Biltmore Estate" label. As new vineyards mature and increase production, the estate grown wines will bear the "Chateau Biltmore" insignia.

In the tradition of excellence evident throughout the Estate, Philippe Jourdain oversees the purchase of only the highest quality fruit. Arranging contractual agreements with growers in California, Washington, and the Finger Lakes of New York, Philippe specifies strict harvesting standards, and sees that fresh fruit and juice are transported by refrigerated railway cars. While not ideal, Philippe is quite satisfied with the process that has resulted.

After the point of delivery, wines are produced at the Biltmore facility, which surpasses, in technological terms, all but the most sophisticated California wineries. Fresh grapes are unloaded directly into low-pressure bladder presses and juice is pumped through a maze of plumbing into the enormous fermentation room. Row upon row of temperature-controlled stainless steel tanks are housed there, so large that an intricate catwalk has been constructed along their tops to provide accessibility. For red wines, large stainless steel tanks (unlike any I've ever seen) are designed to be rotated on their sides so that the cap of crushed grape skins can be mixed with the fermenting *must*. A network of caves and cellars has been dug below ground level for the aging of red wines, where only French Nevers and Limousin oak are utilized. A completely separate temperature-controlled champagne processing room ensures the safe development of sparkling wines during the extended period when they ferment a second time, and then age on their fermentation *lees*, in the bottle. Finally, a high-tech, sterile bottling line can bottle over 3,000 bottles per hour.

Under the direction of Jourdain, Biltmore Estate has produced a string of impressive, solidly-made wines. Appearing under the Biltmore Estate label, three styles of Chardonnay are produced: a *"sur lie"* version aged on its fermentation yeast sediment for seven months; a crisp, dry version; and an unusual sweet rendition bottled with 2.5% residual sugar which, according to Philippe "was needed in this marketplace.

Unlike most parts of this country, a strong preference for sweeter wines persists in the South." Of the three, the limited edition "sur lie" proves most attractive, with yeasty, baked bread aromas mingled with citrus fruitiness.

Two Rieslings are also produced by the winery: one dry and one medium sweet with 2.5% residual sugar. Both are fruity and clean, with the sweeter "Johannisberg" offering more generous floral aromas and a lush, mouthfilling quality. It is produced in the optimal method by stopping the fermentation through an extreme drop in tank temperature, followed by centrifugation and sterile filtration to remove any yeast cells.

Other whites offered include a slightly grassy, low-intensity Sauvignon Blanc, a medium-sweet, somewhat herbaceous Chenin Blanc, and a clean "House White" produced from a blend of grapes.

The "Blanc de Noir" bottled by Biltmore is a curious blend of Carignane, Sauvignon Blanc, Ruby Cabernet, and Pinot Noir. Possessing a pink/salmon color and just 1% residual sugar, the blush wine more resembles a Cabernet blanc (due to its berry fruit and mild herbaceousness) than a white Zinfandel.

The Cabernet Sauvignon is quite impressive. A medium crimson in color, it displays a forward nose of berries, herbs, and allspice, with an attractive menthol note. In the mouth, the wine possesses soft tannins and fleshy fruit, and finishes with creamy, French oak flavors. All in all, it is clearly a California wine made in a drinkable, everyday style. Another house wine, called "Cardinal Crest," is also offered and is a blend of various red grapes.

When you taste the sparkling wine at Biltmore, it quickly becomes very clear that a Frenchman is at the helm. During my visit, a young cuvée of Blanc de Blanc was tasted pre-dosage, i.e., before its final sugar adjustment. Made predominantly from Chardonnay, it presented a fine, persistent mousse of bubbles, was tart and clean, with light citrus flavors surrounded by toasty, yeasty notes.

Finally, and most important, I was allowed the distinct pleasure of tasting a wine produced at Biltmore from its pre-freeze era—the 1983 Chateau Biltmore Cabernet Sauvignon. It displayed very deep berry and cassis fruit flavors and smooth, mellowing tannins. Its low pH/high acid structure was quite Bordeaux-like. This wine truly reflects the promising potential of the area for vinifera grapes and points toward the exciting time in the near future when Biltmore will no longer need to purchase fruit and can, instead, rely on its own patiently awaited harvest.

DIRECTIONS

From Interstate 40, take Exit 50 and follow signs for the Biltmore House and Gardens.

Duplin Wine Cellars

ADDRESS: P.O. Box 756, Hwy. 117 N.
Rose Hill, NC 28458
PHONE: (919) 289-3888
OWNERS: David Fussell &
    stockholders
WINEMAKER: David Fussell
TOTAL ACRES: 400 (leased)
CASES/YR: 40,000
HOURS: Monday-Saturday 9-5

David Fussell is a soft-spoken, polite man who epitomizes the "southern gentleman." He is also, as is evident after only a few minutes of conversation, a very intelligent man with a good head for business. "I'm very proud of our culture and heritage in North Carolina," says Fussell. "You know the state motto here is Est Quam Verite—To Be Rather Than To Seem." David embodies this motto in his approach to winemaking at Duplin. "I've always felt very strongly that it would be a marketing mistake to copy the wines of Europe, California, or New York. We make what cannot be produced outside of the Carolinas, and we will succeed due to the fact that we're different, not because of our similarities to others."

In 1972, David Fussell was a grape grower in rural southeast Duplin County. When prices for his produce dropped that year from $325 per ton picked up from the vineyard to $150 per ton delivered to the winery, he quickly realized that there would be little future for himself and his family if things didn't change.

He decided that it would make more sense to make wine himself than to sell grapes to others. But he couldn't do it by himself. Through effective persuasion and careful negotiation, David convinced enough local growers to join with him to make a go for it. In their first year (1975), just over 1,000 cases were bottled, divided amongst three wines. Fifteen years later, with 120 stockholders and 400 acres from which grapes are purchased, Duplin Wine Cellars now produces over 40,000 cases annually in twelve different bottlings.

Located in rural Rose Hill, Duplin is a modest but charming place to visit. The reason Duplin is different and the reason David Fussell is so proud is due entirely to the grapes from which he makes wine—the vitis rotundifolia or Muscadine. For a discussion of that difference, let's turn to the vineyard.

THE VINEYARD

While first called by the colonial settlers simply the "Big White Grape," the most famous of the Muscadines took on the name Scuppernong around the year 1800 from the Algonquin Indian word "ascopa" or sweetbay tree. The family of grapes to which the Scuppernong belongs grows only in a 70-mile wide band stretching along the coast from North Carolina to east Texas. The key requirement for Scuppernong is that the ground must not freeze for more than three weeks or the vine is killed.

The descriptor "sweetbay" only begins to identify how vitis rotundifolia grapes differ from more familiar varieties. Certainly the first thing you notice about the grapes is their unusually large size. In traditional Tarheel parlance, each grape's size is "about that of a hog's eye." (In other words, pretty big!) Second, Muscadines do not grow in bunches like other varieties. Instead, they grow in very loose clusters. When ripe, white varieties turn greenish-bronze while red varieties are actually a striking purple-black.

At harvest time, instead of cutting whole bunches from the vine, fully ripened grapes fall readily from the clusters when shaken either by hand or by mechanical harvester. Such a ripening progression allows farmers to harvest easily only the fully ripened fruit by making several passes through the vineyard, knowing that only those individual grapes that are ready will fall off.

A word to the wise. If you intend to pick a Muscadine grape to munch on, avoid the grape skin and just eat the sweet pulp. Muscadine skins are extremely tough and thick thereby making the grapes highly resistant to disease, insects, and rot.

Finally, one look at a vineyard planted to Muscadines, and its peculiarities become quickly apparent. Muscadine vines are incredibly vigorous and fast growing, forcing growers to plant vines 20 feet apart. By midsummer, a fully mature Muscadine vine impressively supports four 10-foot long arms (or cordons) trellised in a sort of modified double-curtain where two parallel arms extend in opposite directions from the trunk. This means that Muscadines can be planted at rates of only 180 vines per acre. This is in comparison to vinifera and hybrid vineyards, which can support between 600 and 1,400 vines per acre.

In spite of this drastically smaller number of vines per acre, Muscadine vineyards actually out-produce their vinifera and hybrid cousins. During their vigorous growing season, each acre of Muscadine grapes yields an average of 7 tons, while in good years yields can reach 8 to 10 tons. Conventional production levels for vinifera dictate between 2 and 4 tons per acre.

You won't see the Muscadine farmers plowing their grape rows either, the way hybrid and vinifera farmers do to control weeds in the summer and to hill up a protective mound of insulating earth around the vines in winter. Muscadines, in order to survive the frequent summer droughts, where temperatures peak over 100° quite commonly, spread their roots widely and close to the surface so that rainfall can be immediately soaked in. Plowing would actually tear up Muscadine roots and kill the vine. In contrast, hybrid and vinifera vines are famous for their extremely deep rooting characteristics and have been known to send down roots as far as 30 to 50 feet.

Muscadine grape varieties also have names that are, most likely, unfamiliar to most readers. Like any species growing in the wild, thousands of varieties have developed through unchecked cross-pollination. However, extensive research at institutions like North Carolina State University has helped isolate varieties with the most promising wine characteristics. The most prevalent white variety is called Carlos, followed closely by another white variety, Magnolia. The true Scuppernong variety is still extremely popular, but less common due to its particular growing characteristic of producing nine female flowers to every one male, thus creating a lower yield vine. Finally, the Noble is the most widely grown red variety. Other colorful names such as Nesbit, Tarheel, Stirling, Hunts, Albemarle, and Thompsons (not to be confused with the vinifera Thompson Seedless) crop up in any discussion of Muscadine wine grapes.

With that lesson in basic Muscadine viticulture completed, we turn to Duplin Wine Cellars. Specifically, Duplin purchases all of its grapes from stockholder/growers in the eastern North Carolina region. A full 400 acres, divided between Carlos, Magnolia, Scuppernong, and Noble, currently supply the winery. All growers are held to a "gentleman's contract" to bring in fully ripened fruit and are instructed by David Fussell to pick in the early morning hours so that the actual temperature of the fruit can be kept relatively low. Specifically, David will reject fruit that is delivered at temperatures of 90° F and above due to the high probability that that fruit will have deteriorated and begun to spoil.

GRAPE VARIETIES AND ACREAGE

Vitis Rotundifolia	
Carlos	200.00
Magnolia	100.00
Noble	50.00
Scuppernong	50.00
TOTALS	400.00

THE WINES

In this step of the process, at least there are no dramatic differences between the way Muscadine grapes are turned into wine compared with wines made from other species. As is always the case, it is the individual decisions of the winemaker that dictate style, but as is also always the case, good winemakers "go with the grape" and, with constraints, let the grape character guide the process towards the finished product.

Thus stated, two special characteristics of Muscadine grapes and their wines should be discussed to help prepare the taster for the first encounter. First, unlike vinifera and French-American hybrid wines, finished Muscadine wines taste and smell just like the fresh grapes from whence they came. They taste very strongly grapey and fruity and possess a unique spicy, musky flavor, nearly exactly the same flavors one would experience by picking and eating ripe Muscadine grapes from the vine. This phenomenon is very similar to that experienced with the native-American hybrid variety Concord, in which the grape tastes just like the jelly, which tastes just like the wine. This is not necessarily a criticism, just an observation. However, it is a distinctly different characteristic from vinifera and French-American hybrid wines where the fermentation and aging processes change simple grapey flavors into smells and tastes of other fruits, flowers, soils, herbs, etc. Surely this evolution contributes to the subtlety and complexity of fine wines—Muscadines simply do not evolve in the same way.

A second generalization about Muscadine wines relates more to winemaking decisions and regional style than to grape character. Muscadine wines, as a rule, are sweet, sometimes incredibly sweet. The word "soft" often appears on Muscadine labels and is the Tarheel adjective for sweet.

While Fussell maintained control over Duplin's winemaking for several years, more recent vintages saw responsibility for winemaking given to Jeff Randall. Jeff has a Masters degree in Fermentation Science from North Carolina State University. In February 1988, Randall left Duplin to become the winemaster at the new Southland Estate Winery, leaving Fussell to resume his vintner role.

David Fussell prefers to ferment all his wines in stainless steel tanks at relatively cool temperatures of 60° F. No Muscadines are put through secondary *malolactic fermentation* in order to preserve natural acids and fresh fruitiness. Finally, very little oak is used at Duplin, again in order to emphasize the flavors of the fruit. Red wines, Ports, Sherries, and Brandies all receive varying amounts of relatively short-term aging in American cooperage.

Tastings at Duplin begin with a proprietary blend of Carlos and Magnolia called "Chablis." While the driest white in the lineup, the "Chablis" still retains about 1.5% residual sugar. Next, the winery offers 100% varietal Carlos (about 2% residual sugar) and a 100% Magnolia (between 3 and 4% residual). All three are very clean and well made, and are similar yet subtly different. Grapey, "foxy" flavors are viscous and mouthfilling, sweet yet balanced by good acids. Of the three, the Carlos is extremely interesting with its intense spicy clove and cinnamon flavors; one might refer to it as the Gewurztraminer of Muscadines. The Magnolia, too, is quite delightful with its allspice accents and long, grapey finish.

For dessert or summer sipping, a 100% Scuppernong wine is made with 6 to 8% residual sugar. It, too, is very clean and strongly fruity, a fascinating wine for its history and uniqueness.

The closest thing to a red table wine at Duplin is the "Burgundy," made predominantly from the Noble grape, blended with Magnolia. It is light-bodied and colored, quite grapey, with some evident oak. Still sweet, though, it retains 2% sugar. Due to their organic make-up, red Muscadine wines tend to have color instability and will "brown" earlier than more typical reds. In other words, they're best suited for early drinking and not extended aging.

A "Rosé" blend of Noble, Magnolia, and Carlos and a very sweet (or soft) "Carolina Red" are less appealing due to overly cloying sugar and grapiness.

Duplin's specialty wines are quite interesting. Two méthode champenoise sparkling wines (one 100% Carlos, one 100% Scuppernong) are produced, as well as traditional *flor* Sherry (from Scuppernong), a Port, and two Scuppernong Brandies (one drier than the other). The sparklers are surprisingly pleasant wines, refreshing and well-bubbled. The Brandies, which each receive extended American oak aging, are a terrific twist on an old idea.

A second label fleet of wines is also produced under the "Carolina Wines" designation. Wholly-owned and purchased by Duplin in 1984, grapes of lesser quality are used to produce bulk wines at low prices.

INCIDENTALLY . . .

All in all, the Muscadine experience is a fascinating one—educational, eye-opening, and one that offers a new taste sensation to those devotees of vinifera. True fans of wine are encouraged to be open-minded—visit North Carolina and have fun!

DIRECTIONS

From Interstate 95, take Highway 70 east to Goldsboro. Turn south on Highway 117 and proceed about 40 miles to the town of Rose Hill. Duplin is in the middle of town, on the right side of the road. From Wilmington on the Atlantic coast, just follow Highway 117 north for about 40 miles to Rose Hill.

Germanton Vineyard and Winery

ADDRESS: Route 1, Box 1G
Germanton, NC 27019
PHONE: (919) 969-5514
OWNERS: Nine partners
WINEMAKERS: Jerry Pegram and Scott Lawrence
TOTAL ACRES: 20
CASES/YR: 1,500
HOURS: By appointment only

North Carolina's representative in the French-American hybrid market is the tiny, 1,500 case Germanton Vineyard and Winery. Located a short drive north of Winston-Salem outside the little town of Germanton, this charming operation sits atop a small hillock and commands impressive views of the rugged Blue Ridge to the northwest. Situated in an area where harsh winters prohibit the growing of vinifera (without extreme risk) and located too far west for the cultivation of Muscadines, Germanton Vineyard is a perfect example of how intelligent, flexible individuals can succeed in choosing the appropriate varieties to grow given their topographical and climatological requirements.

The seeds for Germanton Vineyard began with two men, one an ophthalmologist by profession, the other a laboratory technician for a nearby beer brewery. Mallory Chambliss and Jerry Pegram had each been growing grapes and making wine as a hobby for several years. They knew of a number of other individuals in the area doing the same thing and, in order to pool their collective knowledge, started the Piedmont Grape Growers Association. Mallory and Jerry then had the idea that if all of them combined their harvests, they could supply a winery of their own. Letters proposing the plan were circulated among twenty-five individuals and families, ten of whom expressed serious interest, six of whom finally agreed to go into business together.

That was in 1981. Today, Mallory and Jerry are joined by Jack Gillespie, Scott Lawrence, Rick Bagley, David and Judy Simpson, and Mike and Tony McGee (whose late father, Bill, was the first president of the operation and contributed one of the major vineyards and the old dairy barn, which has been converted and serves as the winery facility).

While each partner oversees the development of his own vineyards, Jack Gillespie takes the lead in overall vineyard management; Jerry Pegram and Scott Lawrence share the winemaking responsibilities.

THE VINEYARD

Twenty total acres now supply Germanton. Vineyards are widely distributed from the Winston-Salem region (1,000 feet above sea level) to the nearby Blue Ridge foothills (at an elevation of nearly 3,000 feet). Nearly all grapes grown are French-American hybrids with Seyval taking the lead at 8 acres. Other white hybrids include Villard Blanc, Vidal, and Cayuga—the American hybrid developed in the Finger Lakes of New York by the Geneva Experimental Station. The leading red variety grown is Chancellor (5 acres), followed by Chambourcin, and Foch grown in Mallory's mountain vineyard high in the hills. Finally, a small amount of the native-American grape Niagara is also cultivated.

GRAPE VARIETIES AND ACREAGE

Variety	Rotundifolia	French/Amer. Hybrids
Seyval	—.—	8.0
Chancellor	—.—	5.0
Chambourcin	—.—	2.0
Vidal	—.—	1.5
Cayuga	—.—	1.0
Foch	—.—	1.0
Villard Blanc	—.—	1.0
Niagara	0.5	
TOTALS	0.5	19.5

THE WINES

For such a small operation, a surprisingly large number of wines is produced. To satisfy a variety of tastes, both dry table wines and sweeter aperitif-style wines are made. Winemaking emphasizes blending to achieve balance in both flavors and acid. The major exceptions to this rule are the 100% varietal Seyval, Niagara, and Foch rosé.

The Seyval is a very nicely made wine. Rich appley fruit flavors, crisp citrine acidity, and a deft touch of American oak remind the drinker of a lighter styled Chardonnay.

The "Rosé," made from Foch grapes allowed to stay in contact with the grape skins for only two to three hours, is likewise a very pleasant wine. With a copper/brick hue, a fresh fruity nose, and full flavors of raspberries and cranberries, it is a sweet/tart offering that fits well in the popular blush wine category.

Other wines include a "White Table Wine" (a blend of Villard Blanc, Cayuga, and Vidal), a "Sweet White" (a blend of Cayuga, Seyval, and Vidal), a "Sweet Red" (blending Fredonia and Baco Noir), and an "Apple Wine." A particular favorite of the owners is the dry "Red Table Wine." A blend of Foch, Chancellor, and Chambourcin, the wine is medium-bodied and aged in American oak.

DIRECTIONS

From Winston-Salem, take Highway 52 north. Drive 5 miles to Highway 8 exit. Proceed to the town of Germanton, cross the railroad tracks, and turn left on the road just past the town's gas station. The winery is at the end of the drive.

Southland Estate Winery

ADDRESS: P.O. Box 129
Selma, NC 27576
PHONE: (919) 965-3645
OWNERS: A public stock company
WINEMAKER: Robert Burgin
TOTAL ACRES: 5
CASES/YR: 25,000
HOURS: Monday-Saturday 9-5, Sunday 1-5

NOTE: A more complete discussion of the history of Muscadines, the growing of Muscadine grapes, and the making of Muscadine wines appears under the discussion of Duplin Wine Cellars. Before visiting Southland, the Duplin chapter is required reading!

Building on both the success of Duplin Wine Cellars and their enormous pride in the heritage of Muscadine winegrowing in the south, David Fussell and a large group of committed investors set out to create a showcase for North Carolina wine that could be shared with the rest of the world. Beginning in 1983, their goals in doing so were two-fold: First, they needed to select a location that was easily accessible to the public and, second, they wanted to build not just a winery but a model that would reflect the elegance, heritage, and traditions of winemaking in the south.

After a great deal of planning and strategizing, the group developed a proposal, issued stock, and began raising the money needed to realize this dream. Within just a couple of years, a site was purchased and Southland had become a reality. The winery opened its doors in June 1987 with the investment support of 553 stockholders and with David Fussell acting as its president for the first year. Subsequent years have seen various members of the winery Board of Directors fill this role.

Southland Estate is certainly located ideally to achieve one of its major goals: accessibility. The winery, on its 42-acre site, is within clear view of Interstate 95 near the town of Selma. From a marketing perspective, it is an ideal location—nearly 20,000 cars pass by the property each day on the highway and within a 90-mile radius of the winery live nearly two million people.

Southland has also been constructed to meet its second goal: style, elegance, and history. A classic white wood and brick antebellum mansion has been built to house both the winery facility and visitor center. Perched overlooking a manmade, crystal blue, 8-acre lake, and surrounded by a 5-acre vineyard, Southland truly looks like something out of a vinous *Gone With the Wind*.

Inside, the winery features a large tasting room decorated with antique casks and barrels from Germany and other parts of Europe, a museum stocked with bottles, crushing equipment, and grape presses dating as far back as 1835, a hokey-but-fun film explaining the winegrowing process, and banquet facilities for special occasions. Outside, a special "show vineyard" is planted to old historical varieties no longer cultivated and is trellised in the manner of early North Carolina vineyards (using an overhead, arbor-like structure). Underneath the mansion, a large cellar has been dug for the production and aging of sparkling wine.

THE VINEYARD

Southland Estate produces only Muscadine wines made from vitis rotundifolia grapes. For its supply of produce, Southland purchases grapes from several hundred acres cultivated across rural eastern North Carolina. This acreage is planted primarily to white varieties Carlos, Magnolia, and Scuppernong, and the red variety Noble.

In addition, a 5-acre vineyard has recently been established surrounding the estate. More for experimental purposes than for harvesting, this vineyard has 1.25 acres each devoted to Noble, Nesbit, Carlos, and Sterling.

GRAPE VARIETIES AND ACREAGE

Variety	Vinifera	Rotundifolia
Carlos	—.—	1.25
Nesbit	—.—	1.25
Noble	—.—	1.25
Sterling	—.—	1.25
TOTALS	0.0	5.00

THE WINES

Winemaking at Southland Estate follows similar guidelines as those used at Duplin Wine Cellars, with one important exception: the emphasis is placed on producing blended wines made from various Muscadine varieties, rather than bottling 100% varietals.

Such a direction is followed for several reasons. First and most obviously, Southland is striving to create a product distinct from its neighbor, Duplin. Second, due to the singularly fruity character of Muscadines, the winery aims to produce wines of greater nuance and complexity through blending. Finally, from a marketing standpoint, generic names such as "Blush" will be applied to blends and be more meaningful to consumers, since they describe a style of wine. Just as winemakers in Virginia and Maryland have found that it is hard to sell wines called DeChaunac or Chancellor, the folks at Southland have found no great consumer recognition of wines called Magnolia or Carlos.

Southland's "Chablis" blends together various percentages of Scuppernong, Magnolia, and Carlos and is finished medium sweet with about 2% residual sugar. A pleasing wine, it is crisp and presents a surprisingly dry impression despite the sugar. The wine offers clean, grapey, floral, and spicy fruitiness, and possesses classic Muscadine flavor. A second blend is the "Blush." Displaying a faint copper color, the wine is sweeter still (at about 3% residual) and presents flavors similar to the "Chablis."

One hundred percent varietal bottlings of Magnolia and Scuppernong remain on the Southland wine list as well. While each is very similar in Muscadine grapiness, each is also subtly different. The Magnolia is probably my favorite with more forward fruit, a silky and viscous palate, and an incredibly long, grapey finish. Finally, the Scuppernong is the sweetest (8% residual sugar) and most assertive in flavor, with a distinct blossomy, perfumed character. Like all the Muscadines, it will surprise and even, perhaps, put off those unaccustomed to the experience. But given time and serious consideration, the wine will gain the respect of the truly appreciative for its unique character and quality craftsmanship.

Two reds are offered: the "Soft Red" and the "Robust Red." Now, just to get the southern jargon down, "soft" translates into "sweet." While both are predominantly made from the red variety Noble, they are actually blended with small portions of white varieties Carlos and Magnolia to tone down the overall impression. The "Soft" is cloying in its sweetness. The "Robust Red," however, is surprisingly likeable, with rich berry fruitiness and evident, attractive, spicy oak. While maybe not a perfect match with a sirloin, it certainly could go well with barbecued chicken or ribs.

Southland also bottles two méthode champenoise Champagnes (one blended, one from 100% Scuppernong), an oak-aged Sherry, and a Port. For the teetotaler, Sparkling Non-Alcoholic Scuppernong is also produced. All are well made. The sparklers are clean and lively. Of the fortified wines, the Sherry, especially, is rich and smooth and velvety. Probably the least overtly Muscadine wine in the crowd, the Sherry is impressive with its flavors of coffee, butterscotch, and pecans, and is enhanced by smoky, spicy, bourbony oak throughout aromas and flavors.

DIRECTIONS

From Interstate 95, take Exit 98 at Selma. Head east off of the exit and immediately turn left onto the frontage road adjacent to I-95. The winery is on your right.

ADDITIONAL NOTE ON NORTH CAROLINA

For the adventurer at heart who wants to seek out every possible wine experience in the state of North Carolina, two additional locations require mentioning. One is a bonded winery that is not really producing or bottling wine. The other is a cheese shop selling wine under its own label, though the wine is actually produced elsewhere.

The LaRocca Wine Company is the creation of and retirement business for Sam LaRocca of Fayetteville, North Carolina. A one-man operation, LaRocca has produced Muscadine wine from purchased vitis rotundifolia grapes in the basement of his suburban Fayetteville home since the winery was established in 1978. When bottled, it appears under the "Carolina Pines" label and is a blend of Carlos, Magnolia, and Hunts. At this writing, Sam had not made wine for the last year or so and had a large quantity unbottled. He welcomes visitors by appointment only and can be reached at:

LaRocca Wine Company
408 Buie Court
Fayetteville, NC 28304
(919) 484-8865

In Hickory, North Carolina, Bernard's Waldensian Cheese Shop has North Carolina wine for sale. Back in 1935, under the direction of Mellie C. Bernard, the Waldensian Winery was a thriving operation. Named for the group of northern Italian immigrants who settled in the mountains of western North Carolina in 1893, the winery was put out of business several years later when the county it was located in was declared "dry." Today, however, Lorin Weaver, a descendant of Mr. Bernard, has a contract with Duplin Wine Cellars. Under the arrangement, Duplin produces wine according to Weaver's "recipes," bottles it under the Waldensian label, and then ships it to Hickory. Visitors to Bernard's can sample and purchase a wide variety of Muscadine wines including several versions of Scuppernong. While there is talk of forming a new winery, for now visitors can find the wines at:

Bernard's Waldensian Cheese Shop
2828 Highway 64-70, Southwest
Hickory, NC 28601
(704) 327-2743

A NOTE ON PENNSYLVANIA

Of course, similarities amongst winegrowing regions do not always abide by political boundaries.

When this guide was initially conceptualized, certain decisions had to be made. Namely, it was to be organized by state and, most important, it was designed to be comprehensive, i.e., all wineries in a covered state would be included. So, when I looked at Pennsylvania, which has nearly fifty wineries by itself, I decided that I simply could not cover it. Doing so would have nearly doubled the size of the book and the work involved in producing it.

However, this guide would be remiss if it did not mention the prevalence of fine wineries that exist just north of the Maryland/Pennsylvania border. Recall that, in the introduction to the Maryland section, the so-called "Golden Crescent" was discussed: arching gently from western New Jersey through southeastern Pennsylvania, across central and western Maryland, and finally encompassing eastern West Virginia and the northern piedmont of Virginia. This area is becoming known for its ability to produce fine wine of a particular style. Throughout this book, mid-Atlantic wines have been described, when at their best, as possessing some of the best attributes of both California and French wines: the full-bodied and ripe fruitiness found in Napa and Sonoma, coupled with the tight structure and elegance of Bordeaux. Let it be known that some very impressive wines in this vein can be had if a wine tour of Maryland strays into neighboring Pennsylvania.

Pennsylvania's own wine history dates back over 300 years when William Penn brought French and Spanish grape vines to what is now present day Philadelphia. Today, the state's forty-two wineries are spread throughout the state, but cluster mainly either around the Lake Erie shore in the northwest or in the rolling hills of the southeast. Below is an extremely abbreviated list of some of the better wineries within quick striking distance of the Washington-metro area.

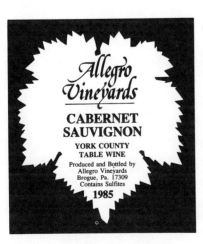

Allegro Vineyards

R.D. #2, Box 64
Brogue, PA 17309
(717) 927-9148

Tim and John Crouch, proprietors, opened the doors of Allegro in the fall of 1981 and have since quickly gained a great deal of respect from peers, critics, and consumers alike. Located just a stone's throw from the mighty Susquehanna River, the winery grows a wide range of vinifera varieties as well as select French-American hybrids.

Allegro's deep, spicy Cabernet Sauvignons are uniformly outstanding, its oak-aged Seyval Blanc is strikingly clean and complex, its Chardonnay buttery and elegant, and its slightly sweet Vidal a ringer for a German Kabinet Riesling.

Naylor Wine Cellars

R.D. #3, Box 424, Ebaugh Road
Stewartstown, PA 17363
(717) 993-2431

A true leader in the Pennsylvania industry, Richard Naylor founded Naylor Wine Cellars in 1978. Located on a 1,000-foot plateau, the winery has 27 acres of vinifera, French-American hybrid, and native- American varieties and, not surprisingly, produces a plethora of wines from them (20 table wines, 5 fruit wines). Especially noteworthy are the Cabernet Sauvignon and Chambourcin, both deeply fruited and wrapped in spicy, forthright oak.

Other wineries in the same general area include:

Chaddsford Winery
Rt. #1, P.O. Box 229
Chadds Ford, PA 19317
(215) 388-6221

Nissley Vineyards
R.D. #1
Bainbridge, PA 17502
(717) 426-3514

A SHORT LIST OF THE AUTHOR'S FAVORITE WINES

VITIS VINIFERA

Chardonnay

MARYLAND:
  Basignani Winery, Estate Bottled
  Boordy Vineyards, Virginia/Maryland
  Byrd Vineyards, Estate Bottled
  Catoctin Vineyards, Oak Fermented and Regular
  Elk Run Vineyards and Winery, Liberty Tavern-Estate Bottled

VIRGINIA:
  Linden Vineyards, Estate Bottled
  Loudoun Valley Vineyards, Reserve and Regular
  Montdomaine Cellars, Barrel Select
  Naked Mountain Vineyard, Estate Bottled
  Oakencroft Vineyard
  Piedmont Vineyards, Winemakers Reserve
  Prince Michel Vineyards, Barrel Select and Regular
  Tarara Vineyard
  Willowcroft Farm Vineyards, Reserve
  The Williamsburg Winery Ltd., Reserve and Regular

Cabernet Sauvignon

MARYLAND:
  Basignani Winery, Estate Bottled
  Byrd Vineyards, Estate Bottled
  Catoctin Vineyards, Reserve and Regular
  Elk Run Vineyards, Liberty Tavern-Estate Bottled
  Montbray Wine Cellars, Estate Bottled

VIRGINIA:
  Ingleside Plantation, Virginia
  Meredyth Vineyards, Virginia
  Montdomaine Cellars, Estate Bottled
  Naked Mountain, Estate Bottled "Claret"
  Oakencroft Vineyard, Virginia

Riesling

MARYLAND:
  Catoctin Vineyards

VIRGINIA:
  Burnley Vineyards
  Dominion Wine Cellars, "Johannisberg"
  Naked Mountain Vineyards
  Rapidan River Vineyard, Semi-dry

Merlot

MARYLAND:
    Basignani Winery, Estate Bottled
    Byrd Vineyards, Estate Bottled

VIRGINIA:
    Misty Mountain Vineyard
    Montdomaine Cellars, Reserve

Other Vinifera Varietals

CABERNET FRANC
    Maryland's Montbray Wine Cellars
GEWURZTRAMINER
    Maryland's Byrd Vineyards
    Virginia's Rapidan River Vineyards
SAUVIGNON BLANC
    Virginia's Linden Vineyards
    Virginia's Naked Mountain Vineyard
SEMILLON
    Virginia's Piedmont Vineyards, Artists Series

FRENCH-AMERICAN HYBRIDS

Seyval

MARYLAND:
    Basignani Winery
    Boordy Vineyards, Sur Lie Reserve
    Catoctin Vineyards
    Montbray Wine Cellars, Seyve-Villard

VIRGINIA:
    Linden Vineyards
    Meredyth Vineyards
    Oakencroft Vineyard

Vidal

MARYLAND:
    Boordy Vineyards, "Nouvelle" and Regular

VIRGINIA:
    Stonewall Vineyards, Dry and Semi-Dry
    Winchester Winery

Chambourcin

MARYLAND:
    Woodhall Vineyards

VIRGINIA:
    Shenandoah Vineyards
    Stonewall Vineyards
    Winchester Winery

Other French-American Hybrids

CHANCELLOR
    Maryland's Ziem Vineyards

CHELOIS
Virginia's Mountain Cove Vineyards, "Harvest Red"
DeChaunac
Maryland's Ziem Vineyards
Foch
Maryland's Boordy Vineyards, "Nouveau"
Maryland's Ziem Vineyards
Rayon d'Or
Virginia's Winchester Winery
Villard Noir
Virginia's Meredyth Vineyards

VINIFERA/FRENCH-AMERICAN HYBRID BLENDS

White Wines

Virginia:
Chateau Morrisette Winery, "White Table Wine"
Blend of 65% Seyval, 20% Vidal, 15% Riesling
Dominion Wine Cellars, "White"
Blend of Seyval and Chardonnay
Ingleside Plantation, "Chesapeake Blanc"
Blend of 90% Seyval, 10% Chardonnay
Linden Vineyards, "Riesling/Vidal"
Blend of 65% Riesling, 35% Vidal
Shenandoah Vineyards, "Shenandoah Blanc"
Blend of 75% Vidal/Seyval/other hybrids, 25% Riesling
Williamsburg Winery Ltd., "Governor's White"
Blend of 55% Riesling, 45% Vidal
Tarara Vineyard, "Charval"
Blend of 60% Seyval, 40% Chardonnay

Red Wines

Maryland:
Loew Vineyards, "Harvest Red"
Blend of 85% Chancellor, 15% Cabernet Sauvignon

Virginia:
Dominion Wine Cellars, "Red"
Blend of Chambourcin and Cabernet Sauvignon
Guilford Ridge Vineyard, "Page Valley Red"
Proprietary Blend of Chambourcin, Chelois, Cabernet Sauvignon
Ingleside Plantation, "Chesapeake Claret"
Blend of 90% Chancellor, 10% Cabernet Sauvignon
Oasis Vineyard, "Virginia Red"
80% Chelois, 10% Cabernet Sauvignon, remainder Foch and Chancellor
Rose Bower Vineyard, "Hampden Forest Claret"
Blend of 65% Chancellor, 35% Cabernet Sauvignon

VITIS ROTUNDIFOLIA

North Carolina
Duplin Wine Cellars, Magnolia
Duplin Wine Cellars, Scuppernong
Southland Estate Winery, "Robust Red"

SELECTED RESTAURANTS AND ACCOMMODATIONS

MARYLAND

Eastern Maryland

RESTAURANTS

Barron's
Hunt Valley, MD
(301) 785-7700

Manor Tavern
Cockeysville, MD
(301) 771-8155

Milton Inn
Sparks, MD
(301) 771-4366

Peerce's Plantation
Towson, MD
(301) 252-3100

BED & BREAKFASTS

Hunt Valley Inn
Hunt Valley, MD
(301) 785-7000

The Shirley-Madison
Inn
Baltimore, MD
(301) 728-6550

Central Maryland

RESTAURANTS

Baugher's Country
Restaurant &
Farm Market
Westminster, MD
(301) 848-7413

Cockey's Tavern
Westminster, MD
(301) 848-4202

Fiore's
Reistertown, MD
(301) 833-6300

Linwood's
Owings Mill, MD
(301) 356-3030

Maggie's
Westminster, MD
(301) 876-6868

McDaniel's
Westminster, MD
(301) 857-1800 or
876-0500

Mt. Airy Plantation
Mt. Airy, MD
(301) 856-1860

Olney Ale House
Olney, MD
(301) 774-6708

BED & BREAKFASTS

Judge Thomas House
Westminster, MD
(301) 876-6686

National Pike Inn
New Market, MD
(301) 865-5055

The Newel Post
Uniontown, MD
(301) 775-2655

Rose Bud Inn
Woodsboro, MD
(301) 845-2221

Strawberry Inn
New Market, MD
(301) 865-3719

Turning Point Inn
Urbana, MD
(301) 875-2421

Western Maryland

RESTAURANTS

Auction House
Boonsboro, MD
(301) 733-3301

Harnish Haus
Hagerstown, MD
(301) 791-6199

The Inn at Blackford's
Crossing
Sharpsburg, MD
(301) 432-8200

The Morel
Hagerstown, MD
(301) 733-6200

Old South Mountain
Inn
Boonsboro, MD
(301) 432-6155

Oliver's
Hagerstown, MD
(301) 790-0011

Richardson's
Restaurant
Hagerstown, MD
(301) 733-3660

BED & BREAKFASTS

Bavarian Inn
Shepherdstown, WV
(304) 876-2551

Carriage Inn
Charles Town, WV
(304) 728-8003

Cottonwood Inn
Charles Town, WV
(304) 725-3371

Inn at Antietam
Sharpsburg, MD
(301) 432-6601

Magnus Tate's Kitchen
Charles Town, WV
(304) 725-8052

Spring Bank Farm
Frederick, MD
(301) 694-0440

Stonebrake Cottage
Shepherdstown, WV
(304) 876-6607

Thomas Shepherd Inn
Shepherdstown, WV
(304) 754-7646

VIRGINIA

Eastern Virginia

RESTAURANTS

Arbuckles
Fredericksburg, VA
(703) 371-0775

Berret's
Colonial Williamsburg,
VA
(804) 253-1847

Big Bill's Captain's
Deck
Nassawadox, VA
(804) 442-7060

Clos de Marchand
Williamsburg, VA
(804) 220-3636

Chimneys
Fredericksburg, VA
(703) 371-9229

Chownings Tavern
Colonial Williamsburg,
VA
(804) 229-1000

Christiana Campbell's
Tavern
Colonial Williamsburg,
VA
(804) 229-1000

Island House
Wachapreague, VA
(804) 787-4242

King's Arms Tavern
Colonial Williamsburg,
VA
(804) 229-1000

Olde Mudd Tavern
Thornburg, VA
(703) 582-5250

La Petite Auberge
Fredericksburg, VA
(703) 371-2727

Port Royal Tavern
Port Royal, VA
(804) 742-5609

Ramparts
Fredericksburg, VA
(703) 373-5526

Shield's Tavern
Colonial Williamsburg,
VA
(804) 229-1000

The Smythe's Cottage
Fredericksburg, VA
(703) 373-1645

The Trellis Restaurant
Colonial Williamsburg,
VA
(804) 229-8610

Wilkerson's Seafood
Restaurant
Colonial Beach, VA
(804) 224-7117

Le Yaca
Williamsburg, VA
(804) 220-3616

BED & BREAKFASTS

Anchor Motel
Nassawadox, VA
(804) 442-6363

The Burton House
Wachapreague, VA
(804) 787-4560

Fredericksburg
Colonial Inn
Fredericksburg, VA
(703) 371-5666

The Inn at Montross
Montross, VA
(804) 493-9097

The Kenmore Inn
Fredericksburg, VA
(703) 371-7622

McGrath House
Fredericksburg, VA
(703) 371-4363

Richard Johnston Inn
Fredericksburg, VA
(703) 899-7606

Northern Virginia

RESTAURANTS

Conyers House
Sperryville, VA
(703) 987-8025

The Depot
Warrenton, VA
(703) 347-1212

Foster Harris House
Little Washington, VA
(703) 675-3757

Green Tree Restaurant
Leesburg, VA
(703) 777-7246

Heritage House
Little Washington, VA
(703) 675-3207

The Inn at Little
Washington
Little Washington, VA
(703) 675-3800

Jordan's Restaurant
Leesburg, VA
(703) 777-1471

Leathercoat
The Plains, VA
(703) 253-5286

Lovettsville Village Inn
Lovettsville, VA
(703) 822-5333

The Rail Stop
The Plains, VA
(703) 253-5644

Smiley's Restaurant
Leesburg, VA
(703) 771-9334

Tuscarora Mill
Leesburg, VA
(703) 771-9300

BED & BREAKFASTS

The Ashby Inn &
Restaurant
Paris, VA
(703) 592-3900

Carradoc Hall
Leesburg, VA
(703) 771-9200

Inn Between the Hills
Hillsborough, VA
(703) 668-6162

L'Auberge Provencale
White Post, VA
(703) 837-1375

Brookside
Basye, VA
(703) 856-3710

Caledonia Farm
Flint Hill, VA
(703) 675-3693

The Gay St. Inn
First Washington, VA
(703) 675-3288

Gibson Hall Inn
Upperville, VA
(703) 592-3514

Hamilton Garden Inn
& Restaurant
Hamilton, VA
(703) 338-3693

Hilltop Manor
Orlean, VA
(703) 364-3292

Little River Inn
Aldie, VA
(703) 327-6742

Luck House
Middleburg, VA
(703) 687-5387

Middleburg Guest
Suites
Middleburg, VA
(703) 687-5510

Pied-A-Terre
Middleburg, VA
(703) 687-5317/5265

The Pink House
Waterford, VA
(703) 882-3453

Red Fox Inn
Middleburg, VA
(703) 687-6301

The 1763 Inn
Upperville, VA
(703) 592-3848

Sycamore Hill House
Little Washington, VA
(703) 675-3046

Welbourne
Middleburg, VA
(703) 687-3201

Windsor House
Middleburg, VA
(703) 687-6800

Culpeper

RESTAURANTS

The Bavarian Chef
Madison, VA
(703) 948-6505

Davis Street Ordinary
Culpeper, VA
(703) 825-3909

Horsefeathers
Orange, VA
(703) 672-2666

La Scala
Orange, VA
(703) 672-5816

The Little Chef
Madison, VA
(703) 948-6908

Orange Gourmet
Orange, VA
(703) 672-3514

Toliver House
Gordonsville, VA
(703) 832-3485

BED & BREAKFASTS

Five Oaks Farms
Orange, VA
(703) 854-5934

Fountain Hall
Culpeper, VA
(703) 825-6708

Graves Mountain
Lodge
Syria, VA
(703) 923-4231

Hidden Inn
Orange, VA
(703) 672-3625

Mayhurst Inn
Orange, VA
(703) 672-5597

Olive Mill
Banco, VA
(703) 923-4664

The Shadows
Orange, VA
(703) 672-5057

Sleepy Hollow Farm
Gordonsville, VA
(703) 832-5555

Stuartfield Hearth
Culpeper, VA
(703) 825-8132

Willowgrove Bed and
Breakfast
Orange, VA
(703) 672-5982

Monticello

RESTAURANTS

The Galerie
Charlottesville, VA
(804) 823-5883

The Ivy Inn
Charlottesville, VA
(804) 977-1222

Historic Michie Tavern
Charlottesville, VA
(804) 977-1234

Mozart Restaurant
Charlottesville, VA
(804) 971-5988

Rhodes Farm Inn
Wintergreen, VA
(804) 325-2200

South Street
Charlottesville, VA
(804) 979-9300

Stoney Creek Cafe
Nellysford, VA
(804) 361-CAFE

BED & BREAKFASTS

Boar's Head Inn
Charlottesville, VA
(804) 291-2181

Chester
Scottsville, VA
(804) 286-3960

High Meadows
Scottsville, VA
(804) 286-2218

Prospect Hill
Charlottesville, VA
(703) 967-0844

Silver Thatch Inn
Charlottesville, VA
(804) 978-4686

200 South Street
Charlottesville, VA
(804) 979-0200

Wintergreen
Wintergreen, VA
(800) 325-2200

Southern Virginia

RESTAURANTS

Armbrusters
Blackstone, VA
(804) 292-5992

The Bank
Lynchburg, VA
(804) 847-8100

Briar Patch Restaurant
Amherst, VA
(804) 946-2249

The Cabochon
Roanoke, VA
(703) 389-1587

Charcoal Steak House
Roanoke, VA
(703) 366-3710

Charley's
Roanoke, VA
(703) 774-7475

Coach & Four
Restaurant
Roanoke, VA
(703) 362-4220

Fesquet's
Roanoke, VA
(703) 362-8803

The Homeplace
Catawba, VA
(703) 384-7252

La Maison du Gourmet
Roanoke, VA
(703) 366-2444

The Library
Roanoke, VA
(703) 985-0811

Luigi's
Roanoke, VA
(703) 989-6277

Rutledge Inn
Amherst, VA
(804) 946-7670

The Wilson-Walker
House
Lexington, VA
(703) 463-3020

BED & BREAKFASTS

Buckingham Springs
Plantation
Dillwyn, VA
(804) 392-8770

Hotel Roanoke
Roanoke, VA
(800) 542-5898

Irish Gap Inns
Vesuvius, VA
(804) 922-7701

Mountain Lake Hotel
Mountain Lake, VA
(703) 626-7121

Shenandoah Valley

RESTAURANTS

Battletown Inn
Berryville, VA
(703) 955-4100

Courthouse Cafe
Winchester, VA
(703) 662-3300

Cork Street Tavern
Winchester, VA
(703) 667-3777

Edinburg Mill
Edinburg, VA
(703) 984-8555

Girard's Cafe and
Bakery
Basye, VA
(703) 856-2196

Morgan's Choice
Winchester, VA
(703) 665-0922

My Father's Moustache
Front Royal, VA
(703) 635-3496

Parkhurst Restaurant
Luray, VA
(703) 743-6009

Spring House
Restaurant
Edinburg, VA
(703) 459-4755

23 Beverley
Staunton, VA
(703) 885-5053

BED & BREAKFASTS

Blue Ridge Bed &
Breakfast
Berryville, VA
(703) 955-1246

Bryce Resort
Basye, VA
(703) 856-2121

Candlewick Inn
Woodstock, VA
(703) 459-8008

The Constant Spring
Inn
Front Royal, VA
(703) 635-7010

Countryside
Summit Point, WV
(304) 725-2614

The Hillbrook Inn
Charles Town, WV
(304) 725-4223

Hotel Strasburg
Strasburg, VA
(703) 465-9191

The Inn at Narrow
Passage
Woodstock, VA
(703) 459-8000

Jordan Hollow Farm
Inn
Stanley, VA
(703) 778-2209

Mary's Country Inn
Edinburg, VA
(703) 984-8286

Mimslyn
Luray, VA
(703) 743-5105

The Pumpkin House
Inn
Harrisonburg, VA
(703) 434-6963

The River House
Boyce, VA
(703) 837-1476

Schlisselsmith
Woodstock, VA
(703) 459-5369

The Sky Chalet
Mt. Jackson, VA
(703) 856-2147

The Wayside Inn
Middletown, VA
(703) 869-1797

Widow Kipp's Inn
Mt. Jackson, VA
(703) 477-2400

NORTH CAROLINA

Eastern North Carolina

RESTAURANTS

Country Squire
  Restaurant and
  Tavern
Keenansville, NC
(919) 296-1727

Josef's
Keenansville, NC
(919) 296-1368

Rose Hill Restaurant
Rose Hill, NC
(919) 289-2151

BED & BREAKFASTS

Eli Olive's Bed &
  Breakfast
Smithfield, NC
(919) 934-0246

Liberty Inn
Wallace, NC
(919) 285-7586

Squire Vintage Inn
Keenansville, NC
(919) 296-1831

Central North Carolina

RESTAURANTS

Brass Kettle
Winston-Salem, NC
(919) 723-4265

Ryan's Restaurant
Winston-Salem, NC
(919) 724-6132

Staley's Steak House
Winston-Salem, NC
(919) 723-8631

BED & BREAKFASTS

Brookstown Mill
Winston-Salem, NC
(919) 722-1818

Western North Carolina

RESTAURANTS

Black Forest Family
  Restaurant
Skyland, NC
(704) 684-8160

Cafe Primavera
Asheville, NC
(704) 254-2349

Fairview Log Cabin
  Restaurant
Asheville, NC
(704) 628-1828

Five Boston Way
Asheville, NC
(704) 274-1111

Steven's Restaurant &
  Pub
Asheville, NC
(704) 253-5348

Stone Soup
Asheville, NC
(704) 255-SOUP

GLOSSARY OF WINE TERMS

Throughout this book, words of special significance to the growing and making of wine have been printed in italics. Below appears a brief glossary of these terms, with short explanations or definitions.

BLANC DE BLANC—A French term meaning, literally, a white wine made from white grapes.

BLANC DE NOIR—A white wine made from red (or black) grapes. Most often applied to either sparkling, "blush," or rosé wines. Certain grape varieties, while possessing a dark skin, actually have clear or lightly colored juice, Pinot Noir being the best example. The term is used to describe the finished product of a winemaking practice in which these types of grapes are pressed and the clear (or slightly tinted) juice is kept separate from the skins during fermentation to produce a lighter and more delicate wine.

BLIND TASTING—When tasting wines for evaluation or judging in a competition, the identity of the wine is often kept anonymous by wrapping each bottle in a brown paper bag. This practice keeps judges objective since they are "blind" to the source and maker of the wine being tasted.

BOTRYTIS CINERA—Often referred to as the "noble rot," botrytis is actually a fungus that can attack ripening grapes in the vineyard around harvest time. Unlike most rots that ruin grapes, botrytis cinera can enhance grape quality by absorbing the juice of the grape, shriveling the berries, thereby concentrating sugars, acids, and other components that lend flavor to wine. Often encouraged in white varieties like Riesling, Gewurztraminer, Semillon, and Sauvignon Blanc, grapes infected with "noble rot" can produce uniquely aromatic, lush, beautiful Late Harvest dessert wines.

BRIX—The French scale that is used to measure the sugar content in grapes. Roughly comparable to a percentage, grapes should optimally ripen to a level between 20° and 24° Brix (or 20% to 24% sugar) before harvesting.

CARBONIC MACERATION—The fermentation process perfected in the Beaujolais region of France. In this process, whole clusters of uncrushed grapes are placed in a tank or bin and allowed to ferment "internally"; i.e., natural yeasts act on the juice within individual berries converting sugars to alcohol. After a period of seven to ten days, the whole clusters are crushed and the young wine can then either be bottled as a fresh, fruity "nouveau" or aged in oak. Typically, wines made through carbonic maceration are intensely aromatic, fresh, and grapey. Since the grape skins are not broken, these wines do not extract the tannin of traditional reds and are thus usually intended for early consumption.

CHAPITALIZATION—If grapes do not ripen optimally, inadequate levels of natural sugar are attained. Chapitalization refers to the process in which cane sugar is added to the fresh juice of crushed grapes to raise sugar levels. Rather than contributing any flavor, this process simply allows for the wine to be finished with an adequate level of alcohol.

CLUSTER THINNING — Grape quality is enhanced if the output of individual vines is controlled and limited. Midway through a growing season, growers often go through the vineyard and cluster thin, that is, snip off clusters of grapes to reduce the overall production of the vineyard in order to improve quality.

COLD STABILIZATION—After completion of fermentation, wines are often put through a process of cold stabilization. Chilling the wine to temperatures of 28-32° for two weeks encourages solids such as tartaric acid crystals (tartrates) to precipitate out of solution and settle at the bottom of the tank. This clarification helps to avoid such a precipitation after the wine is bottled.

CULTIVARS—A word synonymous with grape variety.

CUVÉE—Generally refers to a blend of wines, most often applied to the blend making up a champagne or sparkling wine.

DEGREE DAYS—A measure used to differentiate between climatological growing regions based on the amount of heat vineyards are exposed to during a growing season. Specifically, total degree days are calculated by taking, each day, the mean temperature above 50° F and totalling these means over the entire number of days in the growing season.

DEGOURGEMENT—The next-to-last step in the champagne-making process in which the frozen plug of accumulated yeast sediment is literally blasted out of the bottle under the carbon dioxide pressure that has developed as the champagne has refermented in the bottle.

DOSAGE—The last step in the champagne-making process in which liquid lost during degourgement is replaced in each bottle just prior to corking. For Brut (or dry) sparkling wine, the dosage is usually an addition of the same still wine that was used to make the sparkling wine. For sparkling wine with residual sugar, slightly sweetened brandy is used for the dosage.

ENOLOGY—The scientific study of the process of making wine.

ESTATE BOTTLED—The general term used to identify that the wine in a given bottle is made from grapes grown by the winery.

FERMENTATION—The heart of the winemaking process. Microscopic yeast cells, either naturally existing on grapes or more often a specially selected strain with which fresh grape juice is inoculated, grow and multiply in fresh must by feeding on the sugars present in the juice and producing, as a byproduct, equal parts of alcohol and carbon dioxide. The process produces heat; thus many winemakers work hard to control the temperatures of their fermentations to preserve the delicate nuances of the grape.

FINING—A clarification process whereby various agents such as bentonite (a refined clay), gelatin, or egg whites are added to an aging wine. These agents, which are heavier than the wine, slowly precipitate to the bottom of the tank or barrel, dragging with them certain particles and proteins that make an unfinished wine hazy.

FLOR—A specific type of yeast used in making Spanish-style sherries.

FREE RUN JUICE—After grapes are crushed, a must is created, made up of juice released from the berries, skins, and pulp. When this must is placed in a wine press, that juice which runs out freely before pressure is exerted on the skins and pulp is referred to as "free run juice." It is usually the smoothest, lightest, most delicate juice from the grape. About 60% to 70% of the total yield of juice from grapes is free run. Some wineries' special bottlings are made only from this juice.

FRENCH-AMERICAN HYBRID — That family of grape varieties produced by botanically crossing European vitis vinifera varieties with native-American varieties. The resulting cultivars, which were developed mainly in France earlier in this century, possess many of the "fine wine" characteristics of their European parents, while also sharing the hardier, sturdier characteristics of native grapes. The goal of these hybridizers was to create fine wine grapes that could survive in a harsher, colder climate.

LEES (or Lies)—As yeasts complete fermentation, they die for two reasons: the very alcohol that they have produced becomes toxic to the cells, and they run out of sugar to eat. Dead yeast cells fall to the bottom of the tank or barrel and form a layer of sediment called "lees." For delicate, crisp wines, winemakers try to separate the clarifying wine quickly from these lees. For wines of more complexity, like Chardonnay, the winemaker may leave the wine in contact with the lees so that it may absorb creamy, toasty, baked-bread components from the decomposing yeast.

MACERATION—Refers to the process whereby fermenting wine is in contact with the grape skins.

MALOLACTIC FERMENTATION—A secondary fermentation process that can take place after the completion of the primary sugar/yeast fermentation. Specific bacteria present in the wine can grow and begin to convert naturally present malic acid (which tends to be harsh and bitter) into the softer, milder lactic acid. Most red wines should complete malolactic fermentation, but most whites are prevented from going through the process in order to retain "crisp" acids. Some Chardonnays and Sauvignon Blancs being produced in a full-bodied, complex style are encouraged to complete malolactic fermentation because the process lends a softer, rounder texture to the wine and can also add a buttery note to the flavors and aromas.

MÉTHODE CHAMPENOISE—The classic French process for producing Champagne. Young, slightly underripe grapes are picked and fermented to complete dryness. The wine is then bottled, but before being capped, a sugar solution inoculated with yeast is added to each bottle. Over a period that can last more than two years, the yeast continues to ferment the added sugar, slowly building up the pressure of the trapped carbon dioxide byproduct. The bottles, toward the end of the process, are tilted in special racks to collect the yeast lees sediment into the cap of the bottle. When this sediment is solidly compacted in the cap of the upside-down bottle, the neck is frozen in a glycol solution. During degourgement, the frozen plug of sediment is blown out of the bottle when the cap is removed, a dosage of brandy or wine is added to replace the lost liquid, and a finished cork is secured. When expertly done, the wine achieves a persistent, delicate effervescence of tiny bubbles. Since the wine is allowed to remain in contact with the yeast in each bottle, good sparkling wine often possesses a toasty, yeasty complexity.

MICRO-CLIMATES—A term used to describe the particular climatological conditions in a given vineyard or region.

MUST—The unfermented or fermenting juice created by the process of crushing and pressing fresh grapes.

NÉGOCIANT—A title applied to a person who purchases finished wine from a producer, prepares it for bottling, bottles it, and sells and markets it under his own name.

PRESS JUICE—As opposed to "free run juice," press juice is that juice extracted under pressure from the pulp and skins of unfermented or fermented must. The press juice is usually more bitter, heavier, and more tannic than the free run, but also possesses more intense flavor, color, and aroma derived from the extended skin contact. Winemakers usually handle the press juice separately from the free run, and blend either all or part of it back into a finished wine to create a suitable, desired balance.

PROTEIN STABILITY—All wines naturally possess certain proteins which, if left alone, would create a haze in a finished wine. For red wines, the tannic acid content causes proteins to settle to the bottom of a barrel during aging. For whites, which have much less tannin, the proteins must be removed lest a bottled wine develop an unattractive "fluffy" haze. Bentonite finings are most often used to bond with and precipitate proteins. Please note: Small wineries with less scientific equipment for measurement may occasionally bottle wines that are slightly protein-unstable. If you purchase a bottle with some slightly fluffy particles of protein, this is no cause for alarm—it is a purely cosmetic deficiency. These proteins in no way detract from flavor.

RACKING—The process of siphoning wine from one container to another, usually to remove it from whatever sediment has collected at the bottom of the container during fermentation or aging. Successive rackings during the making of a wine render it clear.

RESIDUAL SUGAR — Sugar content in a finished wine, usually expressed as a percentage.

RIDDLING—That step in the méthode champenoise in which bottles that have completed their second yeast fermentation are placed in racks that tilt the bottles upside-down. By repeatedly riddling, or jolting the bottles in this position, the dead yeast cells slide down the side of the bottle and collect in the cap at the neck of the bottle.

SCION WOOD—The dormant cutting of a grape variety that is grafted onto hardier rootstock.

SETTLED—The general term used to describe solids sinking to the bottom of a must or wine. Most frequently used to describe how fresh juices are initially clarified to render a semi-clear, clean juice just prior to fermentation. Settling is hastened by chilling the must.

STILL WINE—Still wine is any wine that is not carbonated, i.e., most table wines.

"SUR LIE"—The French term meaning "on the lees," it refers to the winemaking practice of leaving a wine in contact with its lees on purpose, in order to develop desirable characteristics of toastiness, yeastiness, or roundness. Wines left on the lees often complete a secondary malolactic fermentation.

SWEET RESERVE — One method of finishing a wine with residual sugar, often employed by winemakers in the mid-Atlantic. Rather than trying to halt a strong fermentation before all the sugar is fermented out (a difficult process involving extensive chilling and tight filtration) or simply adding flavorless cane sugar to a dry wine, winemakers often prefer the "sweet reserve" method to create slightly sweet wine from varieties like Riesling or Gewurztraminer. At crushing, a portion of fresh free run juice is set aside, chilled, settled, filtered, and then frozen. After the main batch of wine is ready for bottling, the frozen batch, which retains all of the natural grape aromas and flavors, is thawed and added back to the dry wine until the desired residual sugar is reached. The blended wine is then filtered carefully to remove any stray yeast cells in order to prevent a resurgence of fermentation and is bottled.

TARTRATES—Actually a truncated word for sodium bitartrate and the same element that can be purchased in grocery stores as cream of tartar. Tartrates or tartaric acid crystals often form while wine is aging and fall to the bottom of the tank or barrel. The process of cold stabilization is employed in an attempt to remove all tartrates from a wine before bottling, as tartrates are encouraged to form and settle at near-freezing temperatures. Like proteins, if a wine is purchased with tartrate crystals at the bottom of the bottle, fear not. This is another cosmetic deficiency and in no way affects flavor.

UNFILTERED—Often appears on labels to inform the consumer that the wine in the bottle was not filtered prior to bottling. Quite an uncommon practice these days, as filtering is one way winemakers can ensure that wine is stable and "sterile" before it is bottled for the consumer. While wines can be over-filtered and thus suffer from being "stripped" of some of their aromatic and flavor components, some filtering is usually a good idea. Some winemakers may not filter wines in order to create the aura of a rustic, home-made product.

UNFINED—Another label term used to identify wines that have been bottled without going through any fining process for clarification. Never seen on white wines (which would almost certainly be protein unstable and thus possess an unsightly haze), red wines can sometimes be unfined because the tannin content causes proteins to fall out during aging. Again, wines that are "unfined and unfiltered" are often appealing to people as being more natural or handcrafted.

VEGETAL—An adjective used to describe characteristics in a wine that remind the taster of vegetables like green peppers or Brussels sprouts. In limited degrees, these characteristics can add an interesting complexity. If excessive, vegetal traits can be very unpleasant.

VITICULTURE—The scientific study of the process of growing and cultivating grapes.

VITIS LABRUSCA—A species of wild grape vine, which grows naturally in North America. Varieties of this species are referred to in this book as native-American hybrids, since most are not pure vitis labrusca, but have instead been cross-pollinated in the wild with other species. All native-American hybrids share a common, very grapey aroma and flavor, often labeled as "labrusca" or "foxy," which is similar to Concord grape juice or jelly. The best known varieties are, besides Concord, Niagara, Catawba, and Delaware.

VITIS ROTUNDIFOLIA—The species of wild grape that grows only in the warmer, southern portions of this country, within a 70-mile radius of the coastline. Extremely different in its growing habits from vitis vinifera, French-American or native-American Hybrids, the vitis rotundifolia are discussed at length in the section of this book describing wineries in North Carolina.

VITIS VINIFERA—The noblest, classic species of grape that is responsible for producing the world's greatest wines. European in origin, the species requires ample heat and a long growing season to ripen fruit optimally. The species is not terribly hardy in harsh, colder climates and is susceptible to numerous killing molds and fungi. In California's mild climate, the vinifera thrive. In the eastern, midwestern, and southern portions of the U.S., special steps must be taken to ensure survival in climates that are often too cold, variable, and humid. As a region, the mid-Atlantic has begun to succeed wonderfully with cultivation of vitis vinifera varieties. Occasionally, winter temperatures dip to killing levels, and late spring frosts have caused damage to early budding varieties. However, advanced technology allows for quite successful growing.

AUTHOR'S NOTE

Several Virginia wineries could not participate in the production of this book. For information, please contact the wineries directly.

Monticello

Chermont Winery
Route 1, Box 59
Esmont, VA 22937
(804) 286-2211

Salzburg Vineyard
Route 1, Box 83-B
Columbia, VA 23038
(804) 375-3207

Shenandoah Valley

Mount Hermon Vineyard
P.O. Box 94
Basye, VA 22810
(703) 856-2196

Southern Virginia

Chateau Naturel Vineyard
Rt. 4, Box 1535
Rocky Mount, VA 24151
(703) 483-0758

INDEX